ENTERPRISE FOUNDATION LAW IN A COMPARATIVE PERSPECTIVE

FUNDING ACKNOWLEDGEMENT

Support from the Novo Nordisk Foundation and the Research Project on Long-Term Ownership and Value Creations in Enterprise Foundations as well as Bielefeld University is gratefully acknowledged. The project is funded by Copenhagen Business School, the Augustinus Foundation, the Carlsberg Foundation, the COWI Foundation, the Interogo Foundation, the Lauritzen Fonden, Leo Holding, the Lundbeck Foundation, the Ramboll Foundation, the William Demant Foundation and Bielefeld University.

An open access online version of this book is also available.
Visit www.intersentiaonline.com for more information.

INTERSENTIA | ONLINE

ENTERPRISE FOUNDATION LAW IN A COMPARATIVE PERSPECTIVE

Edited by
Anne SANDERS
Steen THOMSEN

INTERSENTIA

Cambridge – Antwerp – Chicago

Intersentia Ltd
8 Wellington Mews
Wellington Street | Cambridge
CB1 1HW | United Kingdom
Tel: +44 1223 736 170
Email: mail@intersentia.co.uk
www.intersentia.com | www.intersentia.co.uk

Distribution for the UK and
Rest of the World (incl. Eastern Europe)
NBN International
1 Deltic Avenue, Rooksley
Milton Keynes MK13 8LD
United Kingdom
Tel: +44 1752 202 301 | Fax: +44 1752 202 331
Email: orders@nbninternational.com

Distribution for Europe
Lefebvre Sarrut Belgium NV
Hoogstraat 139/6
1000 Brussels
Belgium
Tel: +32 (0)2 548 07 13
Email: mail@intersentia.be

Distribution for the USA and Canada
Independent Publishers Group
Order Department
814 North Franklin Street
Chicago, IL 60610
USA
Tel: +1 800 888 4741 (toll free) | Fax: +1 312 337 5985
Email: orders@ipgbook.com

Enterprise Foundation Law in a Comparative Perspective

Artwork on cover: Danny Juchtmans

ISBN 978-1-83970-306-5
D/2023/7849/7
NUR 827

British Library Cataloguing in Publication Data. A catalogue record for this book is available from the British Library.

FOREWORD

An enterprise foundation is a nonprofit organization that serves to own and control a conventional for-profit business corporation that produces goods and services for the general market. This ownership structure has been common in the nations of northern Europe for well over a century and was similarly common in the United States until 1969, when controversial changes in U.S. tax law rendered enterprise foundations no longer viable.

Despite (or because of) their unconventional structure and economic success, enterprise foundations (EFs) and the subsidiary operating companies (SOCs) that they control, were long neglected by scholars in law and social sciences. This situation changed profoundly when Professor Steen Thomsen of the Copenhagen Business School began to study these anomalous firms and ultimately persuaded a number of colleagues and students (including, importantly, scholars from other countries) to join him in this project. Although Thomsen has previously published important articles on the subject, written alone or with others, this volume – co-edited by Professor Anne Sanders of the University of Bielefeld – is the first collective fruit of the broader international scholarly coalition that Thomsen has assembled and guided. As is appropriate, the book is essentially a mapping project, setting out the central facts and themes to be explored.

The book concentrates on the legal framework for EFs and leaves it largely to future scholarship to probe economic, political and social forces that might lead to the formation of EFs. Neverthless, it presents sufficient facts to support some broad conjectures that might be fruitful foci for future research.

It is apparent from the statistics presented in the chapters that follow that a disproportionately large number of EFs are located in northwestern Europe in countries that are small, prosperous and technically sophisticated. Why should this be? The patterns described in this book might be taken as potential support for several broad conjectures which are not mutually exclusive.

One of those conjectures is that, by placing a nonprofit organization in control of a for-profit firm, it may be possible to get the best attributes of each form: the competitive striving for efficiency of a profit-seeking firm whose success is measured in simple monetary terms, and the reluctance to exploit opportunistically the incompleteness of markets that arguably characterizes nonprofit entities. This is, however, a complex subject which will require a substantial commitment of time and sophisticated effort to understand. In this short Foreword, therefore, I will focus on a more familiar and simpler type of conjecture, which is that a substantial portion of the support for EFs has its roots in economic nationalism – though this is not to say that it is injurious to the societies involved.

In this regard, it is helpful to begin by looking at the types of special benefits that, in a hospitable legal regime, seem commonly to be available to persons (particularly founders and their families) who pass control of their firm to an EF. Very roughly described, those benefits seem generally to include one or more of the following:

> *Tax Benefits.* The SOC's founder and his or her family may be relieved of a variety of transfer taxes, including gift and inheritance taxes on the value of the controlling shares that the founder transfers to the EF.
>
> *Profits Without Ownership.* A founder may be able to reserve for his or her descendants a share in the future profits of the SOC even though they own no shares in the SOC.
>
> *Non-Pecuniary Private Benefits of Control.* Even if the founder and his or her family retain no rights to a share in the profits of the SOC, the founder may be able to exercise effective control over the SOC by virtue of the right to appoint its initial board, in the reasonable expectation that the persons he or she appoints will manage the firm as he or she would wish, as will the succeeding self-appointing boards. The engagement, status, and influence (both social and political) that the founder thus retains may in itself be an enormous benefit for him or her.

What, beyond the political influence of individual founders, could be the state's motivation for granting such benefits? The most obvious answer is that they serve as incentives, to the firm and its founder, for keeping the SOC located in its country of origin. Highly successful firms that get their start in a small country are often bought by foreign firms from larger and wealthier countries. This may be perceived as an indignity by the smaller country's population and may have negative material consequences for that country as well, including loss of tax revenue, loss of jobs, and loss of support for improving the nation's physical infrastructure and, perhaps more important, its intellectual infrastructure, such as apprenticeship programs and universities.

In these circumstances, ownership of a firm by an EF may have the important result of keeping that firm registered and headquartered, and its operations located, indefinitely in its country of origin, without the compulsion of nationalization or other heavy-handed forms of regulation.

In the US the potential for economic protectionism through encouragement of foundation ownership, though once strong, has largely been eliminated, presumably because the nation's economy is now sufficiently large, diversified and productive to provide sufficient economic and social benefits to successful startups to induce them to remain within the country.

The US tax legislation of 1969, which brought the demise of nearly all of the country's EFs, imposed an upper limit of 20% on the fraction of any company's stock that could be held by a nonprofit foundation without exposure to ruinous financial penalties. That limit, whose rationale was to remove the opportunity for self-dealing between founders and their SOCs, was surely overkill in that respect, as are the 2019 tax reforms that leave EFs viable in principle but require that they own 100% of the stock of their respective SOCs. In short, US tax policy regarding EFs is now concerned primarily with limiting the potential that EFs provide for opportunistic evasion of taxes, and not with preventing privately held firms from leaving the country.

If in fact law favouring EFs is largely the product of economic nationalism, it may be difficult to refine that policy by determining which EFs are in the national interest – and should be encouraged – and which are not. Additionally, it may be even more difficult to implement that distinction through the reform of general organizational law and tax law.

In short, Steen Thomsen and his fellow scholars may have some hard – and very important – work cut out for them.

Henry Hansmann
Yale Law School
October 2022

CONTENTS

LIST OF CONTRIBUTORS

Eugenio Barcellona
Professor of Business Law, DIGSPES (Dipartimento di Giurisprudenza e Scienze Politiche, Economiche e Sociali), University of Eastern Piedmont, Italy

Ofer Eldar
Professor of Law, Economics & Finance, Duke University, United States

Rasmus Feldthusen
Professor, Ph.D., University of Copenhagen, Denmark, Faculty of Law, member of the Danish Committee on Foundation Governance (appointed by the Minister for Industry, Business and Financial Affairs) and chairman of the Foundation Law Committee (appointed by the Minister of Justice)

Dominique Jakob
Prof. Dr. iur., M.I.L. (Lund), Professor of Private Law and Director of the Center for Foundation Law at the University of Zurich, Independent Advisor, Switzerland

Susanne Kalss
Institute of Business Law, University of Economics and Business, Vienna (Austria), Professor, Dr. Dr. h.c., LL.M. (Florence), member of the board of foundations

Katarina Olsson
Professor, Faculty of Law, University of Lund, Sweden, member of the board of the Association of Swedish Foundations and member of the boards of several foundations

Anne Sanders
Chair for Civil law, Company law, the law of Family Businesses and Comparative Judicial Studies at the University of Bielefeld, Germany; Professor II at the University of Bergen, Norway

Steen Thomsen
Center for Corporate Governance, Copenhagen Business School, Denmark, and ECGI

ENTERPRISE FOUNDATION LAW

Introduction

Anne Sanders and Steen Thomsen

Enterprise foundations are foundations that own companies.[1] The term is not widely known, but many will recognize the names of companies like Bosch, Bertelsmann, Carlsberg, Hershey, Rolex, Investor and Tata Sons, which are owned by foundations or equivalent entities – Stiftungen, Trusts, Fonde, Stichtingen, etc. – whose names reflect their legal and national origins.

Although enterprise foundations have been around for more than a century, they have recently attracted attention as embodiments of the purpose-driven company advocated by Colin Mayer (2013, 2018),[2] the British Academy (2019),[3] the World Economic Forum (2020)[4] and others. Many enterprise foundations are non-profit organizations without a personal profit motive, which sets them apart from other corporations.[5] Instead, they are legally bound by their purpose, which is typically to secure the longevity and independence of the companies that they own

---

1 Previously used terms for enterprise foundations include industrial foundations, commercial foundations, Unternehmensträgerstiftungen, Unternehmensstiftungen, fondations actionnaires, erhvervsfonde, erhvervsdrivende fonde, business trusts and others.

2 Mayer, C. *Firm commitment: Why the corporation is failing us and how to restore trust in it*, Oxford: Oxford University Press 2013; Mayer, C. *Prosperity: Better business makes the greater good*, Oxford: Oxford University Press 2018.

3 British Academy, 2019. Principles for purposeful business, https://www.thebritishacademy.ac.uk/publications/policy-and-practice-for-purposeful-business/#:~:text=In%20November%202019%2C%20the%20British%20Academy%20produced%20a,where%20they%20perform%20important%20public%20functions.%20Weitere%20Elemente.

4 World Economic Forum. 2020. Davos Manifesto 2020: The Universal Purpose of a Company in the Fourth Industrial Revolution. World Economic Forum.

5 In family foundations the family members of the founder benefit from the profits of the foundation.

and to contribute to society through philanthropy. As perpetuities which cannot be dissolved, they are long-term business owners. However, not all enterprise foundations are equally altruistic. Some have strong ties to the founding family and continue to donate to family descendants. Others have ties to government organizations, cooperatives or associations which helped to establish them. This book aims to help explore and understand this fascinating diversity.

We know that enterprise foundation law differs greatly around the world. Very few countries have codified civil and tax law on the subject like Denmark. Some, such as until recently the US, have effectively banned them. Others, like Austria or Germany, seek to limit foundation involvement in the underlying businesses. The tax treatment of foundations also varies considerably. Enterprise foundation law therefore has to be constructed from various sources, including in particular foundation law and tax law. Clearly, there is much to be learned by mapping and analysing the diversity across countries.

This book explores enterprise foundation law in seven nations and analyses how the law influences the prevalence and governance of enterprise foundations around the world.

The first chapter, 'Foundation Ownership around the World' by Professor Steen Thomsen, Copenhagen Business School, introduces readers to the general topic and to what we know from the empirical literature. This introduction sets the stage for the following country chapters by defining the topic and providing some background information. The chapter introduces a functional definition of enterprise foundations as foundations which own companies. Foundations are independent legal entities, non-profits created by irrevocable donations, typically from the former business owners. They are governed by their charter and a foundation board. The formal purpose of foundations varies, but often combines a business purpose (being a responsible owner of a business) and philanthropic goals. In some cases (such as family foundations), foundations may also support the members of a founding family.

The chapter then provides descriptive information about enterprise foundations around the world, primarily focusing on listed companies on which there is better information. What are the largest enterprise foundations? Where are they most common?

Thomsen's chapter ends with a discussion of factors limiting or promoting the spread of enterprise foundations, including enterprise foundation governance, i.e. how the foundations are governed and how they exercise their business ownership. Who sits on the foundation boards?

How much stock do they own in the company? Who sits on the company board? What (if any) is the role of the founding family?

After this introduction, *authors from seven different legal systems* outline enterprise foundation law in each of the seven countries with an eye to answering the following questions:

- Does foundation allow enterprise foundations? If yes, with what qualifications?
- Are enterprise foundations commonly used? What are the reasons for their popularity or lack of it?
- What rules are in place regarding the purpose that a foundation must have? Does running an enterprise alone suffice as a purpose for a foundation?
- Does the law impose specific rules on foundation governance?
- Are enterprise foundations subject to supervision by a public body?
- To what extent are foundation enterprises favoured by the tax system?
- What challenges do enterprise foundation face?

In her chapter, Professor Anne Sanders from the University of Bielefeld discusses enterprise foundations in Germany. Enterprise foundations have a long history in Germany, with businesses like Zeiss, Bosch and Mahle either using foundations or their functional equivalents. The chapter describes their legal framework, organization and tax treatment. It takes into account how other legal forms outside foundation law, e.g. the limited company (GmbH), are used for the same purposes as foundations. Tax benefits are not limited to foundations. While a major reform legitimized all kinds of purposes for foundations in 2002, running and developing a business alone is not accepted as the purpose of a German foundation. Moreover, foundation law is still mainly regulated by the Länder, Germany's federal states. However, this is about to change. A major reform of foundation law is going to be passed into law. While the reform will make foundation law more transparent with the introduction of a centralized register and regulation in the German Civil Code, it is doubtful whether the new law should be regarded as a step forward for German enterprise foundations or a lost opportunity.

In her chapter, Professor Susanne Kalss from the Vienna University of Economics and Business discusses enterprise foundations in Austria, focusing on the Law on Private Foundations (Privatstiftungsgesetz) in Austria, which entered into force in 1993. There are about 2,500 enterprise foundations in Austria. The chapter describes the development of law of enterprise foundations, the considerations of the legislator and the main characteristics shaped by the leading decisions of the Supreme Court. The enterprise foundations are registered at the business register, which is operated by the Court. Austrian enterprise foundations are not subject to a permanent supervisory authority. The chapter analyses the flexibility of the legal framework, the layers of legal sources, the governance structure of the foundation and, in particular, the role and the legal position of the founder and the beneficiaries of the foundation. A significant part of the chapter is devoted to analysing the tools of influence and to change the charter of the foundation. The final section of the chapter describes the tax-treatment of enterprise foundations, which was previously quite generous, but is now more restrictive.

The chapter by Professor Dr Dominique Jakob from the University of Zurich covers enterprise foundations in Switzerland. Swiss foundation law follows a classical foundation model: any foundation purpose is permitted that is not contrary to law or morality and no 'special' foundation form is applicable to enterprise foundations. Therefore, enterprise/business foundations are 'normal'/classical private foundations under Swiss law without specific provisions. In practice, various forms of 'business-linked' foundations have developed, especially 'business operating' foundations (the foundation itself operates an economic business for its purpose) and 'holding foundations'. Among the latter, there are pure business foundations (foundation with the sole purpose of holding a business), pure charitable foundations (where the business is only an asset) and mixed foundations (that pursue a holding, a charitable and a family purpose).

The chapter describes the various models with their specific legal questions before going on to address current challenges, such as the admissibility of self-maintaining foundations, the scope of state supervision and how to deal with reduced flexibility. It also discusses how to deal with the unfriendly tax environment for charitable (tax-exempt) foundations with holding companies and the unclear situation for mission-based investments, impact investments and entrepreneurial grant-making schemes (by investments in companies). The general need for good 'foundation governance' and, in a family business context, 'family governance' is highlighted as a crucial success factor for enterprise foundations. The chapter concludes by looking to the future.

In her chapter, Professor Katarina Olsson from Lund University shows the reader that the story of enterprise foundations in Sweden is a remarkable one. In the early 1960s it was revealed that a majority of the large companies in Sweden were owned and controlled by 15 families, in many cases through foundation-structures. During the 1960s and 1970s, there were strong voices advocating against allowing enterprise foundations. The preparatory works to the current 1996 Foundations Act concluded that there should not be a ban on enterprise foundations in the Act. The Swedish definition of an enterprise is an entity which conducts activities of an economic nature with independence and a long duration. This is a very narrow definition compared to, for example, the wide Danish definition. There are many issues concerning enterprise foundations in Sweden that needs to be addressed. Sweden does not have a historical heritage of using the foundation form in connection with enterprises. There is also a general suspicion that foundations are used for money laundering and fraud. More research is needed, but so too is a political discussion on the values of foundations running and/or owning enterprises. Definite answers need to lift the purpose veil from the foundation and look for the real purpose behind the words.

Enterprise foundations in Denmark are then discussed by Professor Rasmus Feldthusen from Copenhagen University. The chapter describes the Danish legal regime of enterprise foundations which are governed by a separate act (The Enterprise Foundation Law). It starts by giving a brief historical overview of the emergence of enterprise foundations and the data on the prevalence and importance of enterprise foundations in Denmark. It then describes the special Danish legislation on enterprise foundations, including definitions, requirements, the allowance of an 'Unternehmens-Selbstzweckstiftung', typical ownership structures, hard and soft law governance rules, rules against perpetuities, the role of state supervision, rules on disclosure and transparency, enterprise foundation registry, etc. It concludes by discussing how industrial foundations are treated for tax purposes.

In his chapter, Professor Eugenio Barcellona from the University of Eastern Piedmont introduces the reader to the fascinating history and law of enterprise foundations in Italy. The Italian market is heavily characterized by family-owned enterprises whose long-term perspective, and the social and economic values that come with it, survive until the firm is sold to a foreign investor or its value is squandered by the founder's heirs fighting over it. Enterprise foundations are similar to family-owned firms from many perspectives – most of all, they are particularly suited to preserving the social and economic value of family-owned firms. One might expect Italy to be a fertile land for enterprise foundations; instead, they are a chimera.

The chapter analyses the legal regime of enterprise foundations in Italy from a historical perspective in order to explore the legal reasons behind the scarcity of enterprise foundations. Five historical moments that led to the current legal framework are analysed: (i) the original 1942 civil code regime; (ii) the legal scholarship shift in the 1960s following the adoption of the republican constitution; (iii) the introduction of banking foundations in the 1990s; (iv) the overhaul of the legal personality regime in 2000 and (v) the third sector reforms in 2017. The impact of the historical evolution on the purposes and governance structure of foundations is addressed, and family foundations are analysed as a special category. The chapter concludes by discussing how legal shortcomings and broader cultural traits have prevented enterprise foundations from thriving

In his chapter, Professor Ofer Eldar from the Duke University School of Law concludes the country reports in this volume with a discussion of enterprise foundations in the US. The chapter first explains the hurdles under US tax law for creating enterprise foundations, particularly taxes on excess business holdings and the unrelated business tax, which may explain why enterprise foundations are rare in the US. It also discusses the policy rationale against enterprise foundations.

The chapter then goes on to discuss the Hershey Trust as one of the few examples of an enterprise foundation and the recently adopted 'Paul Newman Law', which allows enterprise foundations under certain strict conditions. It then considers other alternative mechanisms for implementing a long-term business vision (dual-class stock, benefit corporations, perpetual purpose trusts), examining the advantages and limitations in each case. It concludes by discussing whether US law should be more permissive towards enterprise foundations.

A final, concluding chapter by Anne Sanders and Steen Thomsen compares enterprise foundation law in the seven nations. Although all countries permit enterprise foundations in some form, there are great differences in terms of the relevant civil and tax laws that influence their prevalence and governance.

This book extends the literature on business law beyond its normal focus on corporations. We are confident that this book will be essential reading for officers and directors of foundation-owned companies around the world, as well as for lawyers and government officials who work with enterprise foundations. We also hope that it will be read with interest by advocates and critics of company purpose, as well as by readers with a general interest in corporate governance. Hopefully, it will offer food for thought concerning the development of effective enterprise foundations not only for lawyers but also for legislators and regulators.

FOUNDATION OWNERSHIP AROUND THE WORLD

Steen THOMSEN*

ABSTRACT

A number of important companies around the world are owned by foundations known in the literature as enterprise foundations. In this chapter, we provide a tentative first impression of the extent of foundation ownership around the world by tapping into preliminary research results from an ongoing research project. We find that foundation-owned companies are rare at the global level, accounting for an estimated 0.6% of listed companies, 1.1% of global market capitalization and 0.002% of companies worldwide. However, in some European countries like Denmark, Sweden, the Netherlands and Luxembourg,

* Support from the Research Project on Long-Term Ownership and Value Creations in Enterprise Foundations is gratefully acknowledged. The project is funded by Copenhagen Business School and the Augustinus Foundation, the Carlsberg Foundation, the COWI Foundation, the Interogo Foundation, the Lauritzen Fonde, Leo Holding, the Lundbeck Foundation, the Rambøll Foundation and the William Demant Foundation. Paper prepared for SANDERS, A. and THOMSEN, S. 2022. *Enterprise Foundation Law in a Comparative Perspective*, Cambridge: Intersentia, 2023. Helpful comments and assistance by David Schröder are gratefully acknowledged.

they are economically very significant, in some cases (like notably Denmark) accounting for more than 60% of total market capitalization. The most obvious explanation for such national variations appears to be differences in regulation – for example, differences in foundation law and taxation.

1. INTRODUCTION

Enterprise foundations – also known as industrial foundations – are foundations that own companies. This ownership structure is not widely known, but some well-known companies around the world turn out to be foundation-owned (see below).

Figure 1. 20 Foundation-owned companies around the world

A.P. Møller-Mærsk – Denmark
Anheuser Busch Inbev – Belgium
Bertelsmann – Germany
Robert Bosch – Germany
CaixaBank – Spain
Carl Zeiss – Germany
Carlsberg – Denmark
The Guardian – UK
Hershey – USA
Inter IKEA – Switzerland
Investor (Wallenberg) – Sweden
Kavli – Norway
Kuehne + Nagel – Switzerland
Lloyd's Register – UK
Mahle – Germany
Norske Veritas (DNV GL) – Norway
Novo Nordisk – Denmark
Pierre Fabre – France
Rolex – Switzerland
Tata Sons – India

Source: Thomsen and Kavadis (2022).[1]

Many of these are remarkable companies: A.P. Møller-Mærsk is the world's largest container shipping company; Anheuser Busch Inbev is the world's

1 Thomsen, S. and Kavadis, N. 2022. 'Enterprise Foundations: Law, Taxation, Governance, and Performance', Annals of Corporate Governance: Vol. 6: No. 4, pp 227–333. http://dx.doi.org/10.1561/109.00000031.

largest brewer; Bertelsmann is one of the largest publishing companies in the world; Robert Bosch is one of the largest German manufacturing companies; Caixa in the largest retail bank in Spain; Investor is the holding company of the Swedish Wallenberg companies, the leading Swedish business Group; Tata Sons is the main holding company of the Tata Group, one of the largest and most admired Indian business groups; Inter IKEA is the franchisor of IKEA, while most IKEA stores are owned by the INGKA Foundation. Brand names like Rolex, Carlsberg, Carl Zeiss and *The Guardian* need no further introduction.

Enterprise foundations have ownership control over all these companies. For example, 51.7% of votes in the Danish shipping company A.P. Møller-Mærsk are owned by the A.P. Møller Foundation, which was created in 1953 by the Danish shipping magnate A.P. Møller to 'safeguard the long-term viability of the Group and control by the Mærsk family'.[2]

While enterprise foundations have been studied in Denmark[3] and Germany,[4] we know very little about their whereabouts in the rest of the world. A tentative first step towards an international overview was taken by Schröder,[5] who found that foundation ownership was particularly common in the Nordic countries (Denmark, Sweden, Norway and Finland), in the German-speaking Dach region (Germany, Austria and Switzerland) and (somewhat surprisingly) in India. As a share of market capitalization, he found that foundation owned companies account for about 40% in Denmark, 30% in Austria, 20% in Sweden, 10% in Norway, 5% in Germany and Switzerland and 5% in India.

In this chapter, we extend this work using the same data source for a global mapping of foundation-owned companies around the world. We begin by explaining what enterprise foundations are and then provide a tentative sketch of their global reach. We point to differences in foundation law and taxation as hypothetical explanations for the uneven distribution of foundation ownership around the world.

However, before we engage in this mapping exercise, we owe it to the reader to try to motivate the topic. Why bother with enterprise foundations?

A first, by now rather obvious, answer to this question is that a number of excellent companies around the world are foundation-owned.

---

2 Ibid.

3 Thomsen, S. 2017. *The Danish Industrial Foundations*. DJOEF Publishing.

4 Herrmann, M. and Franke, G. 2002. 'Performance and Policy of Foundation-owned Firms in Germany'. *European Financial Management* 8, 261–279.

5 Schröder, D.J. 2021. 'Publicly Listed Foundation-Owned Firms around the World: An Overview'. Unpublished working paper: https://www.enterprisefoundations.dk/wp-content/uploads/2021/11/Publicly-listed-FoFs-Descriptive-Paper-02112021.pdf.

These companies seem to make a difference to the world, and one wonders whether it is really a coincidence that so many distinct companies are owned by a very particular ownership structure, which few people have heard about before. Could it be that foundation ownership contributes to corporate excellence? If so, how can we have more of it? Certainly, a more comprehensive assessment of the strengths and weaknesses (or costs and benefits) of foundation ownership is warranted before we can jump to policy conclusions, so the objective here is merely to examine why it may be interesting to study this question a little more closely.

A second, closely related motivation is that foundation ownership is an alternative mode of capitalism based on non-profit rather than for-profit ownership.[6] Foundations are governed by a purpose rather than private profit incentives, and in most cases the purpose directly or indirectly obliges the foundation to be a responsible long-term owner. This resonates with recent calls for reform of companies by a corporate purpose[7] and more long-term governance,[8] in which foundation ownership is regarded as a prototype example of a purpose-driven company.[9] Thus, it may be worthwhile to consider foundation ownership as an alternative to conventional capitalist enterprises.

Third, there are other attractive features of foundation ownership which are worth thinking about and may catch the eyes of policy makers. Foundation-owned companies cannot be taken over by hostile raiders. They tend to treat their employees better.[10] Enterprise foundations reduce economic inequality by transferring concentrated private wealth to foundations which in most cases have a charitable purpose. They contribute

6 Non-profit is defined by Hansmann (Hansmann, H. 1980. 'The Role of Non-profit Enterprise'. *Yale Law Review* 89(5), 835–901) to mean that foundations do not have owners or other residual claimants. It does not mean that foundation cannot make a profit.

7 Edmans, A. 2020. *Grow the Pie*. Cambridge University Press; British Academy. 2018. 'Reforming Business for the 21st Century'; British Academy. 2019. 'Principles for Purposeful Business'; Business Roundtable. 2020. 'Statement on the Purpose of a Corporation': https://www.businessroundtable.org/business-roundtable-redefines-the-purpose-of-a-corporation-to-promote-an-economy-that-serves-all-americans; Henderson, R. 2020. *Reimagining Capitalism in a World on Fire*. New York: Public Affairs; Mayer, C. 2019. 'Ownership, Agency and Trusteeship'. European Corporate Governance Institute – Law Working Paper No. 488/2020, 11 December. Available at SSRN: https://ssrn.com/abstract=3522269; Mayer, C., 2020. 'The Future of the Corporation and the Economics of Purpose'. subsequently published in the *Journal of Management Studies*, 51(3) 2022.

8 European Commission. 2020. *Study on Directors' Duties and Sustainable Corporate Governance*. Final Report. Prepared by EY: https://doi.org/10.2838/472901.

9 Mayer, C., above n. 7.

10 Winther Børsting, C. and Thomsen, S. 2017. 'Foundation Ownership, Reputation, and Labour'. *Oxford Review of Economic Policy*. 33(2), 317–338.

funding for research and development (R&D), education, social projects and culture. At the same time, the evidence is that foundation-owned firms perform no worse than the other private firms financially.

Finally, while foundation ownership is rare at a global level, it is sufficiently important in some countries – notably Denmark – to be of national economic importance, and even where it is not – as in the US, the UK or Japan – the foundation model may attract attention as an example of steward ownership, which may be of interest for other long-terms owners like family businesses.

2. WHAT IS AN ENTERPRISE FOUNDATION?

The definition of enterprise foundations as 'foundations that own companies' calls for clarification. By a foundation, we mean an independent non-profit entity. 'Non-profit' in this context does not mean that enterprise foundations cannot make a profit, but that they have no residual claimants, i.e. owners or members.[11] Although the foundation may choose to donate part of its wealth to outside beneficiaries, they do not have a claim on donations. 'Independent' means that the foundation has its own funds and organization separate from the founders or other stakeholders. In particular, an enterprise foundation cannot be a government organization. Enterprise foundations are private entities that operate on market terms. Foundation-owned companies in turn are normal business companies that engage in commercial activities on market terms.

By 'foundation ownership', we mean that one or more foundations have controlling influence in a business company. The foundations do not have to own 100%. Many of the largest foundation-owned companies are publicly listed, as we shall see. But in order to qualify as enterprise foundations, the foundations have to have a controlling influence. It should be noted that controlling influence is focused on voting rights rather than capital shares or dividend rights, and that the definition is functional regardless of the purpose stated in the foundation charter, whether it is philanthropic or not. If a foundation has controlling influence in a business company, it is an enterprise foundation; if not, it is referred to as an ordinary foundation.

What ownership share is regarded as controlling depends on the circumstances – for example, how much other shareholders own or whether the foundation has a special say because of shareholder agreements. It may

11 Hansmann, H., above n. 6.

be practical for empirical analysis to set a minimum voting share (say 50%), but in most cases the foundation can exercise effective control with less than that (for example, with 20%). However, usually, the foundation would be required to be the largest shareholder before we talk about foundation ownership.

To supplement the functional definition – enterprise foundations are foundations that own companies – we identify the following key characteristics as part of an extended definition of a standard enterprise foundation:[12]

- Creation by donation (i.e. irrevocable separation from the founder). Once created, the founder cannot take back the donations; attempting to do so would be an act of theft.
- Independence (a separate legal personality for the foundation). Foundations have no owners. Once created, the founder cannot change the charter or instruct the foundation. Moreover, foundations cannot be dissolved except by government decree. In practice, founders or founding families may be able to exert significant informal influence, but the foundation board has the decision-making power and the responsibility.
- A non-selfish purpose (which goes beyond benefiting the founder). In enterprise foundations, the purpose will often, but not always, involve responsible, long-term ownership of a business company (i.e. a business purpose). Usually, but not always, there will also be a philanthropic purpose served by donations or operating activity.
- A foundation endowment, which includes shares in a company as well as sufficient funds to pay for administrative expenses and philanthropic donations.
- A foundation board of directors or trustees. There may also be an executive management function.
- A foundation charter (including foundation purpose and governance rules).
- Ownership (voting) control of a business company.
- Outside supervision, for example, by a foundation authority, a government organization or a private court.[13]

---

12 Cf. Kronke, Herbert. 1988. *Stiftungstypus und Unternehmensträgerstiftung.* J.C.B. Mohr; Thomsen, S. 1996. 'Foundation ownership and economic performance'. *Corporate Governance* 4, 212–221; Thomsen, S. and Kavadis, N., above n. 1. Ibid.

13 A detailed development of these characteristics can be found in Thomsen, S. and Kavadis, N., above n. 1.

We acknowledge that some enterprise foundations – like the Stichting Anheuser-Busch Inbev which owns the company of the same name or many of the Austrian private foundations – do not fit into this standard definition, although we have included them both in the book (see the chapter on Austria in this volume) and in the statistical overview below. We defined these entities as 'family foundations' since they can be owned, altered and sometimes dissolved by founding family members, and can therefore be considered to be a kind of extended family ownership.

3. DATA SOURCES

One reason why we know so little about enterprise foundations is that it is difficult to find information about them.

This chapter is based on hand-collected data, extrapolation and estimation. Since there is no global register of enterprise foundations or foundation-owned companies, in most cases (except in Denmark) data has to be hand-collected from a range of other sources. We have relatively good information about publicly listed companies which provide a useful, but imperfect starting point for the analysis given below. We also have some (but more limited) information about private companies, since some (but far from all) countries have publicly available company registers. Finally, we have very limited information about the enterprise foundations which are only systematically registered in one country (Denmark), while only a few countries register foundations at all.

We therefore map foundation ownership around the world first by mapping its prevalence among listed companies and second by reporting what we have found so far from studies of private companies in Europe.

4. THEORETICAL RATIONALE FOR FOUNDATION OWNERSHIP

Given the above characteristics, it seems worthwhile to briefly consider the theoretical rationale for foundation ownership compared to other kinds of private ownership.

Economic agency theory stresses the power of individual incentives, which are missing or muted in enterprise foundations and foundation-owned companies. Moreover, foundation-owned firms cannot diversify risk and attract equity capital when the foundation is reluctant to dilute its ownership and give up control to the same extent as investor-owned firms. Hence, according to agency theory,[14] we would under normal circumstances expect foundation-owned companies (non-profits) to underperform and be outcompeted by their more efficient for-profit rivals.

However, in some cases there may be economic as well as social value to ownership commitment, which foundation ownership can more credibly provide.[15] As long-term owners, enterprise foundations can enable companies to focus on the long term while avoiding financial short-termism and family succession issues.[16] Because they are less focused on profit seeking, foundation-owned companies may find it easier to gain the trust of their stakeholders.[17] For example, consumers may be more likely to buy from them because there are less fearful of exploitation.[18] Idealistic employees – and other stakeholders – may be more motivated to work for a company purpose than to maximize profits.[19]

In theory, there will be a rationale for enterprise foundations when the benefits of commitment exceed the incentive and financing costs of foundation ownership.

5. A GLOBAL PERSPECTIVE

As research on this topic continues, it seems likely that more and more cases of foundation ownership will be uncovered. Nonetheless, the data to which we currently have access seems to allow for some broad generalizations. In Table 1, we provide some tentative figures.

Globally, foundation ownership is rare. So far, we have found 237 listed foundation-owned firms around the world with a combined market capitalization of $1.459 billion (or about $1.4 trillion). This is about 0.5% of the world's listed companies (which total around 43,000)[20]

---

14 Fama, E.F. and Jensen, M.C. 1983. 'Agency Problems and Residual Claims. *Journal of Law and Economics* 26, 327–349.

15 Mayer, C., above n. 7.

16 Thomsen, S., Poulsen, T., Børsting, C. and Kuhn, J. 2018. 'Industrial Foundations as Long-Term Owners'. *Corporate Governance: An International Review* 26(3), 180–196.

17 Mayer, C., above n. 7.

18 Hansmann, H., above n. 6.

19 Henderson, R. and van den Steen, E. 2015. 'Why Do Firms Have "Purpose"? The Firm's Role as a Carrier of Identity and Reputation'. *American Economic Review* 105(5), 326–330.

20 The OECD counted 41.000 companies in 2019: https://www.oecd.org/corporate/who-are-the-owners-of-the-worlds-listed-companies-and-why-should-we-care.htm#:~:text=17%2F10%2F2019%20%E2%80%93%20There,to%20a%20new%20OECD%20report.

and a little more than 2% (2.1%) of global market capitalization of about $93 trillion at the end of 2019.[21]

Table 1. Foundation-owned companies around the world

	2019	% of total
Listed foundation-owned companies around the world	237	0.6%
Global market capitalization of listed foundation-owned companies ($ billions)	1,459	1.6%

Source: The Foundation Project (2022).[22]

This observation immediately raises the following question: if foundation ownership is so great, why is there so little of it? The answer[23] could be that foundation ownership requires founders to make the ultimate economic sacrifice – to give away all (or most of) their wealth to a foundation, a sacrifice very few people are willing to make, except in special circumstances like the absence of close relatives or very high tax rates on private wealth. This implies that foundation ownership is likely to be in permanently short supply, which constitutes a market failure in cases where it is the optimal ownership structure.

Another, less favourable explanation is that foundation ownership is not so great after all. The limited literature on the subject indicates that foundation-owned companies perform no differently than companies with other ownership structures – i.e. they neither systematically underperform or overperform financially.[24]

6. COUNTRY DISTRIBUTION

The geographical spread of foundation ownership around the world appears to be very uneven. In Table 2 we provide a country distribution of the 237 listed foundation-owned companies that we have been able to locate up to now.

---

21 World Federation of Exchanges (2021): https://www.marketsmedia.com/global-market-capitalisation-passed-100-trillion/#:~:text=In%20November%202020%2C%20global%20market,with%20the%20end%20of%202019.

22 The Foundation Project 2022: https://www.enterprisefoundations.dk/.

23 Thomsen, S. and Kavadis, N., above n. 1.

24 Thomsen, S., above n. 3.

The first observation is that foundation-owned companies and enterprise foundations can be found around the world, but usually in very small numbers, as noted above. Second, foundation-owned companies tend to be cluster in a few, mainly European countries. One-third of the 238 companies (34%) are from the Nordic countries (Denmark, Sweden, Norway, and Finland) and three-quarters are from Europe. Nevertheless, it is possible to find a few examples in many if not most countries around the world – in particular, India has quite a few (mainly Tata companies). As mentioned earlier, it seems likely that we will find many more examples as research in the area progresses.

Table 2. Country distribution of listed foundation-owned companies (2019)

Country	Firms	Market capitalization (US$ billion)	% of country market capitalization
Denmark	35	303.4	63.0%
Sweden	32	175.1	18.9%
India	27	127.5	6.1%
Germany	22	83.8	3.8%
Austria	17	36.7	26.1%
US	11	291.2	1.1%
Norway	9	24.0	7.9%
Spain	9	1.8	0.2%
Switzerland	8	97.3	5.0%
Netherlands	7	181.7	14.2%
Luxembourg	6	29.6	61.7%
Belgium	5	2.7	0.7%
Finland	5	9.7	3.0%
Italy	4	47.7	6.3%
Pakistan	3	0.0	0.0%
Poland	3	0.1	0.0%
Brazil	3	1.3	0.1%
China	3	4.2	0.1%
Chile	3	3.4	1.6%
UK	2	24.8	0.7%
Turkey	2	4.3	3.5%
Croatia	2	0.2	1.0%

(continued)

Table 2 *continued*

Country	Firms	Market capitalization (US$ billion)	% of country market capitalization
Bosnia	2	0.0	0.0%
France	1	1.0	0.0%
Romania	1	0.0	0.1%
Japan	1	0.3	0.0%
Bangladesh	1	1.1	3.1%
South Korea	1	0.0	0.0%
Malawi	1	0.0	0.0%
Bermuda	1	0.3	10.9%
Zambia	1	0.1	NA
Iran	1	0.0	0.0%
North Macedonia	1	0.0	0.0%
Ecuador	1	1.8	22.6%
Nigeria	1	0.2	0.7%
Peru	1	0.0	0.0%
Iceland	1	3.3	33.8%
Faroe Islands	1	0.2	NA
Montenegro	1	0.0	0.0%
Liechtenstein	1	1.1	NA
Total	237	1,459.8	2.4%

Sources: Euromonitor International, The World Bank, The Foundation project.[25]

In terms of market value, enterprise foundations appear to be most important in Denmark, Sweden, Austria, the Netherlands and Luxembourg.

7. PRIVATE FOUNDATION-OWNED COMPANIES

There are many more private (unlisted) than listed foundation-owned firms. Data collection for private foundation-owned firms is still ongoing, but Table 3 below gives an overview of the private foundation-owned firms that we have identified so far.

25 Euromonitor International 2022: https://www.euromonitor.com/; World Bank of Listed Domestic Companies 2022: https://data.worldbank.org/indicator/CM.MKT.LCAP.GD.ZS; The Foundation Project 2022: https://www.enterprisefoundations.dk/.

Table 3. Number of private foundation-owned firms and asset volume

	Firms	Asset volume (balanced panel) bill (€)								
Country	**2020**	**2012**	**2013**	**2014**	**2015**	**2016**	**2017**	**2018**	**2019**	**2020**
Austria	394	28.2	32.3	38.2	41.2	48.1	50.7	55.8	59.5	58.3
Germany	383	100.5	111.9	113.7	140.9	144.4	156.2	167	181.5	161.9
Finland	11	0.4	0.5	0.4	0.3	0.4	0.4	0.4	0.4	0.4
The Netherlands	414	33.8	36.2	36.2	39.6	52.8	66.2	74.4	83.2	79.3
Norway	39	2.5	4.2	4.5	4.6	5.5	5.5	6	6.5	6.5
Sweden	85	3.5	9.1	9.4	10.1	10.6	23.2	26.2	26.5	29
Denmark	721	32.8	36.0	38.7	73.1	67.3	78.0	75.6	80.9	81.5
Total	2,047	201.7	230.2	241.1	309.8	329.1	380.2	405.4	438.5	416.9

Source: The Foundation project.[26]

Compared with the number of listed companies in Table 2, these figures indicate that there are 17 times more private than listed foundation-owned companies in these countries, which have 120 listed foundation-owned companies compared to the 2,047 private foundation-owned companies identified in Table 3 (2,074/120 = 17).

We also note that asset volumes appear to be steadily increasing over time and in fact almost doubled over the period covered. The decline in 2020 may have been caused by the COVID-19 pandemic. However, the figures suffer from survival bias since we identified foundation-owned companies in 2019 and tracked them backwards in time, so the table does not account for companies which have exited during the period.

If the proportions are the same across the world, there should be 4,000+ foundation-owned companies globally and an estimated 2,500 enterprise foundations (see Table 4).[27] Although country sources seem to indicate much higher numbers, foundation ownership probably constitutes substantially less than 1% of the global total. Enterprise foundations also seem to be rare compared to philanthropic foundations. According

26 Ibid.

27 Since some foundations own many companies, we estimate there are fewer enterprise foundations than foundation-owned companies. On Danish data, the ratio of holding foundations (which own companies) to foundation-owned companies is about 400:720. If this ratio holds universally, it can be used to estimate the number of enterprise foundations for a given number of companies.

to the Global Philanthropy Report (2018),[28] there are about 260,000 philanthropic foundations worldwide, so 2,500 private foundation-owned companies account for less than 1% of all foundations worldwide.

Table 4. Estimated number of foundation-owned companies and enterprise foundations worldwide

	N	% of total	Total
Private foundation-owned companies in Europe	2,958	0.01%	22,400,000
Private foundation-owned companies worldwide	4,046	0.002%	213,609,000
Foundation-owned companies worldwide	4,284	0.002%	213,650,000
Enterprise foundations worldwide	2,448	0.8%	260,000

Sources: Foundation Project, Statista, OECD, Global Philanthropy Report.[29]

It should be noted that the proportion of private foundation-owned companies relative to the population of private companies seems to be lower than the proportion of listed foundation-owned companies compared to the number of listed companies globally. For example, the estimated number of foundation-owned companies in Europe is 2,958, which accounts for about 0.01% of the European Commission's estimated number of private companies in Europe (22.4 million). The share of the global proportion is even smaller (0.002%). Therefore, it would appear that foundation-owned companies tend to be larger and more frequently listed than companies with other ownership structures. An obvious explanation is that succession to foundation ownership tends to be more common for mature companies, but it is also possible that foundation-owned

28 Harvard Institute for Civil Society. 2018. 'Global Philanthropy Report': https://cpl.hks.harvard.edu/publications/global-philanthropy-report-perspectives-global-foundation-sector.

29 The Foundation Project 2022: https://www.enterprisefoundations.dk/; Statista. 2022. 'Estimated Number of Companies Worldwide from 2000 to 2020 (in Millions)': https://www.statista.com/statistics/1260686/global-companies/#:~:text=Number%20of%20companies%20worldwide%202000%2D2020&text=There%20were%20estimated%20to%20be,in%20the%20provided%20time%20period; OECD. 2022. 'Who are the Owners of the World's Listed Companies and Why Should We Care?' https://www.oecd.org/corporate/who-are-the-owners-of-the-worlds-listed-companies-and-why-should-we-care.htm#:~:text=17%2F10%2F2019%20%E2%80%93%20There,to%20a%20new%20OECD%20report; Harvard Institute for Civil Society. 2018; Global Philanthropy Report, above n. 28.

companies particularly benefit from additional stock market monitoring because foundations lack the strong incentives of private ownership.

Obviously, these numbers are very tentative and should be taken with a very large pinch of salt. Nevertheless, there is little doubt that foundation ownership and enterprise foundations are relatively rare phenomena at the global level.

8. REGULATION AS A CAUSE OF NATIONAL VARIATIONS IN FOUNDATION OWNERSHIP

The highly uneven distribution of foundation ownership around the world indicates that national characteristics strongly influence the spread of enterprise foundations.

An obvious hypothesis is that that the international differences are caused by (national) differences in regulation. Apparently, enterprise foundation law differs from company law, where legal scholars have identified a range of generic legal attributes that are common to most jurisdictions.[30]

Legality. Some countries have liberal foundation laws. For example, the Danish Enterprise Foundations Act allows 'free access to establish enterprise foundations with any kind of purpose', provided that the purpose is sufficiently well defined, legal and not contrary to common decency. In particular, running a particular kind of business or 'owning and ensuring the survival' of a company are legitimate purposes.[31]

Other nations have actively set up enterprise foundations though 'privatization privation to foundations.[32] The Italian government transferred more than 80 savings banks and credit institutions to newly established charitable foundations by the so-called Amato Act.[33]

---

30 Hopt, K. J. and von Hippel, T. (2010). Comparative Corporate Governance of Non-Profit Organizations. Cambridge University Press.

31 Thomsen, S. and Kavadis, N., above n. 1.

32 See Salamon, Lester M. (2014), 'Philanthropication thru Privatization: Building Permanent Assets for the Common Good'. Bologna: Il Mulino. Also available at: bit.ly/PtP_FinalReport. See also Megginson, William L. and Salamon, Lester M. (2018). 'How to Apply PtP to State-owned Enterprises Philanthropication thru Privatization Building permanent endowments for the common good', PtP How-To Booklet no. 2. East-West Management Institute.

33 Leardini, C., Rossi, G., and Moggi, S. (2014). Board Governance in Bank Foundations. Springer, Berlin.

However, a third group of countries – like Lithuania, Slovenia and (until recently) France – appear not to permit enterprise foundations at all[34] or, as in the Czech Republic, allow them only in exceptional circumstances.[35]

Taxation. It is perhaps no accident that foundation ownership is particularly prevalent in the Nordic countries, which have the highest wealth taxes in the world. Germany and Austria also have relatively high tax rates. This may have incentivized entrepreneurs to establish enterprise foundations to evade estate and capital gains taxes. In contrast, some countries, like the US, have effectively banned foundation ownership through the use of severe tax penalties.

Governance constraints. Foundation governance rules may also influence the formation and growth of enterprise foundations. Some countries, like Germany, require foundations to have purely charitable goals unless they want to be taxed as companies. Accordingly, German or French foundations are barred from active ownership of business companies, which could make them less efficient owners. Governance rules can also make foundation ownership more or less flexible. In some countries, like Denmark, charters can be changed (by so-called permutation), in other countries, this is virtually impossible. In some countries, foundations are mainly regulated by the tax authorities (the US), while in others, they are regulated by a government agency (Denmark) or by the courts (the Netherlands). Finally, governance rules may make foundation ownership more or less attractive from a family business perspective. For example, in some countries, like Sweden, it is acceptable that the founding family occupies a majority of the board, while in others, like Denmark, it is not.

9. SOFT VARIABLES

It is also possible that cultural and political variables play a role in fostering enterprise foundations. For example, the Nordic countries are

---

34 Hopt, Klaus J., von Hippel, Thomas, Anheier, Helmut, Then, Volker, Ebke, Werner, Reimer, Ekkehard, and Vahlpahl, Tobias (2008). Feasibility study on a European foundation statute: final report. URL: http://www.ub.uni-heidelberg.de/archiv/18688. pp. 90–91.

35 Ibid.

characterized by high levels of trust and low levels of corruption, which may have facilitated the preponderance of enterprise foundations in this part of the world.

As a preliminary test of this hypothesis, we plot the proportion of foundation ownership (the share of market capitalization) against levels of trust and levels of corruption in Figures 2 and 3 below respectively. We observe a positive correlation which is also statistically significant in each case. In other words, countries with high levels of social trust and corruption control tend to have higher levels of foundation ownership. Social trust and corruption control tend to be mutually correlated and correlated with other factors like the rule of law, some of which are reported in the World Bank Governance Indicators. Therefore, it seems premature to explain foundation ownership with any particular indicator; instead, it may be preferable to regard them as expressions of 'good governance', 'social capital' or 'institutional quality'.

Figure 2. Corruption control and foundation ownership

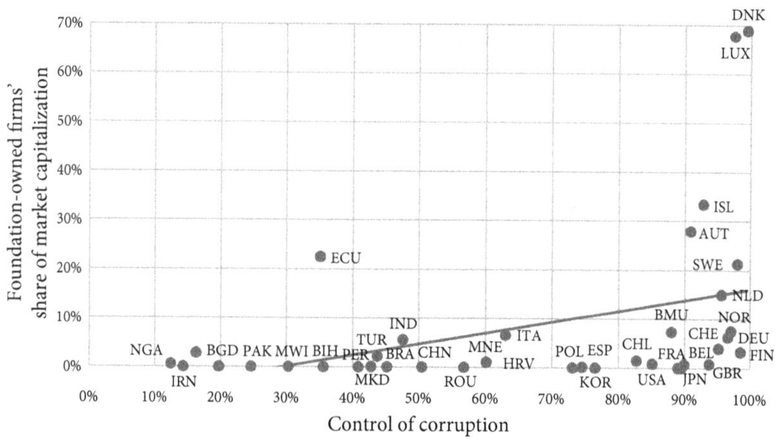

Source: World Bank – Worldwide Governance Indicators, The Foundation Project.[36]

[36] World Bank Corporate Governance Indicators. 2021. https://databank.worldbank.org/source/worldwide-governance-indicators; The Foundation Project 2022. https://www.enterprisefoundations.dk/.

Figure 3. Trust in public institutions and foundation ownership

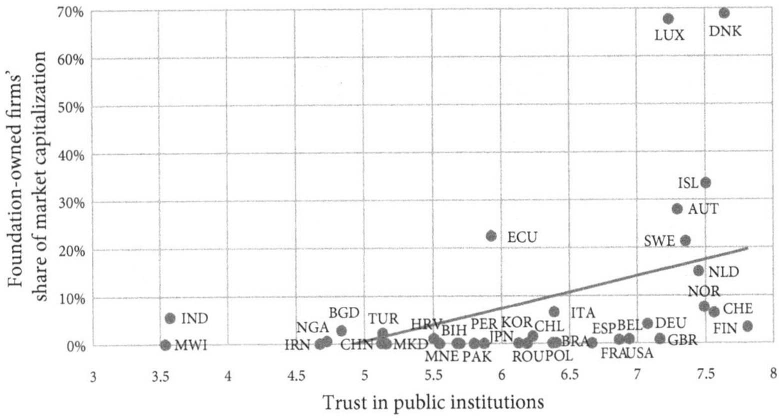

Sources: World Happiness Report, The Foundation Project.[37]

10. CONCLUSION

A number of important companies around the world are owned by foundations known as 'enterprise foundations'. In this chapter, we have provided a tentative first impression of their global reach. We found that foundation ownership is a rarity, accounting for only about 0.5% of listed company assets globally, although in some European countries like Denmark, Sweden and Belgium, they are economically very significant. The most obvious explanation of such national variations appears to be differences in regulation – for example, differences in foundation law and taxation.

We can particularly single out the following factors as hypothetical determinants of the legality of enterprise foundations around the world:

- Legality: in some countries (like, historically, France) it is illegal to illegal to establish enterprise foundations. In others (like the US) regulations exist that are specifically intended to limit foundation ownership.

[37] World Happiness Report. 2020: https://worldhappiness.report/; The Foundation Project. 2022: https://www.enterprisefoundations.dk/.

- Relative taxation of private wealth and foundation ownership: high taxation of private wealth which can be avoided by donating to foundations provides a powerful motive to establish them.
- Regulatory constraints: excessive regulation can deter founders and impede the efficient operation of enterprise foundations – for example, by preventing foundations from exercising active ownership or from adapting to new circumstances by charter changes.

ENTERPRISE FOUNDATIONS IN GERMANY

Anne SANDERS*

* I would like to express my gratitude to my research assistant Shkelqim Berisha for the inspiration and help he provided for this chapter.

ABSTRACT

This chapter discusses the history, terminology and legal framework of enterprise foundations in Germany. Despite its long tradition with enterprise foundations like Zeiss and Bosch, the legal framework is surprisingly complicated. While a major reform legitimized all kinds of purposes for foundations in 2002, running and developing a business alone is not accepted as the purpose of a German foundation. Moreover, foundation law is still mainly regulated by the Länder, Germany's federal states. However, this is about to change. A major reform of foundation law was passed into law on 16 July 2021[1] and will come into force on 1 July 2023. While the reform will make foundation law more transparent with the introduction of a centralized register and regulation in the German Civil Code, it is doubtful whether the new law is a big step forward for German enterprise foundations or – in part – a lost opportunity.

1. INTRODUCTION AND HISTORICAL CONSIDERATIONS

Enterprise foundations have a long history in Germany, with businesses like Zeiss, Bosch and Mahle either using foundations or their functional

[1] BGBl. 2021 I 2947. For an overview, see R. Hüttemann and P. Rawert, 'Das neue Bundesstiftungsrecht – Darstellung und Analyse sowie Vorschläge für notwendige Reformen der Landesstiftungsgesetze,' *Zeitschrift für Wirtschaftsrecht* (33) 2021, 3; B. Weitemeyer, 'Das Gesetz zur Vereinheitlichung des Stiftungsrechts – Zur Reform des Stiftungsrechts in Deutschland', *Zeitschrift für Erbrecht und Vermögensnachfolge* 2021, 54; K. Lorenz and J. Mehren, 'Das neue Stiftungsrecht ist da – Kernpunkte der gesetzlichen Neuregelungen und deren Bedeutung für bestehende und noch zu errichtende Stiftungen', *Deutsches Steuerrecht* 2021, 1774; M. Pruns, 'Ein Überblick über das neue Stiftungsrecht', *Zeitschrift für Steuer- und Erbrechtspraxis* 2021, 301; R. Werner, 'Der Regierungsentwurf eines Gesetzes zur Vereinheitlichung des Stiftungsrechts', *Zeitschrift für die gesamte erbrechtliche Praxis*, 2021, 482; S. Schauhoff and J. Mehren, 'Die Reform des Stiftungsrechts', *Neue Juristische Wochenschrift* 2021, 2993.

equivalents. This chapter discusses the legal framework of enterprise foundations.

This introduction will explain basic concepts and terms, the historical developments and importance of enterprise foundations, and the different structures used to organize them. Section 2 focuses on the legal framework after the 2021 reform, discussing the founding of enterprise foundations, their purpose, property, foundation governance and the future German foundation register. Section 3 provides a very brief overview of tax treatment. Section 4 summarizes regulatory challenges such as the need to further develop foundation governance and the new movement of steward ownership.

1.1. INTRODUCTION: THE FOUNDATION UNDER GERMAN LAW

Foundations are formed to dedicate property to the pursuit of a long-term goal. Under German law, a number different legal forms such as trusts and companies are used for such purposes, which will be discussed in detail in section 1.3 below. However, at the centre of this discussion is the legal foundation (rechtsfähige Stiftung des bürgerlichen Rechts) regulated in §§80 et seq. of the German Civil Code (Bürgerliches Gesetzbuch (BGB)). As of 31 December 2020, there were a total of 23,876 legal foundations in Germany, 92% of which pursued charitable purposes.[2]

Foundations are legal persons that may hold rights, conclude contracts and be liable in tort and contract. Such foundations do not have shareholders or members with the right to decide its fate but only directors with the power to act for the foundation in order to pursue its purpose. A foundation's legal objective or purpose must be prescribed by its founder, which – at least in principle – cannot be changed later on.[3] The foundation authority (Stiftungsaufsicht) oversees the realization of this purpose. Foundations are founded by a unilateral declaration of the founder (Stiftungsgeschäft) and the formal recognition (Anerkennung) of the respective foundation authority.

For the first commentary of the new law, see M. Orth and M. Uhl, *Stiftungsrechtsreform 2021*, Dr. Otto Schmidt, Cologne 2021; K.J. Schiffer, M. Pruns and C.J. Schürrmann, *Die Reform des Stiftungsrechts*, Zerb Verlag, Bonn 2022.

2 See: https://www.stiftungen.org/stiftungen/zahlen-und-daten/statistiken.html.

3 See B. Weitemeyer in F.J. Säcker, R. Rixecker, H. Oetker and B. Limperg (eds), *Münchener Kommentar zum BGB*, 9th ed., C.H. Beck, Munich 2021; BGB §80 para. 2.

Foundations running businesses, so-called enterprise foundations, have a long tradition in Germany.[4] Today, they usually do not run enterprises directly, but hold the shares of companies.

1.2. HISTORICAL DEVELOPMENT

There is a long history of charitable foundations in Germany, which, often provided services to fulfil their mission, for example a hospital. However, the history of foundations holding and running enterprises started later. In 1889 the Carl-Zeiss Foundation was founded, which ran the Schott and Zeiss enterprises and is still regarded as the archetype of the German enterprise foundation.[5]

From the start, the federal structure of Germany state had a significant influence on the regulation of foundations.[6] Even after the unification of German civil law under the BGB in 1900, the foundation largely depended on the foundation laws of the federal states (Landesstiftungsgesetze).[7] While the declaration to found a foundation, its representation by its directors, the change of its purpose and the legal effect of its dissolution were regulated in the BGB from the start, the prerequisites of the formal recognition by the respective authorities were regulated by the laws of the federal states. The BGB did not make any demands in relation to the purposes being pursued, but left that crucial function to the federal states. However, the draftsmen of the BGB agreed that the long-term pursuit of a special purpose required public permission of some kind.[8]

---

4 S. Thomsen, *Industrial Foundations*, DjOfs Publishing, Copenhagen 2017, pp. 85–90; on the development of corporate foundations in Germany since the 19th century, see H. Berndt, *Stiftung und Unternehmen*, 5th ed., Nwb Verlag, Berlin 1995, pp. 285–317.

5 D. Jakob, *Schutz der Stiftung*, Mohr Siebeck, Tübingen 2006, p. 17; see also H. Fleisch, 'Unternehmensverbundene Stiftungen', *Stiftung&Sponsoring* Rote Seiten (4) 2018, 2.

6 For a historical overview, see R. Hüttemann and P. Rawert in J. von Staudingers, *Kommentar zum Bürgerlichen Gesetzbuch*, Sellier/de Gruyter, Berlin 2017; BGB Vorbem. zu §§80 et seq., para. 61 et seq.

7 For more details, see R. Hüttemann, A. Richter and B. Weitemeyer, *Landesstiftungsrecht*, Dr. Otto Schmidt, Cologne 2006.

8 B. Mugdan, *Die gesamten Materialien zum Bürgerlichen Gesetzbuch für das Deutsche Reich*, vol. I, 1899, p. 961; R. Hüttemann and P. Rawert, above n. 6; BGB Vorbem. zu §§80 et seq., para. 71.

At the beginning of the 20th century, foundations could only be founded for charitable purposes. Thus, a manual for laypeople in 1902 summarized the prerequisites of founding a foundation as follows:

> Sie setzt voraus: Erlaubten Stiftungszweck (Wohlthätigkeit, Förderung gemeinnütziger Bestrebungen, z.B. Wissenschaft, Kunst-Gewerbe); 2. Stiftungsakt (einseitige schriftliche Erklärung unter Lebenden oder Testament; 3. Vermögen, das für den Stiftungszweck dienen soll; 4. Genehmigung der Landesregierung.[9] [It requires: permissible foundation purpose (charity, support of a public beneficial purpose such as science or decorative art); 2. the declaration to found a foundation in writing or in a will; 3. foundation property to serve the foundation's purpose; 4. authorization by the government of the federal state].

While the draftsmen of the BGB believed in the need to control foundations and their purposes through the requirement of public acknowledgement, foundations and their private money for beneficial purposes were increasingly seen as an opportunity in the second half of the 20th century. In this context, other foundations that did not pursue a public benefit were also increasingly accepted.[10] At this time, the purpose of every permissible foundation was to be approved by the foundation authorities and the foundation law of the states. This could cause considerable differences and discussions as to the permissibility of different foundation purposes. For example, in the federal state of Baden-Württemberg, a foundation with the sole purpose of administrating a business was permissible in the 1980s. Moreover, the purpose of supporting members of a certain family was considered problematic as well. The federal state of North Rhine-Westphalia, for example, did not accept such foundations, so founders chose other federal states for their foundations.[11] In this context, enterprise

---

9 *Neuestes Gesetzbuch für den praktischen Gebrauch*, commented by A. Korn, F. Ebstein, A. Kurnicki, P. Plinzner, P. Schwarz and R. Haenschke, Verlag E Globig Berlin, 1902, pp. 13–14.

10 See D. Jakob, above n. 5, p. 13, p. 19; U. Burgard, 'Das neue Stiftungsprivatrecht', *Neue Zeitschrift für Gesellschaftsrecht* 2002, 699–700.

11 R. Hüttemann, 'Unternehmensnachfolge mit Stiftungen', *Der Betrieb* 2017, 591, 594; on the old practice, see B.-H. Hennerkes, K.J. Schiffer and M. Fuchs, 'Die unterschiedliche Behandlung der unternehmensverbundenen Familienstiftung in der Praxis der Stiftungsbehörden', *Betriebs Berater* 1995, 209.

foundations were also under discussion.[12] In this situation, the call for reform became louder and louder.[13]

A first unification was achieved in 2002[14] by the first federal foundation reform since 1900. In this reform, in section 80(2) BGB, federal law regulated foundation purposes for the first time.

> §80 (2) 1 Die Stiftung ist als rechtsfähig anzuerkennen, wenn [...] die dauernde und nachhaltige Erfüllung des Stiftungszwecks gesichert erscheint und der Stiftungszweck das Gemeinwohl nicht gefährdet. [§80 (2) 1 A foundation is to be recognised as having legal personality if (...) if the long-term and sustained achievement of the object of the foundation appears guaranteed and if the object of the foundation does not endanger the common good.][15]

With this reform, the BGB established a right to have a foundation acknowledged as long as its purpose did not violate the common good. The 'all-purpose foundation' ('gemeinwohlkonforme Allzweckstiftung') was now explicitly accepted by law.[16] It only requires that a foundation pursues a benefit that is not *harmful* to public benefit rather than beneficial. With this reform, the unclear legal situation in relation to a number of enterprise foundations was settled. The law sparked a 'boom' of new foundations, which became increasingly interesting for legal advisors as tools to organize succession within family businesses.

However, at least since 2014, a new reform of federal foundation law was debated.[17] For this purpose, a working group of federal and Länder representatives organized by the federal Ministry of Justice and Consumer Protection was established.[18] In late November 2016, it presented

---

12 H. Gummert in V. Beuthien, H. Gummert and M. Schöpflin (eds), *Münchener Handbuch des Gesellschaftsrechts*, vol. V, 5th ed. 2021, §81 para. 33–37. G. Schwarz, 'Die Stiftung als Instrument der mittelständischen Unternehmensnachfolge', *Betriebs Berater*, 2001, 2381; K.J. Schiffer, 'Die unternehmensverbundene Stiftung ist im Gerede', *Zeitschrift für Erbrecht und Vermögensnachfolge*, 1999, 424; P. Rawert, 'Der Einsatz der Stiftung zu stiftungsfremden Zwecken', *Zeitschrift für Erbrecht und Vermögensnachfolge*, 1999, 294.

13 See with further references D. Jakob, above n. 5, pp. 16–20.

14 BGBl. 2002 I 2634, in force since 1 September 2002.

15 Translation by a team of translators of Langenscheidt Langenscheidt's translation service: https://www.gesetze-im-internet.de/englisch_bgb/englisch_bgb.html#p0236.

16 BT-Drs- 14/8765, p. 9.

17 For an overview of the reform, see R. Hüttemann and P. Rawert, above n. 1, pp. 3–4.

18 Established by the 85. Konferenz der Justizministerinnen und Justizminister on 25 and 26 June 2014 and by the 198. Sitzung der Ständigen Konferenz der Innenminister und -senatoren der Länder on 11–13 June 2014.

far-reaching proposals.[19] After a hearing with scholars and practitioners, the working group presented a discussion draft on 27 February 2018.[20] The draft recommended a complete regulation of foundation law, but refrained from proposing the establishment of a national foundation register.

The draft was fiercely discussed and a group of the most eminent German foundation scholars even presented an alternative draft.[21] The following draft of the federal Ministry of Justice highlighted important aspects, especially the demand for a foundation registry,[22] but also considered some less convincing suggestions, especially some that would seriously limit the founder's freedom to design the foundation charter. Fortunately, the next governmental draft amended some important points.[23]

The federal reform was approved by the Federal Parliament (Bundestag) on 16 July 2021 and will come into force predominantly on 1 July 2023. It unifies foundation law and aligns federal law in the BGB with the law as commonly accepted by scholars and practitioners. However, it was not meant to change the law in a fundamental way. The opportunity for a more thorough reform was not taken. However, the new law brings improvements, especially a federal foundation register in 2026. While the reform did not address enterprise foundations directly, the reform is also of crucial importance for them and will be taken into account in the general discussion of the legal framework in section 2 below.

1.3. DIFFERENT KINDS OF 'FOUNDATIONS'

When discussing German foundations and especially enterprise foundations, the coverage should not be limited to the foundation that is a legal person, the rechtsfähige Stiftung. Other legal forms are also used

---

19 See: www.innenministerkonferenz.de/IMK/DE/termine/to-beschluesse/20161129-30.

20 https://www.innenministerkonferenz.de/IMK/DE/termine/to-beschluesse/2018-06-08_06/anlage-zu-top-46.pdf?__blob=publicationFile&v=2.

21 A. Arnold, U. Burgard, M. Droege, R. Hüttemann, D. Jakob, L. Leuschner, P. Rawert, G. Roth, S. Schauhoff, U. Segna and B. Weitemeyer, 'Professorenentwurf zur Stiftungsreform', *Zeitschrift für Wirtschaftsrecht*, (10) 2020, 3.

22 Referentenentwurf des Bundesministeriums der Justiz und für Verbraucherschutz, Entwurf eines Gesetzes zur Vereinheitlichung des Stiftungsrechts vom 28.09.2020 (RefE): https://www.bmj.de/SharedDocs/Gesetzgebungsverfahren/Dokumente/RefE_Stiftungsrecht.pdf;jsessionid=515B6D42BBED4A10BAE7B7003A94A630.2_cid324?__blob=publicationFile&v=2.

23 Gesetzesentwurf der Bundesregierung, Entwurf eines Gesetzes zur Vereinheitlichung des Stiftungsrechts vom 03.02.2021 (RegE): https://www.bmj.de/SharedDocs/Gesetzgebungsverfahren/Dokumente/RegE_Stiftungsrecht.pdf;jsessionid=515B6D42BBED4A10BAE7B7003A94A630.2_cid324?__blob=publicationFile&v=2.

to achieve the goal of dedicating property to a purpose, especially in the context of enterprise foundations.

1.3.1. The Foundation which is a Legal Person – Rechtsfähige Stiftung

The rechtsfähige Stiftung, the legal foundation regulated in §§80 et seq. BGB (§§80 et seq. BGB-new) has already been introduced. This chapter focuses on this form of foundation, but it should be kept in mind that the practice uses functional equivalents as well.

1.3.2. The Nichtrechtsfähige Stiftung/Fiduciary Foundation

Besides the rechtsfähige Stiftung, which is a legal person and is regulated in §§80 et seq. BGB, there is also the nichtrechtsfähige Stiftung, the fiduciary foundation. It is set up like a trust in a common law system by transferring property to a trustee who promises to administrate it for a certain purpose.[24] It is more flexible and can be set up much more quickly, but has no legal personality and thus lacks the durability many founders desire.

1.3.3. The Limited Liability Company (GmbH)

The German limited liability company, the Gesellschaft mit beschränkter Haftung (GmbH) is also used as a more flexible alternative to the foundation.[25] It is a company with legal personality and was introduced in Germany in 1892 as a cheaper, more flexible alternative to the Aktiengesellschaft (AG, stock company or stock corporation).[26] The GmbH allowed the owners of smaller businesses to exclude their personal liability by founding a company.[27] Today, the GmbH is much more popular than the AG, with 1,376,420 registered GmbHs and only 13,883 AGs on 1 January 2021.[28] The reasons for this popularity are the GmbH's flexibility,

---

24 A. Westebbe, *Die Stiftungstreuhand*, Nomos, Baden-Baden 1993; K.-H. Muscheler, 'Die unselbstständige Stiftung von Todes wegen und unter Lebenden', *Zeitschrift für die gesamte erbrechtliche Praxis* 2016, 358; V. Kuhn, 'Überblick über zivilrechtliche Grundlagen und ausgewählte Aspekte der Beratungspraxis', *Zeitschrift für Erbrecht und Vermögensnachfolge* 2020, 535.

25 H. Fleisch, above n. 5, p. 3.

26 For major characteristics in English, see M. Schulz and O. Wasmeier, *The Law of Business Organizations*, Springer, Berlin 2012, pp. 38–40.

27 M. Schulz and O. Wasmeier, above n. 26, pp. 4–5.

28 U. Kornblum, 'Bundesweite Rechtstatsachen zum Unternehmens- und Gesellschaftsrecht', *GmbH-Rundschau* 2021, 681.

which makes it useful for small businesses as well as a corporate subsidiary under a holding.[29]

The GmbH, just like the AG, is usually founded to pursue entrepreneurial purposes, but is open for other objectives as well. GmbHs pursuing charitable purposes are quite common and enjoy the same tax benefits as foundations.[30] In the event that a charitable purpose is pursued, tax benefits require that profits are not distributed to shareholders. This goal can be achieved by amendments to the articles of association. However, even the best legal design does not change the most important difference between a foundation and a company that must be taken into account: while a foundation is property with legal personality dedicated to a purpose, a company has shareholders who decide what it does. The articles of association can be changed at any time[31] and shareholders may liquidate the company and keep the proceeds for themselves, even if this means that tax benefits have to be repaid.

Nevertheless, GmbHs are often found in the context of enterprise foundations, whether as an alternative to a foundation, as in the case of Bosch, or to run a business with a foundation as its shareholder.

1.4. THE CONCEPT AND IMPORTANCE OF ENTERPRISE FOUNDATIONS

Before the introduction of a national, centralized foundation register in 2026, it is still difficult to assess the exact number of German enterprise foundations. However, it is assumed that about 700–2,000 out of the estimated 23,300 foundations in Germany may be described as enterprise foundations holding shares to enterprises worth more than €100 billion.[32]

---

29 J. Rosengarten, F. Burmeister and M. Klein, *The German Limited Liability Company*, 9th ed., C.H. Beck, Munich 2020, pp. 13–15.

30 See with further references A. Gilberg, 'Die gemeinnützige GmbH in der notariellen Praxis', *Rheinische Notar-Zeitschrift* 2020, 193; B. Weitemeyer, 'Fallstricke der gGmbH', *GmbH-Rundschau* 2021, 57.

31 See with further references A. Schlüter, *Stiftungsrecht zwischen Privatautonomie und Gemeinwohlbindung*, C.H. Beck, Munich 2004, pp. 266 et seq.

32 H. Fleisch, above n. 5, p. 4; J. Bothello et al. 'Families, Firms and Philanthrophy: Shareholder Foundation Responses to Competing Goals' in L. Roza, S. Bethmann, L. Meijs and G. von Schnurbein (eds), *Handbook on Corporate Foundations*, Springer, Berlin 2019, p. 73, give the number as 500–1,000. For examples, see G. Brandmüller and T. Klinger, *Unternehmensverbundene Stiftungen*, 4th ed., Erich Schmidt Verlag, Berlin 2014, pp. 26–30; H. Gummert in: V. Beuthien, H. Gummert and M. Schöpflin (eds), above n. 12, §81 para. 38; on the international significance

In Germany, founding an enterprise foundations is a well-known but rarely used option for organizing business succession of family businesses.[33] The reasons for this may be that founding a foundation is not that easy – practitioners usually recommend it only for larger enterprises. Moreover, entrepreneurs fear a lack of flexibility. However, the experiences of those businesses making the transfer seem to be positive.[34]

The reasons to choose a foundation as a tool to organize business succession include the wish to keep an enterprise independent, by supporting family members without actually making them holders of shares. A foundation as the main shareholder can also prevent shares from becoming smaller and smaller with the growth of the family. Moreover, the goal of supporting good causes can also be important.[35]

A number of different terms are used in the context of enterprise foundations,[36] which, although given in German, will be mentioned here. Though the terminology is not universal, the following terms are most commonly used:

Unternehmensverbundene Stiftung, which may be translated as 'a foundation which is connected to an enterprise', is the most common term used for different kinds of foundations relevant for this chapter and may be roughly translated as enterprise foundation.

Unternehmensträgerstiftung means a foundation which directly administrates a business.[37] The *Carl Zeiss Stiftung* was the most famous example of this kind of enterprise foundation. However, today, direct enterprise foundations have (almost) vanished. The reason for this is that the foundation regulated in the BGB is simply not designed to run a

---

of corporate foundations today, see L. Roza, S. Bethmann, L. Meijs and G. von Schnurbein (eds), *Handbook on Corporate Foundations*, Springer, Berlin 2019, pp. 85 et seq.

33 See M. Habersack in Stiftung Familienunternehmen (ed), *Stiftungsunternehmen in Deutschland*, Munich 2021; see also H. Fleisch, M. Eulerich, H. Krimmer, A. Schlüter and S. Stolte, *Modell unternehmensverbundene Stiftung*, Erich Schmidt Verlag, Berlin 2018; T. Dahlmanns, 'Errichtung einer rechtsfähigen Stiftung – zugleich Modell der Unternehmensnachfolge', *Rheinische Notar-Zeitschrift* 2020, 417; R. Hüttemann, 'Unternehmensnachfolge mit Stiftungen', *Der Betrieb* 2017, 591; J. Ihle, 'Stiftungen als Instrument der Unternehmens- und Vermögensnachfolge', *Rheinische Notar-Zeitschrift* 2009, 557 (part 1) and *Rheinische Notar-Zeitschrift* 2009, 621 (part 2).

34 H. Fleisch, above n. 5, p. 6.

35 See G. Brandmüller and T. Klinger, above n. 32, pp. 10–18; see also T. Dahlmanns, above n. 33, 417, 418–419.

36 See H. Gummert in V. Beuthien, H. Gummert and M. Schöpflin (eds), above n. 12, §81 para. 4.

37 G. Brandmüller and T. Klinger, above n. 32, p. 93; A. Godron in M. Feick (ed), *Stiftung als Nachfolgeinstrument*, C.H. Beck, Munich 2015, §32 para. 1.

business.[38] Among other reasons, its charter may only be changed with the approval of the foundation authority and it has no rules designed to secure the interests of creditors.

The *Beteiligungsträgerstiftung*,[39] which may be translated as 'holding foundation', is a foundation which holds shares of a company, usually a flexible GmbH, which runs a business. Today, this is the usual form of German enterprise foundations.[40] The company has its own management, and its articles of association may be changed easily to adjust the company to new challenges.

Sometimes, the term *Unternehmensstiftung* is also used in the discussion.[41] This term, which may be translated simply as 'enterprise foundation' or 'corporate foundation', is mostly used for a foundation founded by a company primarily as an instrument of corporate social responsibility, but that is not running a business or holding shares of a company.[42]

1.5. DIFFERENT ENTERPRISE FOUNDATIONS

Federal foundation law does not provide special rules on enterprise foundations. However, different motives and wishes of founders have motivated legal practitioners to develop a number of different types of enterprise foundations. Often, a founder chooses a foundation strategy if no family member or other potential successor is considered trustworthy or qualified enough to take over the business. However, the founding of an immortal legal person as the businesses owner is not enough to guarantee the survival of a business – motivated and competent people are irreplaceable.[43]

---

38 H. Fleisch, above n. 5, p. 3.

39 G. Brandmüller and T. Klinger, above n. 32, pp. 117–120.

40 D. Jakob and M. Uhl in B. Gsell, W. Krüger, S. Lorenz and C. Reymann (eds), *Beck-online.Großkommentar*, C.H. Beck, Munich 2020; BGB §80 para. 476.

41 For example, Geibel uses the term for all kinds of enterprise foundations: S. Geibel, 'Unternehmenstiftungen und Governance', in B. P. Paal, D. Poelzig and O. Fehrenbacher (eds), *Deutsches, Europäisches und Vergleichendes Wirtschaftsrecht – Festschrift für Werner F. Ebke zum 70. Geburtstag*, C.H. Beck, Munich 2021, pp. 251, 254.

42 M. Hoffmann-Becking, 'Unternehmensverbundene Stiftung zur Sicherung des Unternehmens', *Zeitschrift für das gesamte Handels- und Wirtschaftsrecht* 178 (2014), 491, 492.

43 R. Hüttemann, above n. 11, 591, 596–597.

1.5.1. *Charitable Enterprise Foundations*

Founders without a family may wish to keep their businesses independent and commit them to a long-term strategy. However, as will be discussed more fully below, according to the predominant view in the academic literature and foundation authorities, a foundation must have a purpose beyond the administration of a business. This – and possibly tax benefits – can be achieved by choosing a charitable purpose.[44] Founders may also wish to support their families through the foundation. Even a charitable foundation does not make this impossible. However, this kind of support does not go beyond a founder's grandchildren and is therefore not enough to guarantee long-term family security.[45]

1.5.2. *Family Enterprise Foundations*

Founders with the main goal of supporting their families may found a family foundation,[46] the purpose of which is to support a specific family or families.[47] Such a purpose is a valid foundation purpose under §80 (2) BGB (§82 (1) BGB-new version).

There are different ways to structure such a foundation. A foundation's beneficiaries do not have any rights against the foundation and no influence over either the foundation or the business, unless the founder explicitly provides so. This may be exactly what a founder who does not believe that the family could have a beneficial influence on the business wants. In this case, scholars assume that the true motivation for the founder may have been ensuring the long-term wellbeing of the enterprise rather than of the family.[48] However, it is also possible to assign considerable influence to family members.[49]

---

44 T. Dahlmanns, above n. 33, 417, 425–427.

45 A. Schlüter and S. Stolte, *Stiftungsrecht*, 3rd ed., C.H. Beck, Munich 2016, Chapter 7, para. 53.

46 See C. von Löwe, *Familienstiftung und Nachfolgegestaltung*, 2nd ed., C.H. Beck, Munich 2016; H. Gummert in V. Beuthien, H. Gummert and M. Schöpflin (eds), above n. 12, §80; R. Pauli, 'Die Familienstiftung', *Zeitschrift für das gesamte Familienrecht* 2012, 344; W. Blumers, 'Die Familienstiftung als Instrument der Nachfolgeregelung', *Deutsches Steuerrecht* 2012, 1.

47 G. Brandmüller and T. Klinger, above n. 32, part 6; T. Dahlmanns, above n. 33, 417, 424–425.

48 R. Hüttemann, above n. 11, 591, 595.

49 K.W. Lange, 'Sicherung des Familieneinflusses durch Stiftungen', in K. Lange and K. Windthorst (eds), *Sicherung des Familieneinflusses in Familienunternehmen*, Baden-Baden, Nomos 2017, pp. 95–115; C. von Oertzen and M. Reich, 'Family

1.5.3. *Double Foundations*

With a double foundation, a founder may combine the advantages of a charitable foundation and a family foundation.[50] The enterprise is administrated by a company, usually a GmbH because of its flexibility. The shares of this company are split between a charitable foundation and a family foundation. The family foundation receives shares with voting rights, while the charitable foundation receives shares with capital. In this way, family foundations pay less tax but retain influence over the business. Nevertheless, both foundations may receive an equal amount of dividends, or the family foundation may receive even higher dividends than the charitable foundation.

Usually, tax law is the reason for such constructions. However, other reasons might also be found, for example, the internationally known Robert Bosch enterprise, a producer of household appliances.[51] The enterprise is run by the Robert Bosch GmbH. Shares holding dividend rights are held by the Robert Bosch Stiftungs gGmbH, a charitable company, while the voting rights are held in a partnership whose shareholders change every seven years and include former managers and respected members of the community. This construction uses a GmbH and partnership instead of foundations and combines actual partners with voting rights and the long-term orientation of a foundation.[52]

1.5.4. *Foundations as a Liable Partner in a Limited Partnership*

The limited partnership (Kommanditgesellschaft (KG)) is very popular among family businesses. While the tax advantages that made this form attractive have gone, it still offers other benefits, such as a higher degree of confidentiality and great flexibility.[53]

Business Governance – Sicherstellung der DNA als Familienunternehmen bei von Familienstiftungen gehaltenen Unternehmen', *Deutsches Steuerrecht* 2017, 1118.

50 T. Dahlmanns, above n. 33, 427; J. Ihle, above n. 33, 621, 634 et seq.; B. Theuffel-Werhahn, 'Fallstricke bei der Gestaltung einer Doppelstiftung', *Zeitschrift für Stiftungs- und Vereinswesen* 2015, 201; V. Auwera, *Die Doppelstiftung*, Centaurus Verlag, Munich 2008, p. 51; A. Godron in M. Feick (ed), above n. 37, §32.

51 For the structure of the Bosch-group, the so called 'Bosch-Modell', see R. Kögel and D. Berg, 'Die Unternehmerverfassung des Hauses Bosch als Grundmodell der Doppelstiftung', *Zeitschrift für Familienunternehmen und Strategie* 2011, 13.

52 See R. Kögel and D. Berg, above n. 51, 13.

53 A. Sanders and S. Berisha, 'Der persönlich haftende Gesellschafter', *Neue Zeitschrift für Gesellschaftsrecht* 2020, 1290, 1298; regarding the advantages and disadvantages in addition J. Lieder in C. Bochmann, J. Scheller and J. Prütting (eds), *Münchener Handbuch des Gesellschaftsrechts* Vol. IX, 6th ed., C.H. Beck, Munich 2021, §3 para. 33–37.

A KG has at least one partner who is personally liable and at least one limited partner. While traditionally the liable partner was the senior partner running the business and other family members received limited positions, today, the liable partner is usually a limited company, a GmbH (GmbH & Co. KG). The shares of the GmbH are then held by the limited partners and every change among the partners needs to be replicated among the shareholders of the GmbH. In order to avoid such difficulties from arising, there are now constructions where the KG is the shareholder of the GmbH (Einheits-GmbH & Co. KG), a construction that is described as odd, but that is now accepted by jurisprudence.[54]

Another way to structure a business is to use a foundation as personally liable partner (Stiftung & Co. KG).[55] The KG then has an eternal liable partner whose members do not need to be kept aligned with that of the KG because a foundation has no members. While forbidden in Austria and Liechtenstein,[56] this construction (which is used, for example, by Lidl, a supermarket chain) is possible in Germany. It provides stability to a business while still involving the founder's family.[57] However, given current foundation law, which will be discussed in more detail below, such foundations must have a purpose going beyond acting merely as a liable partner.

2. THE LEGAL FRAMEWORK

Basic principles of German foundation law have already been explained in section 1 above. In this section, the legal framework will be discussed in more detail in light of the 2021 reform and its effects on enterprise foundations.

---

54 See B. Grunewald in I. Drescher, H. Fleischer and K. Schmidt, *Münchener Kommentar zum HGB*, 4th ed., C.H. Beck, Munich 2019, HGB §161 para. 99 et seq.; R. Werner, 'Die GmbH & Co. KG in der Form der Einheitsgesellschaft', *Deutsches Steuerrecht* 2006, 706; A. von Bonin, 'Die Einheits-GmbH & Co. KG in der notariellen Praxis', *Rheinische Notar-Zeitschrift* 2017, 1.

55 See U. Delp, *Die Stiftung & Co. KG*, R. v. Decker, Heidelberg 1991; P. Höfner-Byok, *Die Stiftung & Co. KG*, Peter Lang, Frankfurt am Main 1996; T. Dahlmanns, above n. 33, 417, 428–429; G. Brandmüller and T. Klinger, above n. 32, pp. 102–116.

56 See for the Austrian private foundation (*Privatstiftung*) §1 (2) nr. 1 of the Austrian law of the private foundation (PSG) and for the foundation in Liechtenstein Art. 552 §1 (2) s. 1 PGR, in detail: C. von Löwe, above n. 46, §8 para. 24 et seq. (for Austria) and §10 para. 19 et seq. (for Liechtenstein); B. Weitemeyer, above n. 1, 54, 56 argues in favour of a ban in Germany, which has not happened yet. However, see the legislative draft of the Green and Liberal Parties: BT-Drs. 13/9320, p. 3 and BT-Drs. 14/336, p. 2.

57 M. Pawlytta and P.A. Pfeiffer in M. Feick (ed), above n. 37, §31 para. 18; T. Dahlmanns, above n. 33, 417, 429.

2.1. THE FOUNDATION AND ITS PURPOSE

Since the BGB of 1900, the prerequisites for founding a foundation have not changed: there needs to be a declaration of a founder in writing to set up a foundation with a property to pursue a certain purpose. Then as now, the acknowledgement of a public body – the foundation authority – is necessary to bring the foundation into being. This has not changed as a result of the 2021 reform. However, for the first time, federal law now includes a definition in of the foundation in §80 (1) 1 BGB-new version:

> Die Stiftung ist eine mit einem Vermögen zur dauernden und nachhaltigen Erfüllung eines vom Stifter vorgegebenen Zwecks ausgestattete, mitgliederlose juristische Person. [A foundation is a legal person without members which has been provided with property for the perpetual and sustainable pursuit of a purpose set by the founder.]

The 2021 reform has not changed the commitment to the 'all-purpose foundation' in §80 (2) BGB (§82 s. 1 BGB-new version). The administration of the foundation's property was and still is not considered an appropriate purpose for a foundation. A purpose must not be self-serving, but must achieve a benefit for third parties (Verbot der Selbstzweckstiftung); a foundation must not be set up to support (only) the founder (Verbot der Stiftung für den Stifter).[58]

This principle is understood by the majority of scholars and practitioners to mean that a foundation may not be set up only to run and develop a business, because this purpose would be limited to the administration of the foundation's property (Verbot der Unternehmensselbstzweckstiftung).[59]

---

58 With further references, see B. Weitemeyer, above n. 3; BGB §80 para. 126–127.

59 P. Rawert, 'Die Selbstzweckstiftung oder: Vom Zwecklosen', in M. Fischer, R. Geck and W. Haarmann (eds), *Zivilrechtliches Ordnungsgefüge und Steuerrecht – Festschrift für Georg Crezelius zum 70. Geburtstag*, Dr. Otto Schmidt, Cologne 2018, pp. 87 et seq.; R. Hüttemann and P. Rawert, above n. 6, BGB §80 para. 9; B. Weitemeyer, above n. 3, BGB §80 para. 127; W. Backert in W. Hau and R. Poseck, *Beck'scher Online.Kommentar zum BGB*, 60th ed., CH Beck, Munich 2021, BGB §80 para. 6; S. Geibel, above n. 41, pp. 251, 254–255; D. Markworth, 'Der Entwurf eines Gesetzes zur Vereinheitlichung des Stiftungsrechts aus unternehmensrechtlicher Perspektive', *Neue Zeitschrift für Gesellschaftsrecht* 2021, 100, 107; A. Sanders, 'Vermögensbindung und „Verantwortungseigentum" im Entwurf einer GmbH mit gebundenem Vermögen', *Neue Zeitschrift für Gesellschaftsrecht*, 2021, 1573, 1577 with further references.

Therefore, under German law, foundations must be founded for another purpose, whether charitable or, for example, for the long-term support of a family.

This understanding has not always been accepted everywhere in Germany. Before the first federal foundation reform in 2002, the federal states were free to regulate foundations and their purposes. Therefore, in the 1980s, founding a foundation with the sole purpose of holding the shares of a business was acceptable in the federal state of Baden-Württemberg. In 1986, for example, the Wala Foundation was founded.[60] It holds the shares to two GmbHs: the Wala Heilmittel GmbH, which produces and distributes organic medicine, and Dr Hauschka, a well-known pioneer of organic cosmetics since 1935. The foundation's purpose reads as follows:[61]

> §2 (1) Es ist Aufgabe der Stiftung, der „WALA HEILMITTEL GMBH" und der „WALA Agrikultur GmbH" eine gedeihliche Entwicklung zu sichern. [Article 2 (1) The object of the Foundation is to safeguard the successful development of the company 'WALA HEILMITTEL GMBH' and 'WALA Agrikultur GmbH'.]

Today, it is unlikely that a foundation with this clear purpose of corporate preservation would be accepted.

While the prohibition of foundations with the sole purpose of managing businesses is discussed by academics, practitioners do not see it as a major obstacle, but simply combine other purposes, such as preserving the graves of the founders and supporting a family, with the purpose of managing the business in question.[62] Foundation authorities usually accept such constructions.[63] The founder may name preserving and developing the business as one of a number of purposes and may provide rules, including under which circumstances the business may be sold to and how much in dividends should be paid out to support other purposes (e.g. a charitable purpose).

However, there are different opinions in relation to how free the founder is in this respect. Some academics demand that the charitable

---

60 https://wala-stiftung.de/en.

61 See the articles of association: https://wala-stiftung.de/files/wala-stiftung/downloads/Satzung_Stiftung_EN.PDF.

62 According to A. Richter in A. Richter (ed), *Stiftungsrecht*, C.H. Beck, Munich 2019, §10 para. 134, it is a mere problem of finding the right phrasing to escape the prohibition of a (*Unternehmens-*)*selbstzweckstiftung*.

63 D. Jakob and M. Uhl, above n. 40, BGB §80 para. 483 point out that nowadays the regulatory practice is basically open-minded towards enterprise foundations.

purpose must always be first, otherwise the foundation may be classified as a 'verdeckte Selbstzweckstiftung' – a foundation which in reality pursues a forbidden purpose.[64] While foundation authorities have been rather lenient in relation to these, this could change any time.[65]

It might well be argued that the whole doctrine is not convincing.[66] There are considerable differences between foundations simply administering property without any interaction with the outside world and an enterprise providing goods or services to consumers. Such an enterprise necessarily interacts with the world not only because it provides employment to its employees, but also because every business that survives in the market pursuing a lawful objective offers something of value to society. Managing a business is not mere administration because it is always changing and developing, interacting with the market and society.

However, in the official governmental materials of the new law, the doctrine seems to have been reaffirmed, even if it was not included in the text of the law. In the material, the following explanation of the new legal definition of the foundation in §80 (1) 1 BGB-new version, the following sentence can be found:

> Aus dieser für die Stiftung typischen Verknüpfung von Zweck und Vermögen folgt, dass als Stiftungszweck nur ein solcher Zweck in Betracht kommt, der sich durch Nutzung eines Vermögens erfüllen lässt. Der Zweck einer Stiftung kann sich nicht in der Erhaltung des eigenen Vermögens erschöpfen. Auch wenn für die Erfüllung eines Zwecks die Nutzung eines Vermögens nicht erforderlich ist, wie etwa für die Übernahme der Komplementärstellung in einer Personenhandelsgesellschaft („Stiftung und Co. KG"), kann dieser Zweck nicht in der Rechtsform der Stiftung verfolgt werden.[67] [This typical link between the foundation and its purpose means that only a purpose is acceptable that can be achieved by using property. Preserving the foundation's property is no

---

64 For more details, see B. Weitemeyer, above n. 3, BGB §80 para. 206; R. Hüttemann and P. Rawert, above n. 6; BGB Vorb. zu §§80 et seq. para. 225 et seq. Among the indications for this, see P. Rawert, above n. 59, pp. 87, 95–97.

65 R. Hüttemann, above n. 11, 591, 593; H. Fleisch, above n. 5, p. 5 argues in favour of long-term orientation of enterprise foundations in the interest of the German economy.

66 K.J. Schiffer and M. Pruns, 'Zum Lehrsatz vom Verbot der Selbstzweckstiftung', *Zeitschrift für Stiftungs- und Vereinswesen* 2012, 1; K.J. Schiffer and M. Pruns in T. Heidel, R. Hüsstege, H.-P. Mansel and U. Noack (eds), *Bürgerliches Gesetzbuch: BGB, Band 1: Allgemeiner Teil – EGBGB*, 4th ed., Nomos, Baden-Baden 2021, §80 para. 54; D. Markworth, above n. 59, 100, 107–108.

67 BT-Drucks 19/28173 p. 46.

sufficient purpose. Even if the property is not necessary to pursue the purpose as when a foundation takes on the position as a liable partner in a partnership, this purpose cannot be pursued with a foundation.]

This statement is discussed as possibly meaning that foundations acting as liable partners in a limited partnership (KG – see section 1.5.4 above) might not be accepted in the future either.[68] However, it is more convincing to assume that the legislator wanted to affirm that foundations may not be founded (only) to perform a certain function or administrate property.[69] However, such foundation constructions probably do not occur in practice in any case.[70] If the legislator had wished to ban foundations acting as liable partners, it would have been necessary to say so explicitly,[71] as is the case in Austria and Liechtenstein, for example.

2.2. DECLARATION TO FOUND A FOUNDATION: STIFTUNGSGESCHÄFT

Setting up a foundation requires the declaration of a founder in a special document (Stiftungsgeschäft unter Lebenden) or as part of a will (Stiftungsgeschäft von Todes wegen).[72] Part of this declaration is the first charter of the foundation. Practitioners and academics agree that the declaration requires careful drafting,[73] but there are relatively few minimum requirements: the founder needs to state at least the foundation's

---

68 See M. PRUNS, above n. 1, 301, 302; R. WERNER, above n. 1, 482–483; U. BURGARD, 'Anerkennungsvoraussetzungen und Grundlagenänderungen', *Zeitschrift für das Recht der Non Profit Organisationen* 2021, 78, 79.

69 D. MARKWORTH, above n. 59, 100, 107; K. LORENZ and J. MEHREN, above n. 1, 1774, 1775; M. FEICK and J. SCHWALM, 'Korrektur bei der Stiftungsreform – Gibt es noch ein happy End?', *Neue Zeitschrift für Gesellschaftsrecht* 2021, 525, 532; see also B. WEITEMEYER, above n. 3, BGB §81 para. 13.

70 F. SCHUCK and J. MEDINGER, 'Stiftungsreform in der entscheidenden Phase: Die geplanten Neuregelungen im Überblick für die Praxis', *Zeitschrift für Erbrecht und Vermögensnachfolge* 2021, 298, 299; K. LORENZ and J. MEHREN, above n. 1, 1774, 1775.

71 So also U. BURGARD, 'Die Kritik an dem Referentenentwurf eines Gesetzes zur Vereinheitlichung des Stiftungsrechts im Überblick mit Fallstudien', *Zeitschrift für das Recht der Non Profit Organisationen* 2021, 1; G. PONATH and G. TOLKSDORF, 'Was lange währt, wird nicht immer gut: Diskussionsfelder des neuen Stiftungsrechts', *Zeitschrift für Erbrecht und Vermögensnachfolge* 2021, 605, 606.

72 In detail, see C. STUMPF in A. RICHTER (ed), above n. 62, §4; T. DAHLMANNS, above n. 33, 417, 421.

73 J. IHLE, above n. 33, 557, 568; S. SCHAUHOFF and J. MEHREN, above n. 1, 2993, 2995.

purpose and the property the foundation shall receive to pursue its purpose. Moreover, the founder needs to make provision for the appointment of the first director of the foundation and where the foundation should have its seat.[74]

According to the old and new laws, the declaration needs to be in writing. However, there was a dispute before the reform over whether the declaration required another form (for example, notarization) in certain cases.[75] A number of different assets (e.g. land and shares of a GmbHs) require notarization both for their transfer and to create enforceable legal claims for their transfer (§311b BGB and §15(4) Act on the private limited company, GmbHG). Therefore, before the 2021 reform, there was a discussion as to whether the declaration of the founder required notarization if the founder wanted the foundation to receive assets such as land or shares of a GmbH. For an enterprise foundation, which usually holds share to a GmbHs in Germany, this question was of crucial importance. A 2020 decision of the Higher Regional Court of Cologne (OLG Köln)[76] held that notarization was indeed also necessary for the declaration of the founder and not only for the transfer of the property to the foundation (on this, see §82 BGB/§82a BGB-new version).[77] Now, this question is resolved.[78] According to the official explanation of §81 (3) BGB-new version, writing is enough.[79]

74 With examples: G. Brandmüller and T. Klinger, above n. 32, pp. 34–41.

75 For a detailed discussion, see K.W. Lange in B. Gsell, W. Krüger, S. Lorenz and C. Reymann (eds), *Beck-online.Großkommentar*, C.H. Beck, Munich 2022, BGB §81 para. 8 et seq.; R. Hüttemann and P. Rawert above n. 6, BGB §81 para. 16.

76 Higher Regional Court of Cologne, 5 August 2019, *Zeitschrift für Erbrecht und Vermögensnachfolge* 2019, 729. For an account that agrees with this, see J. Schwake in V. Beuthien, H. Gummert and M. Schöpflin (eds), above n. 12, §79 para. 146; T. Wachter, 'Stiftungsgründung mit Einbringung eines Grundstücks bedarf der notariellen Beurkundung', *Betriebs-Berater* 2019, 2705, 2706. For a critical view of this decision, see J. Schwalm and M. Thiele, 'Die Form des Stiftungsgeschäfts unter Lebenden: Ausnahmsloser "Vorrang" des §81 Abs. 1 S. 1 BGB', *Zeitschrift für Erbrecht und Vermögensnachfolge* 2020, 523, 525 et seq.; R. Werner, 'Formbedürftigkeit der Übertragung von Immobilien und GmbH-Geschäftsanteilen im Rahmen der Stiftungseinrichtung?', *Zeitschrift für Steuer- und Erbrechtspraxis* 2021, 131; M. Pruns, 'Notarielle Form des Stiftungsgeschäfts bei Zusicherung von Immobilienvermögen?', *Zeitschrift für die gesamte erbrechtliche Praxis* 2020, 163.

77 See R. Hüttemann and P. Rawert above n. 6, BGB §81 para. 17.

78 R. Werner, above n. 1, 2021, 482, 483; R. Hüttemann and P. Rawert, above n. 1, pp. 3, 9.

79 BT-Drs. 19/28173, p. 50.

2.3. FOUNDATION PROPERTY

Unlike many other legal systems, German company law still requires minimum capital for the founding of companies such as the GmbH[80] and the AG. However, there are no special capital requirements for founding a foundation, let alone an enterprise foundation.[81] §80 (2) BGB (§82 s. 1 BGB-new version) requires only that the long-term and sustained pursuit of the foundation's purpose must appear guaranteed.

The 2021 reform introduced in §§83b and 83c BGB-new version for the first time unified federal rules on foundation property and its administration. The new rules replace the legislation of the Länder on the federal level, defining different kinds of foundation property and its administration. The law now distinguishes clearly between basic property of the foundation (Grundstockvermögen), which must be preserved for the future, and 'other' property (sonstiges Vermögen) that may be spent pursuing the foundation's purpose. While most foundations have both kinds of property, there are foundations which only have 'other property'. These are foundations for consumption (Verbrauchsstiftung),[82] which are meant to spend all their assets.[83] For example, a foundation may be set up to renovate a church and given money to be spent completely until the church is renovated.

While a number of open questions remain,[84] the new law helps to clarify a number of problems. This means that the founder has to provide fewer rules on the foundation property in the foundation's charter.[85]

It is now officially allowed to redeploy the foundation's property and use the proceeds to pursue its purpose. While this position has been widely held by scholars and practitioners before, the new law offers more legal certainty. While the foundation's basic property (Grundstockvermögen) has to be retained in full, the legislator also allows more flexibility in the

---

80 In 2008, however, the legislator introduced a subform of the GmbH which can be founded with a minimum capital of EUR 1 (see §5a GmbHG).

81 B. Weitemeyer, above n. 3, BGB §80 para. 34; A. Schlüter and S. Stolte, above n. 45, Chapter 1 para. 50; J. Schwake, 'Zum Mindestkapital bei rechtsfähigen Stiftungen bürgerlichen Rechts', *Neue Zeitschrift für Gesellschaftsrecht* 2008, 248.

82 In detail, see B. Weitemeyer, above n. 3, BGB §80 para. 139 et seq.; J. Tielmann, 'Die Familienverbrauchsstiftung', *Neue Juristische Wochenschrift* 2013, 2934, 2935 et seq.

83 BT-Drs. 19/28173, p. 46.

84 See, for instance, U. Burgard, 'Nach der Reform ist vor der Reform', *GmbH-Rundschau* 2021, R244, R245.

85 BT-Drs. 19/28173, p. 47.

administration of foundation property in §83c (2) BGB-new version. A foundation may now tap into its basic property if it is planned that it will be replenished soon.[86]

2.4. FOUNDATION GOVERNANCE

Foundation governance is a topic of special importance for enterprise foundations.[87] A foundation has no members directing its path, but must pursue a theoretically unchanging purpose set by its founder. Thus, the foundation's purpose may be described as the most important guiding principle in foundation governance.[88]

The larger the foundation's property, the greater the risk that others – its directors, the founder's family and potential beneficiaries – will use it for their own goals rather than for the purpose of the foundation. Just like in company law, the necessity of proper governance mechanisms may be explained with the classical principal-agent theory, which sees economic actors as self-interested and possibly opportunistic.[89] Without members looking out for their interests and that of their legal entity, the foundation may be said to be 'helpless'[90] and in need for protection[91] from different

---

86 BT-Drs. 19/28173, p. 58.

87 In detail, see B. Schmidt-Schmiedebach, *Stiftung und Governance Kodex*, Springer, Wiesbaden 2015; D. Jakob, above n. 5, pp. 528 et seq.; U. Burgard, 'Foundation Governance', *Zeitschrift für Stiftungs- und Vereinswesen* 2015, 1. For details specifically concerning enterprise foundations, see H. Fleisch and S. Stolte in H. Fleisch, M. Eulerich, H. Krimmer, A. Schlüter and S. Stolte (eds), above n. 33, pp. 154–161; S. Geibel, above n. 41, p. 251.

88 S. Geibel, above n. 41, p. 251, pp. 253–254; H. Hof in A. Freiherr, V. Campenhausen and A. Richter, *Stiftungsrechts-Handbuch*, 4th Ed, C.H. Beck, Munich 2014, §7 para. 1; D. Jakob and M. Uhl, above n. 40, BGB §80 para. 112.

89 In the context of (enterprise) foundations in detail, see B. Schmidt-Schmiedebach, above n. 87, pp. 57 et seq.; S.J. Mühlbauer, *Stiftungsverbundene Unternehmen und Agency-Theorie*, Mohr Siebeck, Tübingen 2018, pp. 59 et seq.; K.W. Lange, 'Die Bedeutung institutionenökonomischer Erkenntnisse für das Verständnis von Herrschaft und Kontrolle in der Stiftung', *Archiv für die civilistische Praxis* 214 (2014), 511.

90 H. Liermann, *Handbuch des Stiftungsrechts*, J.C.B. Mohr (Paul Siebeck), Tübingen 1963, p. 281.

91 See the name of D. Jakob's book – *Schutz der Stiftung* (above n. 5) – which may be translated as 'protection of the foundation'; see also N. Thymm, *Das Kontrollproblem der Stiftung und die Rechtsstellung der Destinatäre*, Carl Heymanns, Cologne 2007, pp. 37 et seq., 79 et seq.

parties wishing to use the foundation's means for their own interests. It is the goal of foundation governance to supply this necessary protection.

2.4.1. Board

German law only requires that a foundation has a board with at least one director (Vorstand) who can act for the foundation (§§81 (1) 2 Nr. 5, 86 s. 1 and 26 BGB).[92] In the 2021 reform, there was no change to the required foundation governance or the number of required directors (§§81 (1) Nr. 1 lit. d) and 84 (1)–(2) BGB-new version). However, at least §84 (4) BGB-new version now clearly states that the founder may regulate additional bodies (for example, a supervisory board) in the charter.

However, there is now a small debate as to whether additional by-laws regulating the work of such bodies outside the charter are permissible because §84 (4) BGB-new version prescribes that the composition, duties and rights of such bodies must be set out in the charter.[93] Such by-laws are especially important for the work of enterprise foundations. Nevertheless, it may well be argued that such by-laws are permissible if the charter allows them. This was the practice until now[94] and should not be changed in the future.

The rules with respect to the foundation's directors used to refer to the law of associations (§86 BGB). After 2023, federal foundation law will provide its own rules in §§84–84c BGB-new version on the foundation's board and the basic rights and duties of its members. Some scholars have criticized this separation of foundation law from the law of associations with good reason.[95] Germany hosts an impressive number of associations,

92 B. Weitemeyer, above n. 3, BGB §86 para. 3.

93 Critical about this point: U. Burgard, above n. 84, R244, R245; A. Arnold, 'Teil 3: Die Rechtsstellung der Organe und das Stiftungsregister', *Zeitschrift für das Recht der Non Profit Organisationen* 2021, 84, 86.

94 With further references, see R. Hüttemann and P. Rawert, above n. 6, BGB §86 para. 66; J. Schwake in V. Beuthien, H. Gummert and M. Schöpflin (eds), above n. 12, §79 para. 369.

95 A. Arnold et al., above n. 21, pp. 3, 4; B. Weitemeyer, 'Professorenentwurf zur Stiftungsrechtsreform 2020', *Neue Zeitschrift für Gesellschaftsrecht* 2020, 569, 571; U. Burgard, 'Der Stand der Stiftungsrechtsreform nach dem Regierungsentwurf', *Zeitschrift für Stiftungs- und Vereinswesen* 2021, 45–46; K. Gollan and A. Richter, 'Der Referentenentwurf zur Stiftungsrechtsreform – So nicht, bitte!', *Zeitschrift für das Recht der Non Profit Organisationen* 2021, 29. For a different opinion, see D. Markworth, above n. 59, 100, 104.

but relatively few foundations. The greater number of associations results in more legal procedures and thus more case law clarifying open questions. With the separation of the law of associations and foundations, scholars and practitioners working on foundations may have to wait a long time before the courts have a chance to decide difficult questions.

According to the law, directors and other members of a foundation's governmental bodies work pro bono, unless the charter provides otherwise (§84a (1) 3 BGB-new). Moreover, the new law includes important rules as to the liability of foundation directors, clearly stating that their liability may be limited. According to §31a BGB, which is applicable to directors of an association as well as of a foundation, the liability of directors working pro bono is limited.[96] However, this rule may be excluded (§84a (3) BGB-new).

For directors of enterprise foundations, the new §84a (2) 2 BGB-new version is of special importance.[97] It establishes a business judgment rule similar to the one used in German company law (§93 (2) 1 Aktiengesetz). It states that directors do not violate their duties if they make a decision on the basis of appropriate information reasonably expecting to act for the benefit of the foundation.[98] Without such a rule, directors incur considerable risks, especially when making financial decisions for foundations with considerable wealth, especially enterprise foundations.

German law does not require that foundation boards be independent of their founders and their family members.[99] Founders or members of their families may even become directors of their own foundations.[100] Unless so

---

96 A. Sanders and S. Berisha, 'Die Haftung des fehlerhaft bestellten Stiftungsvorstands', *Zeitschrift für Stiftungs- und Vereinswesen* 2021, 50, 58–59 with further references; L. Leuschner, 'Das Haftungsprivileg der §§31 a, 31 b BGB', *Neue Zeitschrift für Gesellschaftsrecht* 2014, 281.

97 See A. Sanders and S. Berisha, above n. 96, 50, 56 et seq.; on the reform in detail, see K.U. Willy, 'Die Stiftungsreform 2021 – Überblick und haftungsrechtliche Fragestellungen', *Versicherungsrecht* 2022, 79, 80 et seq.; K. Uffmann, 'Haftung des Stiftungsvorstands – auch nach der geplanten Stiftungsreform herausfordernd', *Zeitschrift für Wirtschaftsrecht* 2021, 1251; P. Scholz, 'Vorstandshaftung in der Stiftung und Gesellschaftsrechtsdogmatik: Rezeption und Reflexion', *Zeitschrift für Wirtschaftsrecht* 2021, 1937.

98 BT-Drs. 19/28173, p. 61.

99 D. Jakob in V. Beuthien, H. Gummert and M. Schöpflin (eds), above n. 12, §119 para. 110.

100 U. Burgard, *Gestaltungsfreiheit im Stiftungsrecht*, Dr. Otto Schmidt, Cologne 2006, pp. 447 et seq.; T. Wernicke, 'Vorstandskontrolle in der Stiftung', *Zeitschrift für Erbrecht und Vermögensnachfolge* 2003, 301, 303; I. Saenger, 'Die Rolle des Stifters in der Binnenverfassungsstruktur von Stiftungen', *Zeitschrift für Stiftungs- und Vereinswesen* 2012, 94, 96.

provided in the charter, the founder has no position in the foundation, but remains an external force.[101]

2.4.2. The Foundation Authority (*Stiftungsaufsicht*)

German foundations are subject to the supervision of the supervisory authority of the respective federal state where the foundation has its seat. The work of the foundation authority is limited to legal supervision (Rechtsaufsicht),[102] which especially includes checking and approving changes to foundations' charters, rather than supervision with respect to the expedience of the board's actions. Therefore, the administration of a foundation's property, including a company of which a foundation may hold shares, is usually not reviewed by the foundation authority. However, this may be different, even though it is usually not the case in practice, if a company does not distribute enough profits to support a charitable foundation's purpose. After all, as explained above, according to German law, the foundation's purpose rather than the wellbeing of the enterprise must be its focus. While most foundation authorities do not enforce these principles in the same way, Rainer Hüttemann stresses that founders should not rely on this restraint.[103]

In many foundation laws of the Länder, legal supervision of foundations with a private rather than a charitable purpose, especially family foundations, is limited, as in North Rhine-Westphalia (§7 (4) Stiftungsgesetz NRW) or was completely abolished, as in Bavaria (Article 10 (1) Stiftungsgesetz Bayern).[104] The foundation authority may limit its supervision if the founder has installed an internal governance mechanism such as a supervisory board.[105]

There have been no studies on the foundation authority's effectiveness. However, anecdotal evidence suggests that practitioners have to wait

---

101 H. Hof in A. Freiherr, V. Campenhausen and A. Richter, above n. 88, §8 para. 99. On the role of the founder in the foundation in detail, see D. Jakob, above n. 5, pp. 103–166; I. Saenger, above n. 100, 94 with further references.

102 BVerwG 22.09.1972, BVerwGE 40, 347, 350; BGH 22 January 1987, BGHZ 99, 344, 348; on the preventive and repressive means of foundation supervision, see B. Weitemeyer, above n. 3, BGB §80 para. 68 et seq.

103 R. Hüttemann, above n. 11, 591, 594.

104 For critical accounts of this special treatment, see B. Weitemeyer, above n. 3, BGB §80 para. 197; R. Hüttemann and P. Rawert, above n. 6, BGB Vorb. zu §§80 et seq. para. 136–137 with further references.

105 J. Ihle, above n. 33, 557, 566; F. Rösner, *Die Konzernierung der Stiftung und ihr Einfluss auf die Pflichten des Stiftungsvorstands*, Nomos, Baden-Baden 2012, pp. 90 et seq; see also U. Burgard, above n. 100, p. 214.

several months for the approval of changes of foundation charters by the foundation authorities. This suggests a lack of human resources.[106]

While most practitioners do not see public supervision – where it exists – as a great obstacle,[107] there is agreement that public supervision is no substitute for bespoke governance within the foundation, especially in the case of family foundations.[108]

So far, a foundation's beneficiaries have no right to bring a claim against the foundation unless the charter explicitly provides for this. By law, there is also no third party who could enforce the foundation's claims effectively in the event that the board has no interest in doing so – for example, if the liability of board members is in question. In company law, shareholders have a right to bring such claims. In a foundation, which has no members or shareholders, other genuinely interested parties could be found who can bring such claims or can force the foundation authority to act. However, the 2021 reform denied the introduction of a 'actio pro fundatione' or legal rights for beneficiaries, as demanded, for example, by the 2020 scholarly draft.[109]

2.4.3. Additional Governance Bodies

As mentioned above, despite its practical importance, German federal foundation law only requires that the foundation has at least one director to act for it. Given the size and importance of many foundations, especially enterprise foundations, these requirements are highly limited and the supervisory authority is not enough to compensate for such limited foundation governance. This is especially true in the case of family foundations due to the very limited supervision exercised over them.

Therefore, both scholars and practitioners recommend bespoke governance concepts. It is possible to include directors with supervisory duties on the board so that they can check the actions of their colleagues.[110]

---

106 B. Schmidt-Schmiedebach, above n. 87, pp. 76–77; T. Dahlmanns, above n. 33, 417, 421.

107 S. Schauhoff, 'Stiftungen als Unternehmensträgerin' in Gesellschaftsrechtliche Vereinigung (ed), *Gesellschaftsrecht in der Diskussion 2018*, Dr. Otto Schmidt, Cologne 2019, p. 83, 90.

108 U. Burgard, above n. 87, 1, 3.

109 See §85 (3) of the scholarly draft; see also U. Burgard, above n. 95, 45, 47; B. Weitemeyer, above n. 3, BGB §85 para. 31 with further references.

110 U. Burgard, above n. 100, pp. 427–428; A. Godron in A. Richter (ed), above n. 62, §6 para. 105; I. Saenger, above n. 100, 94, 96.

Moreover, it is also possible to introduce additional bodies (for example, a supervisory board) to supervise a foundation's directors.[111] Such an additional body may have a strong position, like the supervisory board required by law in a stock corporation (AG), but it can also have merely advisory competences.[112] However, especially for large foundations, including enterprise foundations, a strong supervisory body is advisable.[113]

Besides advising and controlling directors, competences of the additional board may also include the selection, appointment, removal and evaluation of directors, and representing the foundation in interactions with the directors. It is also possible that a supervisory body has veto powers for certain transactions and a duty to organize the annual financial statement with the help of an accountant.[114] An additional board can also be invaluable in terms of helping to prevent and solve conflicts.[115] While the foundation authority is limited to legal supervision, a supervisory board should be qualified to and ready to provide competent advice on questions of expedience.[116]

In family foundations, family members often serve as members on an additional board.[117] However, such family influence should be balanced out with competent persons from outside the family. Since there are no rules concerning a foundation's governance, neither the family nor the foundation is necessarily well protected. In this context, it is important to bear in mind that supervisory authorities have almost completely withdrawn from the supervision of private-benefit foundations.[118] Therefore, such a board[119]

---

111 R. Hüttemann, 'Gemeinnützige Stiftungen in der Nachfolgeplanung', in C. von Bar, H. Hellwege, J. M. Mössner and N. Winkeljohann (eds), *Recht und Wirtschaft: Gedächtnisschrift für Malte Schindhelm*, Carl Heymanns, Cologne 2009, pp. 377, 384; J. Ihle, above n. 33, 557, 571; U. Burgard, above n. 100, pp. 267 et seq.

112 On the possibilities in detail, see U. Burgard, above n. 100, pp. 267–272; D. Jakob, above n. 5, pp. 232–239.

113 R. Hüttemann, above n. 111, p. 377, 384; A. Godron in A. Richter (ed), above n. 62, §6 para. 85–89 with further references.

114 See H. Hof in A. Freiherr, V. Campenhausen and A. Richter, above n. 88, §8 para. 51 et seq. on a possible combination of a board of directors and supervisory bodies – for different competences, see para. 80 et seq.; see also U. Burgard, above n. 100, pp. 267–268.

115 For instance: D. Jakob, above n. 5, p. 476 recommends a second body to avoid conflict; see also A. Godron in A. Richter (ed), above n. 62, §6 para. 86.

116 A. Godron in A. Richter (ed), above n. 62, §6 para. 88.

117 H. Gummert, above n. 12, §80 para. 38; C. von Oertzen and M. Reich, above n. 49, 1118, 1120–1123.

118 R. Hüttemann, above n. 11, 591, 595.

119 T. Wernicke, above n. 100, 301, 302.

should include beneficiaries, like family members, who have a vital interest in a foundation's administration, but also qualified experts with sufficient independence from the foundation's directors.[120] It is also possible to set up a family council exclusively composed of family members to complement a supervisory board of experts.[121]

2.5. CHANGING THE FOUNDATION'S CHARTER

A major reason not to found a foundation to organize business succession is the perceived inflexibility of foundations. According to the Allensbach/ BDO AG study[122] of 2015, 23% of family businesses could imagine using a foundation to organize succession, but only 1% actually chose it, due to a fear of inflexibility and bureaucracy.[123] While changes to the articles of association of a partnership or limited company require little or no formality, every change to a foundation's charter in principle needs to be approved by the foundation authority.[124] Such authorities have limited resources and are not always quick in responding. This is one of the reasons why a foundation itself is not an appropriate entity to hold a business, but better acts as a shareholder. Nevertheless, a change of a foundation's charter can be important.

Changes to a foundation's charter were an important point of discussion before the 2021 reform. Some scholars argued that founders should be able to change the charter during their lifetime.[125] However, the discussion

---

120 See H. Kronke, *Stiftungstypus und Unternehmerträgerstiftung*, Mohr Siebeck, Tübingen 1988, pp. 113 et seq., who sees the respective independence as the most important problem.

121 H. Gummert in V. Beuthien, H. Gummert and M. Schöpflin (eds), above n. 12, §80 para. 37; C. von Oertzen and M. Reich, above n. 49, 1118, 1121.

122 O. Bruttel, K. Schweinsberg and if D Allensbach in BDO AG Wirtschaft Sprüfungsgesellschaft (ed), *Nachfolgeregelung in großen Familienunternehmen: Option Stiftungslösung?*, Hamburg 2015, pp. 25, 30: https://www.bdo.de/getattachment/08e6288a-681f-4d74-a601-23f2608a51d6/attachment.aspx?disposition=attachment.

123 According to H. Fleisch, above n. 5, p. 6, in practice, experiences with enterprise foundations are positive.

124 B. Weitemeyer, above n. 3, BGB §85 para. 12; T. Dahlmanns, above n. 33, 417, 433.

125 See, for instance, with further references P. Rawert, 'Öffnung der Stiftung für körperschaftliche Strukturen? – Der noch lebende Stifter und die Verfassung "seiner" Stiftung' in R. Hüttemann, P. Rawert, K. Schmidt and B. Weitemeyer (eds), *Non-profit Law Yearbook 2012/2013*, Bucerius Law School Press, Hamburg 2013, pp. 51–61; D. Jakob, 'Freiheit durch Governance. Die Zukunft des Stiftungsrechts aus rechtsvergleichender Perspektive' in C. Bumke and A. Röthel (eds), *Autonomie*

draft of 2018 did not pursue this goal any further. The 2021 draft explained that such a right would violate the 'nature of the foundation',[126] which has no members constantly changing and adapting its course, but merely a purpose as its lodestar.

The new §§85, 85a BGB-new version establish a three-step approach with increasing prerequisites for changes of increasing importance.[127] The purpose of the foundation can only be changed in a fundamental way in the event that the purpose becomes impossible to pursue or threatens the common good (§85 (1) BGB-new). An adaption of the foundation's purpose and major changes to its organization are possible to align the foundation with new challenges and circumstances (§85 (2) BGB-new). Other changes can be made as long as they facilitate the pursuit of the foundation's purpose (§85 (3) BGB-new). Changes can be made by the board of directors or another body. The approval of the foundation authority is always necessary (§85a BGB-new).

The founder can establish different rules for changes in the original charter and even preclude all changes (§85 (4) BGB-new). If the founder wants to make changes easier, this is also possible. However, the founder must still give guidance in the original charter in relation to the content and extent of the changes. The more important such changes are, the more detailed the original charter should be.[128] No founder may give carte blanche to the board and it directors or other body of the foundation. Moreover, founders may not retain any right to change the charter themselves after the founding.[129] The charter is to be interpreted in light of the historical or hypothetical will (see also §83 (2) BGB-new version) rather than the actual will of the founder.

Therefore, a careful drafting of the foundation's original charter remains of crucial importance, especially for enterprise foundations.

---

im Recht, Mohr Siebeck, Tübingen 2017, pp. 225–246; B. Weitemeyer, 'Von der Stifterfreiheit zur Stiftungsautonomie. Weiterentwicklung oder Sackgasse?' in C. Bumke and A. Röthel (eds), *Autonomie im Recht*, Mohr Siebeck, Tübingen 2017, pp. 201–224. For a right of founders to change the foundation during their lifetime, see U. Burgard, above n. 100, pp. 370 et seq.

126 BT-Drs. 19/28173, pp. 30 f.

127 See in detail T. Schienke-Ohletz and R. Junius-Morawe, 'Möglichkeiten zur Satzungsänderung bei rechtsfähigen Stiftungen nach der Stiftungsrechtsreform', *Betriebs Berater* 2021, 1886; R. Hüttemann and P. Rawert, above n. 1, pp. 3, 23 et seq.

128 BT-Drs. 19/28173, p. 68.

129 BT-Drs. 19/28173, pp. 30 f.

2.6. THE FOUNDATION REGISTER

The 2021 reform finally included the introduction of a national foundation register in §§82b et seq. BGB-new version and a separate Foundation Register Act (Stiftungsregistergesetz (StiftRG)). The register requires much preparation and will start work on 1 January 2026. It will be administrated by the Bundesamt für Justiz[130] in Bonn.[131] All legal foundations need to register there. Foundations founded before 2026 can do so until 31 December 2026. The new law shall increase transparency and facilitate the work of foundation boards, liquidators and foundation authorities.[132] At the moment, persons acting for a foundation need to prove their power of representation with certificates issued by the respective foundation authority. After the introduction of the national registry, foundation authorities can stop issuing such certificates.[133]

Registration in the national register does not convey legal personhood to a foundation;[134] this still requires the approval of the respective foundation authority. However, the register legally protects parties relying on it (§82d BGB). Thus, the national register can help to increase the attractiveness of the foundation, and society's trust and acceptance of foundations.[135]

However, there is a point of discussion which is of special importance for enterprise foundations. According to §15 s. 1 StiftRG, everybody has the right to access the foundation register; there is no need to prove a special interest. This right of access also includes access to the documents on which the registration is based – among others, the original foundation and changed charters. Even a printed version may be requested (§15 s. 3 StiftRG). §15 s. 2 StiftRG provides that if there is a legitimate interest of the foundation or a third party (e.g. a founder or beneficiary), the possibility of inspection is limited (probably by making the relevant offices unidentifiable) or completely excluded.[136]

---

130 For a critical view on the constitutionality of the register, see J.A. Kämmerer and P. Rawert, 'Fallstricke des Stiftungsföderalismus', *Zeitschrift für das Recht der Non Profit Organisationen* 2020, 273, 275 et seq.; A. Arnold, above n. 93, 84, 88–89; D. Markworth, above n. 59, 100, 108; R. Hüttemann and P. Rawert, above n. 1, pp. 3, 37.

131 For the reasons, see BT-Drs. 19/28173, pp. 32 et seq., 81 et seq., 87 et seq.

132 BT-Drs. 19/28173, p. 81.

133 S. Stolte, 'Reform des Stiftungsrechts – Neuregelung zur Vermögensbewirtschaftung und Einführung eines öffentlichen Stiftungsregisters', *Betriebs Berater* 2021, 1026, 1028.

134 BT-Drs. 19/28173, p. 81.

135 See D. Markworth, above n. 59, 100, 108; M. Habersack, above n. 33, p. 95.

136 BT-Drs. 19/28173, p. 101.

Scholars and practitioners have criticized this broad right of access during the legislative process and continue to do so now,[137] especially with respect to family enterprise foundations.[138] In this respect, it must be taken into account that family enterprise foundations in particular often contain information about the beneficiaries and also about the company in the foundation statutes. It is true that §15 s. 2 StiftRG provides for possibilities of restriction. However, the concrete prerequisites are reserved for a separate regulation (see §19 Nr. 4 StiftRG). However, due to the broad right to inspect the foundation statutes and thus gain access to such information, the business foundation could lose some of its attractiveness as a succession model, especially for family businesses.[139] Of course, it will also depend on how high the requirements for the possibility of restriction will be. In any case, future founders will have to give more thought to what information should be apparent from the foundation statutes in future.[140]

The transparency of foundations is a sensitive topic indeed. In Germany, transparency has already been increased since 2017 by the transparency register (Transparenzregister) based on two European money laundering directives.[141] However, with the new right of access to the foundation register, the situation might now change again. It remains

---

137 See J. Schwalm, 'Stiftungsrechtsreform ante portas? – Kernbotschaften für die Stiftungspraxis', *Zeitschrift für Erbrecht und Vermögensnachfolge* 2021, 68, 73–74; M. Feick and J. Schwalm, above n. 69, 525, 529; D. Markworth, above n. 59, 100, 109; K. Lorenz and J. Mehren, above n. 1, 1774, 1779–1780; K. Lorenz and J. Mehren, 'Der Referentenentwurf zur Vereinheitlichung des Stiftungsrechts', *Deutsches Steuerrecht* 2020, 2547, 2557; K. Lorenz, 'Publizitätspflichten bei Familienunternehmen und Familienstiftungen – Neues von Gesetzgeber, Verwaltung und Rechtsprechung', *Die Unternehmensbesteuerung* 2021, 386, 392; S. Stolte, above n. 133, 1026, 1029; M. Habersack, above n. 33, p. 95. For even greater transparency, see A. Arnold, above n. 93, 84, 88–89; U. Burgard, above n. 95, 45, 49.

138 I am thankful to my research assistant Shkelqim Berisha for pointing out this problem to me. He is discussing it in his PhD in detail.

139 D. Markworth, above n. 59, 100, 109.

140 K. Lorenz, above n. 137, 386, 392.

141 See M. Jurawitz, *Das Transparenzregister*, Berliner Wissenschaft-Verlag, Berlin 2021; specifically concerning foundations, see J. Schwalm, 'Das Transparenzregister im stiftungsrechtlichen Kontext – Alte und neue Herausforderungen (auch) nach der GwG-Novelle', *Zeitschrift für Stiftungs- und Vereinswesen* 2020, 52; J. Kotzenberg and K. Lorenz, 'Bedeutung des Transparenzregisters für Stiftungen – Ein Zwischenbericht', *Zeitschrift für Stiftungs- und Vereinswesen* 2020, 29.

to be seen whether the legislator will change the law before the register comes into force or whether practitioners will find other ways to deal with this issue.

3. TAX TREATMENT

Tax treatment is a major aspect for anyone choosing a legal regime to organize a business, including a founder setting up an enterprise foundation. This is a vast topic which will only be briefly discussed here.[142]

It is important to note that a foundation does not enjoy any tax benefits simply because of its legal form. If a founder transfers property to a foundation, whether while alive or after their death, the foundation is usually liable to gift and inheritance tax. However, founding a charitable foundation (see section 1.5.1 above) can be privileged.[143] Charitable foundations receive the same tax benefits regarding the income they receive as charitable companies.

The family foundation (see section 1.5.2 above) is set up with the purpose of supporting the founder's family.[144] The legislator reasoned that such a foundation should not be used to dodge inheritance taxes for property still used to provide benefits to the founder's family. Therefore, a foundation set up for the benefit of a certain family needs to pay a special tax every 30 years (Erbersatzsteuer) according to §1 (1) nr. 4 Inheritance and gift tax Act (Erbschaft- und Schenkungsteuergesetz, ErbStG).

Double foundations (see section 1.5.3 above) are an example of how foundations are designed to avoid exceeding tax liability. Since the shares holding the capital of the respective company are transferred to the charitable foundation, the transfer is tax-privileged. Nevertheless, the

142 For more details, see A. RICHTER in A. RICHTER (ed), above n. 62, §10 para. 196–216; G. BRANDMÜLLER and T. KLINGER, above n. 32, part 4; T. DAHLMANNS, above n. 33, 417, 438–440.

143 See, for instance, §13 (1) Nr. 16 lit. a) ErbStG, §5 (1) Nr. 9 KStG, §10b (1a) EstG, §3 Nr. 6 GewStG and §3 (1) Nr. 3 b) GrStG. In all these norms, the foundation or a donation to the foundation is completely or predominantly privileged under tax law.

144 On the tax law treatment of the family foundation, see in particular A. RICHTER in A. RICHTER (ed), above n. 62, §11 para. 50–146; an overview is given in T. SCHIENKE-OHLETZ and J. MEHREN, 'Die inländische Familienstiftung – ein Steuersparmodell?', *Zeitschrift für Stiftungs- und Vereinswesen* 2022, 1.

founder's family may be supported by the dividends of the company paid to the family foundation.[145]

4. REFORM AND OUTLOOK

In this final section, current regulatory challenges shall be addressed. Section 4.1 addresses questions still left open after the 2021 reform. Section 4.2 provides brief coverage of the movement of steward ownership.

4.1. AFTER THE 2021 REFORM: GOVERNANCE

The 2021 law did not aim at fundamental reform. Therefore, it is necessary to identify regulatory challenges of the future. David Markworth's ideas are especially interesting in this respect.[146] He argues that the foundation's 'entrepreneurial role' should receive greater attention of the legislator.

In this context, foundation governance should be the focus of new legislative reform. The foundation authority is not qualified, nor does it have the necessary legal competence and resources to monitor enterprise foundations adequately. It is indeed possible that the future may bring special rules for enterprise foundations in this respect. At the moment, foundations do not fall under the same rules of co-determination as companies. It is possible that the legislator – dominated by a social democrat, green and liberal coalition – may change this in the future.

In a study on the importance and future of enterprise foundations as a means to organize business succession, Mathias Habersack demanded a mandatory supervisory board to improve the governance of enterprise foundations.[147] This suggestion to improve internal governance mechanisms deserves support.[148] The foundation authority is not equipped to provide competent and timely supervision. Therefore, additional tools of foundation governance are absolutely crucial. While the development of bespoke governance is now left exclusively to founders and their lawyers, the law should demand some basic provisions to secure a minimum level of effective and independent governance.

---

145 A. Godron in M. Feick (ed), above n. 37, §32 para. 75 et seq.

146 D. Markworth, above n. 59, 100.

147 M. Habersack, above n. 33, passim.

148 See S. Geibel, above n. 41, p. 251; see also D. Jakob and M. Uhl, above n. 40, BGB §80 para. 165 et seq.; U. Burgard, above n. 87, 1.

Another point deserving detailed discussion is the introduction of an 'actio pro fundatione', the right of certain third parties (in particular, beneficiaries) to bring claims for the foundation[149] and the suggestion to introduce a right to sue the foundation authority in the event of inaction.

4.2. STEWARD OWNERSHIP

Another future challenge may be the movement of so-called steward ownership – 'treuhänderisches Unternehmertum', 'Verantwortungseigentum' or 'Gesellschaft mit gebundenem Vermögen' in German. This is linked to the international purpose debate, criticism of shareholder value primacy and new legal forms such as the US benefit corporation and French société à mission. Steward ownership has developed a unique approach focusing on corporate structure and business ownership. Rather than combining the pursuit of a prescribed beneficial purpose with profits for shareholders as dual-purpose companies like the benefit corporation, steward owners lead and develop a business without having a right to its profits (the so-called asset or capital lock).[150] In this way, entrepreneurs wish to legally secure a long-term orientation of businesses and show their fundamental commitment to pursue purpose rather than shareholder value.

The so-called 'capital lock' is similar to a foundation. Therefore, under current German law, foundation structures are used to establish steward-owned businesses. Like directors of a foundation, steward owners are paid for their work, but do not receive dividends from the business. Profits shall be reinvested or kept for hard times. The major difference between steward-owned businesses and foundations is that steward owners have voting rights as members and thus constantly develop the business rather than focusing on a founder's foundation purpose that is different from that of the business.

The coalition agreement of the political parties that formed the German government elected in 2021[151] contains the promise to provide a new

---

149 See also §85 (3) of the scholarly draft; U. Burgard, above n. 95, 45, 47; D. Markworth, above n. 59, 100, 104; B. Weitemeyer, above n. 3, BGB §85 para. 31 with further references.

150 In detail, see A. Sanders, above n. 59, 1573.

151 'Mehr Fortschritt wagen – Bündnis für Freiheit, Gerechtigkeit und Nachhaltigkeit, Koalitionsvertrag 2021–2025 zwischen der Sozialdemokratischen Partei Deutschlands (SPD), Bündnis 90/Die Grünen und den Freien Demokraten (FDP)', 2021, p. 30: https://www.bundesregierung.de/resource/blob/974430/1990812/04221173eef9a6720059cc353d759a2b/2021-12-10-koav2021-data.pdf?download=1; see also T. Wachter, 'Zukunft des deutschen Erbschaftsteuerrechts: Der Koalitionsvertrag 2021–2025', *Der Betrieb* 2022, 284, 286.

legal basis for steward-owned businesses. A draft prepared by a group of scholars – among them the author of this chapter – was already prepared in 2020 and revised in 2021.[152] Some eminent foundation scholars in particular have criticized the concept and the idea of creating a hybrid between a foundation and a company.[153] However, some practitioners and scholars see the new legal form as an opportunity to found a more flexible alternative to a traditional foundation.[154]

---

152 A. Sanders, B. Dauner-Lieb, A. von Freeden, S. Kempny, F. Möslein and R. Veil, Entwurf eines Gesetzes für die Gesellschaft mit beschränkter Haftung mit gebundenem Vermögen, 2021. The draft with explanations in German can be downloaded from https://www.gesellschaft-mit-gebundenem-vermoegen.de/der-gesetzesentwurf); see also A. Sanders, B. Dauner-Lieb, S. Kempny, F. Möslein and R. Veil, 'Gesetzesentwurf GmbH mit gebundenem Vermögen – Verantwortungseigentum 2.0', *GmbH-Rundschau* 2021, 285; A. Sanders, above n. 59, 1573; S. Kempny and A. Sanders, 'Zum Entwurf einer GmbH mit gebundenem Vermögen', *NWB Steuer- und Wirtschaftsrecht* 2021, 3117; G.R. Rolfes and S. Berisha, 'Der Schutz der Gläubiger des Gesellschafters einer GmbH mit gebundenem Vermögen', *GmbH-Rundschau* 2022, 23; H. Fleischer, 'Ein Schönheitswettbewerb für eine neue Gesellschaftsform mit Nachhaltigkeitsbezug: Zur rechtspolitischen Diskussion um eine GmbH mit gebundenem Vermögen', *Zeitschrift für Wirtschaftsrecht* 2022, 345.

153 See, for instance, A. Arnold, U. Burgard, G. Roth and B. Weitemeyer, 'Die GmbH im Verantwortungseigentum – eine Kritik', *Neue Zeitschrift für Gesellschaftsrecht* 2020, 1321; R. Hüttemann, P. Rawert and B. Weitemeyer, 'Zauberwort "Verantwortungseigentum"', *Zeitschrift für das Recht der Non Profit Organisationen* 2020, 296; U. Burgard, 'Verantwortungseigentum in Stiftungsform de lege lata und de lege ferenda', *Zeitschrift für Stiftungs- und Vereinswesen* 2021, 1. See also B. Grunewald and J. Hennrichs, 'Die GmbH in Verantwortungseigentum, wäre das ein Fortschritt?', *Neue Zeitschrift für Gesellschaftsrecht* 2020, 1201; M. Habersack, '"Gesellschaft mit beschränkter Haftung in Verantwortungseigentum" – ein Fremdkörper im Recht der Körperschaften', *GmbH-Rundschau* 2020, 992; B. Weitemeyer, B.E. Weissenberger and G.T. Wiese, 'Eine GmbH mit ewigem Gewinnausschüttungsverbot – Bahnbrechende Innovation oder volkswirtschaftlich bedenkliche Perpetuierung?', *GmbH-Rundschau* 2021, 1069; K.-G. Loritz and P.S. Weinmann, 'Die GmbH mit gebundenem Vermögen – Kreative Idee oder Legitimation zum Betreiben eines Unternehmens ohne typische Unternehmerpflichten?', *Deutsches Steuerrecht* 2021, 2205.

154 See, for instance, H.-J. Fischer and K. Fischer, 'Die GmbH in Verantwortungseigentum (VE-GmbH) im Rahmen der Umsetzung globaler Nachhaltigkeitsziele – eine mögliche neue Rechtsform für den Mittelstand', *Betriebs Berater* 2020, 2122; H.-J. Fischer, 'Die GmbH mit gebundenem Vermögen als eine mögliche neue Rechtsform für den Mittelstand', *Betriebs Berater* 2021, 2114; W. Servatius, 'Verantwortungseigentum – in dubio Gesellschaftsrecht!', *Neue Zeitschrift für Gesellschaftsrecht* 2021, 569; M. Reiff, 'Entwurf eines Gesetzes für die GmbH in Verantwortungseigentum (VE-GmbH) vorgelegt', *Zeitschrift für Wirtschaftsrecht* 2020, 1750; A. Sanders, above n. 59, 1573; S. Kempny and A. Sanders, above n. 153, 3117; A. Sanders, 'Eine Gesellschaft in Verantwortungseigentum im GmbHG', *Zeitschrift für Rechtspolitik* 2020, 140.

While there will always be high demand for the traditional foundation, a new legal form for steward ownership may indeed offer interesting new options for a diverse economy.

4.3. CONCLUSION

In Germany, enterprise foundations hark back to a long tradition supported by scholars and practitioners. With the new foundation register, their numbers and economic importance will become even clearer. The 2021 law has clarified much and the new foundation register will increase transparency. This might increase trust in the foundation, but could also make it less attractive to founders who are anxious to protect their privacy. However, the 2021 law was not a real reform, but chiefly an update to the status quo. In particular, questions concerning foundation governance remain the responsibility of founders alone. Therefore, it is unlikely that the discussion will stop now. It also remains to be seen to what extent the discussion about a new legal form for steward ownership will have an impact on foundation law, especially with regard to enterprise foundations.

THE AUSTRIAN FOUNDATION

Susanne KALSS

ABSTRACT

In Austria two different types of foundations exist, mainly the Federal Foundation and the Austrian Foundation. The Austrian Foundation Act was set in force 30 years ago and allows foundations to hold shares and run and to be the head of a group of companies. This type of foundation plays a vital role in the Austrian economy. The law is quite liberal and these require a careful drafting of the legal framework.

1. LEGAL BASIS AND SIGNIFICANCE

1.1. THE FEDERAL FOUNDATION AND FUND ACT

Austrian foundation law is split into two parts and has two completely different legal bases.

On the one hand, there is the Federal Foundation under the Federal Foundation Act (Bundes-Stiftungs- und Fondsgesetz BStFG 2015).[1] The Federal Foundation Act applies exclusively to non-profit foundations. In addition, there are also nine provincial foundation acts, which also apply only to non-profit foundations. The provincial foundation acts apply to foundations that operate exclusively within the sphere of influence of a state (Bundesland). Non-profit foundations must have a non-profit purpose. The foundation is promoted to the public if it benefits the common good. The regulation is based on section 35 (2) of the Federal Fiscal Code (BAO).[2]

This type of foundation plays a minor role in Austria. About 700 foundations are organized exclusively as non-profit foundations under the Federal Foundation Act or one of the provincial foundation acts. They are subject to public supervision.[3] The supervisory system is similar to that of an association. At the same time, when a federal foundation is set up, the founder must submit a founding declaration and confirmation to the Vienna Tax Office, and there has to be a notice that the founding declaration meets the requirements for non-profit status.

1.2. THE AUSTRIAN FOUNDATION ACT

The second main legal basis for foundation law is the Austrian Foundation Act of 1993,[4] which has thus been in force for almost 30 years. This Act forms the legal basis for Austrian foundations. The purpose of the

1 BGBl I 2015/106; Paus/Haslwanter, Kommentar zum BStFG (2015); Melzer/Petritz, Die gemeinnützige Stiftung und der gemeinnützige Fonds (2015).
2 Kalss in Kalss/Nowotny/Schauer, Österreichisches Gesellschaftsrecht[2] (2017) Rz 7/8.
3 See for this Kalss in Kalss/Nowotny/Schauer, Österreichisches Gesellschaftsrecht[2] Rz 7/11.
4 BGBl 1993/694.

foundation is not limited to non-profit purposes; rather, all permissible purposes can be pursued by the Austrian foundation, so not only non-profit purposes but also self-interested purposes. Since it came into force, the Austrian Foundation Act has only been slightly amended in terms of its organizational framework.

From a tax law perspective, numerous changes were made and tax relief originally granted was withdrawn and brought into line with the general regulations of corporations. After about 30 years, the opportunity should be taken to evaluate the performance of the law and to make some adjustments (see section 9).

1.3. TAX MOTIVES WHEN THE ACT CAME INTO FORCE

Originally, the popularity and use of the foundation for organizing participations was primarily tax-motivated. It was a clear concern of the Austrian Foundation Act (PSG) and its accompanying tax laws to make the tax situation particularly attractive for entrepreneurs. Owners of enterprises should be offered an attractive tax framework. The legislator even aimed to attract entrepreneurs and owners to come to Austria from the neighbouring countries and establish a foundation which acts like a holding. Undertakings should be held in Austria and brought to Austria from neighbouring countries, such as Germany and Liechtenstein.[5]

In the past foundations had[6] noticeable tax advantages compared to corporations. The essential ones were as follows:

- At the time that the Austrian Foundation Act came into force, inheritance and gift tax was active in Austria. The amount of inheritance and gift tax was based on the value of the assets and the 'degree' of the relationship between the transferor and transferee. The tax rate was different if the assets were transferred from mother to daughter in comparison to a transfer between a great-aunt and great-nephew. Therefore, in the case of a transfer of a business or assets, the tax burden could be up to 58% of the value of the taxable base. The transfer of assets to a private foundation, on the other hand, was only subject to

5 Cerha, Die Vertreibung des Vermögens österreichischer Privatstiftungen ins Ausland, in Kalss, Aktuelle Fragen des Stiftungsrechts – Acht wesentliche Kernthemen (2014) 1 ff, 3 ff.

6 Most of them have been abolished in the meantime.

a foundation transfer tax (Stiftungseingangssteuer) of 2%, i.e. a small fraction compared to the very high inheritance tax.

- Moreover, contributed companies and participations could be sold practically tax-free. The hidden reserves then disclosed were not subject to subsequent taxation. The increase in value did not have to be taxed; instead, only the low acquisition value was taken as the basis for taxation.[7]
- For beneficiaries, contributions have always been taxed only at the capital gains tax (Kapitalertragsteuer) rate of originally 25% (now 27.5%). Grants from the private foundation are treated as dividend income and are not subject to income tax (Einkommensteuer), which measured with different progression steps can rise up to 50% and even higher for managers.The above-mentioned tax advantages have been massively reduced during the last two decades.

1.4. ECONOMIC DATA

According to the 'Stifterverband',[8] there are 3,028 private foundations as of 1 February 2022. Currently, the number of foundations is slightly decreasing. A few years ago, there were more than 3,300 foundations in Austria. The reason for the decreasing number of foundations is first of all the lack of new tax incentives. However, it is also due to the fact that the original founders of many foundations have died or are no longer compus mentis. In many cases, the successors of the founders, unless they themselves assume the role of founder, have a limited legal position that restricts their options. Therefore, foundations are dissolved and the foundation assets are distributed to the beneficiaries. The 'price' for this is the tax burden on the donated – currently valued – assets through the imposition of capital gains tax. The competence to decide about the dissolution depends on the statute. In most cases the founder has reserved the right to revoke the foundation. The right to revoke according to §34 of the Foundation Act is a personal right that cannot be transferred and ends with the death of the founder. Besides this personal right of the founder, the management

[7] Kalss, Die Leistungskraft der österreichischen Privatstiftung für Familienunternehmen, Zeitschrift für vergleichende Rechtswissenschaft (2018) 117.

[8] The 'Stifterverband' is an association that represents in particular the interests of private foundations.

board has the right to dissolve the foundation unanimously if the purpose of the foundation has been accomplished or has become unattainable. In a family business the beneficiaries have to decide after a hundred years whether they want the foundation to be continued. The foundations deed may state other reasons. The qualification of the entity as a foundation is not contested in these cases (see also section 2.2.1 below).

When new private foundations are established, their main purpose is to reorganize the family assets and to allocate them to the individual family lines (Familienstämme) by establishing individual foundations, so-called sub-foundations (Substiftungen), from the main foundation of a family for the various branches of the family. The establishment of a sub-foundation is functionally to be understood as the splitting-off of a foundation. This form of organization aims to settle internal family disputes or to reorganize assets without disputes and to replicate the division under inheritance law. Thus, both influence and economic participation rights are reorganized.[9] Foundations have in total assets in the triple-digit billion range. In 2016, assets were still around €70 billion.[10] Of these assets, 60% are participations, with an increasing number of around 25% in real estate and securities. Significantly less is invested in private equity and art. Other assets play no role.[11]

Around one-fifth of the Austrian stock corporations (Aktiengesellschaften) listed on the Regulated Market of the Vienna Stock Exchange is held by private foundations. Private foundations hold shares of between 10% and over 96% in these companies.[12] In general, these companies are quite successful in economic terms. They have seen enormous growth during the last ten years, in particular the last three years[13] before the invasion of Ukraine.

---

9 Kalss, Die Gestaltung von Substiftungen, in FS Eccher (2017) 425 ff; C Nowotny, Substiftungen und ihre Probleme, in FS Helbich (2014) 111.

10 Kalss, Zeitschrift für vergleichende Rechtswissenschaften 117 (2018) 1 ff, with reference to a study presented by economist Helmenstein on December 4, 2015, at the Plattform Familienunternehmen der Industriellenvereinigung.

11 Stiftungsmonitor 2021, a joint empirical study of the Verein Stiftung Next Gen and the Johannes-Kepler-University, Kraus and a financial services company specializing in asset management.

12 www.stiftungsverband.at.

13 Ibid.

1.5. NO DIRECT BUSINESS ACTIVITY

Pursuant to section 1 PSG, the private foundation itself may not engage in entrepreneurial activities. It may therefore only hold participations and exercise ownership rights. As such, it may be at the head of a company, a group of companies or manage a group of companies. However, the private foundation may not intervene too intensively in the subsidiaries. The Supreme Court (Oberste Gerichtshof) prohibits it from so-called tight group management (straffe Konzernführung).[14] The private foundation may therefore exercise group management that is not too far-reaching and encompasses all essential management powers. The limit is maintained if the private foundation, as the principal (Hauptgesellschafter) or sole shareholder (Alleingesellschafter), exercises its statutory shareholder rights.[15] It may also exercise veto rights or typical approval rights in the limited liability company (Gesellschaft mit beschränkter Haftung). The strategic decisions close to the owner may be made by the private foundation and a procedure may also be established to implement them in the associated companies.[16] Since the private foundation is not allowed to manage a company itself, Austrian law prohibits the direct corporate foundation (unmittelbare Unternehmensträgerstiftung). It is only permitted within a very narrow framework as a secondary activity, such as the operation of a museum store at a museum foundation (e.g. the Leopold Museum Private Foundation) or the operation of a small canteen in addition to other foundation activities, such as the exhibition of paintings or other works of art. The reason for this was that the interests of the beneficiaries should be protected from claims by creditors against the foundation running the business. A simple entrepreneur (Einzelunternehmen) or a personal partner of the partnerships is directly liable to the creditors of the enterprise or the partnership. Therefore, the assets of the foundation should be protected to the benefit of the beneficiaries. The creditors of a subsidiary of the foundation (Tochter-GmbH) cannot hold the foundation directly liable as a shareholder of the company.

However, since the private foundation may hold shares and – as already explained above – may also manage a group of companies, an

---

14 OGH 6 Ob 217/05b, GesRZ 2006, 82.

15 Kalss/Müller, Die Stiftung als Instrument der Vermögensweitergabe, in Gruber/Kalss/Müller/Schauer, Erbrecht und Vermögensnachfolge² (2018) §26 Rz 41, 902.

16 Kalss/Müller in Gruber/Kalss/Müller/Schauer, Erbrecht und Vermögensnachfolge² §26 Rz 41; Zwick, Die Privatstiftung als Konzernspitze, GesRZ (2009), 278, 284.

indirect corporate foundation is possible. This is also the typical case of a private foundation. In this case, shares or participations are held directly or indirectly. Often, a holding company is placed directly under the private foundation, which in turn holds and directly manages the other participations. According to the different assets, there are different types of private foundations, namely those that actively manage a group of companies and in which the decisive management decisions are made in the private foundation. Other foundations only hold investments as a portfolio and act only as defensive or passive investors without active involvement (portfolio management). Finally, it is also possible to operate a relatively reduced shareholding management, while the operational group management is organized in a subordinate holding company.[17]

1.6. THE PRIVATE FOUNDATION: A LEGAL ENTITY WITHOUT SHARES

The private foundation is a legal entity which exists on a continuing basis and in which no shares can be held. Therefore, there are also no membership rights. As a result, shares and memberships in a private foundation cannot be transferred.

This is because the relevant performance of the private foundation lies in the secure space for the assets – in particular the shares – which have been contributed to it. Neither inter vivos nor upon death is a transfer required. On the occasion of the death of a founder or a beneficiary, a share in the private foundation therefore does not have to be transferred. As such, the private foundation is even more stable than a share transfer restriction in a company, more stable than a syndicate agreement (voting agreement) and also more stable than a holding company in which shares or participations are held.

It is precisely this stability and avoidance of division by the shareholder that is a decisive achievement of the private foundation institution. A majority can always be secured without fear of an immediate danger of division if the share is transferred by a child of an heir.[18]

---

17 Kalss, Zeitschrift für vergleichende Rechtswissenschaften 117 (2018) 1, 14.

18 Kalss/Probst, Handbuch Familienunternehmen (2013) Rz 7/159.

2. THE CONCEPT OF THE PRIVATE FOUNDATION

2.1. THE CONTRACTUAL FREEDOM FOR THE FOUNDATION: NECESSARY CONTROL

The concept of the Austrian foundation is very simple. It is characterized by a high degree of contractual freedom. On the one hand, the Austrian Foundation Act provides only a few requirements and gives the founder merely a few regulatory mandates to regulate certain questions and topics in the foundation's declaration (Stiftungserklärung). This is an advantage for contractual freedom and the adaptability to different needs. On the other hand, many questions remain unregulated and therefore, in the absence of a good regulatory by forward-thinking advisors, must first be clarified in a costly legal proceeding. When the law came into force, consulting competence was often lacking and poorly prepared foundation declarations were entered into the commercial register (Firmenbuch), which also explains the high number of court decisions.

The private foundation plays a major role in the economy. It also plays a major role in the jurisdiction. Currently, eight to ten decisions of the Supreme Court (Oberste Gerichtshof) deal with private foundations. This is significantly more than for stock corporations (Aktiengesellschaften) and for partnerships (Personengesellschaften). Only for limited liability companies (Gesellschaften mit beschränkter Haftung) are more Supreme Court decisions handed down per year. This is not surprising, given that there were around 166,000 limited liability companies at the beginning of February 2022. However, this also shows how highly conflict-prone the private foundation is. This is not surprising, given that it is a young law. It is a legal form that is very successful, but one where conflicts usually involve large amounts of money.

2.2. THE ESTABLISHMENT OF THE PRIVATE FOUNDATION AND HOW THE PRIVATE FOUNDATION BECOMES A LEGAL ENTITY

2.2.1. Foundation Deeds

The private foundation is established by a foundation deed, which must be drawn up by one or more founders. Pursuant to section 39 PSG, a notarial act is required – i.e. a notary must be involved in the establishment. This elaborate form serves to protect the founder, who is advised by the notary.

The notarial act also protects the beneficiaries, who are also to be the addressees of the foundation's purpose.

The foundation deed must contain the essential elements of a private foundation, namely the founder, the purpose of the foundation and the bodies of the private foundation. A number of other matters may be regulated in the foundation deed, such as the individual beneficiaries or the detailed description of the purpose of the foundation, the activity of the foundation and the appointment of the individual bodies. In any case, the private foundation deed, if so desired, must also contain the most important founder rights, namely the right of amendment (Änderungsrecht) pursuant to section 33 PSG and the right of revocation (Widerrufsrecht) pursuant to section 34 PSG, if the founder wishes to exercise them.[19] In addition to the foundation deed, the founder(s) may also draw up a supplementary foundation deed (Stiftungszusatzurkunde).

The foundation deed shall be filed for registration in the commercial register (Firmenbuch) by the first board of directors. The foundation deed becomes part of the collection of documents kept by the Commercial Register Court (Firmenbuchgericht). The Commercial Register (Firmenbuch) is the register kept by the Court of First Instance in which all corporations, partnerships and other selected legal entities and companies are also registered. The private foundation is therefore part of the general commercial register and general register for companies. All private foundations and the foundation deeds are public.

In addition to the foundation deed, the founder may also draw up a supplementary foundation deed. This is also a deed in the form of a notarial act. The main difference is that the supplementary foundation deed is not public. Therefore, it does not have to be registered in the commercial register in order to be effective. Each foundation may have only one supplementary foundation deed. However, it is possible that a supplementary foundation deed consists of several parts, which are drawn up at different times.[20] In addition, there are sometimes also memoranda of understanding (Absichtserklärung) by the founder, in which the founder explains their motivation for the foundation. A memorandum of understanding does not develop any direct normative force and is not directly enforceable. This document can only be used for the interpretation of the foundation deed.[21]

---

19 OGH 6 Ob 72/11y.

20 Zentrum für Stiftungsrecht, Resümeprotokoll des Fachgesprächs mit Firmenbuchrichtern, GesRZ 6/2021, 380 (385).

21 Kalss in Kalss/Nowotny/Schauer, Österreichisches Gesellschaftsrecht² Rz 7/45; Nowotny in Gassner/Göth/Gröhs/Lang, Privatstiftungen (2000) 125 ff.

In addition to this memorandum of understanding, which is not directly effective, syndicate agreements are concluded by or in private foundations, which bind the founders to each other or bind the private foundation to other partners. They are to be strictly distinguished from the memorandum of understanding.

With the registration of the foundation in the commercial register (Firmenbuch), the private foundation, which had already been established with the foundation deed, has actually become an independent legal entity. The period between the establishment of the private foundation by the notarial act and the registration of the foundation in the commercial register (Firmenbuch) is the period of the pre-foundation (Vorstiftung).[22] The Austrian foundation comes into legal existence with the registration in the commercial register. No further official permit is required.[23] The foundation's declaration (Stiftungserklärung) is a unilateral legal transaction that does not require acceptance or access. The private foundation can be established by one or more individuals or legal entities. The establishment of the foundation consists of two parts, namely the organizational part, in which the foundation constitution and the organization of the private foundation are determined, and the circumscription of the obligations of the founders, namely the obligation to dedicate assets to the foundation. Thus, the foundation transaction and the establishment of the foundation have an organizational part and a pecuniary part.[24]

2.2.2. Commercial Register (Firmenbuch): In Control

The Commercial Court (Firmenbuchgericht) is the only authority that controls the foundation, namely the compliance with the legal regulations when shaping the deed of foundation and when appointing the members of the boards of the foundation. The law does not require a more intensive ongoing control. Thus, there is no authority (Stiftungsamt). The Commercial Court has functions similar to supervision in part, and exercises its supervisory duties[25] within the scope of its duty to monitor – for example, whether the foundation deed complies with the legal

22 Arnold, PSG³ (2013) §7 Rz 5ff.

23 Kalss in Kalss/Nowotny/Schauer, Österreichisches Gesellschaftsrecht² Rz 7/36.

24 Zollner, Die eigennützige Privatstiftung (2011) 41 ff; Kalss in Kalss/Nowotny/Schauer, Österreichisches Gesellschaftsrecht² Rz 7/37.

25 Kalss/Schauer/Winner, Allgemeines Unternehmensrecht und Wertpapierrecht (2022) Rz 6/8.

requirements or whether there is an important reason for the premature dismissal of a board member pursuant to section 27(2) PSG or approval of transactions between a member of the board of directors and the private foundation pursuant to section 17(5) PSG.

3. THE PURPOSE OF THE AUSTRIAN FOUNDATION

Pursuant to section 1 PSG, any permitted purpose is permissible for a foundation. The Austrian foundation may pursue both non-profit purposes, such as the financial support of a university or a research institute, and social purposes (such as Concordia Private Foundation). However, the Austrian foundation may also pursue exclusively self-interested purposes, such as supporting the members of a family or supporting certain selected persons who meet certain qualifications circumscribed in the foundation's declaration. A private foundation may also combine self-interested and non-profit purposes. Only a few private foundations exclusively pursue a non-profit purpose. In 2020, for example, there were only 17 private foundations in Upper Austria with an exclusively non-profit purpose. About one-third of all Austrian foundations are resident in Upper Austria. A total of 83% exclusively pursue a self-interested purpose, 5% (17 in absolute terms) pursue a non-profit purpose, and 12% of Austrian foundations pursue both self-interested and mixed purposes. Non-profit purposes include the promotion of the economy, technology, science or the support of humanitarian and non-profit organizations, the promotion of education and schools, and the support of sick people. In the case of mixed foundations, the promotion of culture and tradition, ecclesiastical purposes or disaster relief can be found.[26]

Simply preserving and developing the business would not be an adequate purpose. The purpose must go further than this – at least to support the founder or the founder's family or other people or the public or special groups of the public (for example, students of a university, inhabitants of a region or members of an association).

The limit is merely unlawful projects such as the promotion of drug trafficking or the facilitation of arms trafficking or smuggling across the border. In addition, there is a prohibition of self-purpose foundations

---

26 Lammer, Empirische Datenerhebung für Privatstiftungen in Oberösterreich im Jahr 2021, Masterarbeit an der Wirtschaftsuniversität Wien (Masterstudium Wirtschaftsrecht 2022) 12.

(Selbstzweckstiftung), i.e. those where the sole purpose of the foundation must not be to merely exist and maintain its assets.[27] It follows from the purpose definition that the foundation must be externally directed and must have a purpose addressee and thus beneficiaries. The law assumes the existence of beneficiaries.[28] The general public may also be beneficiaries. The beneficiaries may be generally circumscribed or specifically designated. Thus, they do not yet have to be specified in the foundation deed (Stiftungsurkunde) or in the supplementary foundation deed (Stiftungszusatzurkunde). The foundation can also designate a body in accordance with section 9 PSG, which specifies the beneficiaries by name and also the amount of the respective contribution.

4. THE ACTIVITY OF THE FOUNDATION

As already explained, the activity of the private foundation (Unternehmensgegenstand) is limited. It may not directly manage a company pursuant to section 1 PSG, nor may it assume the position of a partner in a general partnership (Offene Gesellschaft), nor may it become a general partner in a limited partnership (Kommanditgesellschaft) as a personally liable party. The reason for this is simple: there would be a risk of unlimited liability in favour of the creditors of the registered partnership. This would be in conflict with the legal position and protection of the beneficiaries. As already explained, the private foundation may hold participations. Thus, it may be an indirect corporate foundation (mittelbare Unternehmensträgerstiftung) and is also entitled to group management (Konzernleitung). The private foundation may also manage its own assets. It may also sell assets and carry out other activities. The functions of the entrepreneurial private foundation are as follows:

- Holding function: it has a holding function and can hold a stable participation in a company (for example 100% or 60% majority).
- Bridging function: if one generation is unable or lacks suitable persons to manage a company, the private foundation can continue to hold the shares and manage them for the next generation.
- Moderation and mediation function for the family: this provides a permanent institution for discussion and action, and gives the

27 OGH 6 Ob 93/06d; OLG Wien 28R 274/04a; Kalss in Doralt/Nowotny/Kalss, Kommentar zum PSG (1995) §1 Rz 33 f; Arnold, PSG[3] (2013) §1 Rz 13.

28 Kalss in Kalss/Nowotny/Schauer, Österreichisches Gesellschaftsrecht[2] Rz 7/28.

opportunity to keep in touch with the different family members of a family business.
- Entrepreneurial function: the Austrian foundation typically pursues the function of strategic owner (the core shareholder (Kernaktionär) or anchor shareholder (Ankeraktionär)) and may also assume the function of group management.
- Non-profit function: finally, the Austrian foundation may pursue non-profit purposes.

The Austrian foundation as a whole can therefore realize the will of the founder and act as a custodian of the will (Testamentsvollstreckung). At the same time, it can also act like a syndicate agreement among the family members.

5. THE ASSETS OF THE FOUNDATION

The initial minimum assets of the foundation are €70,000. The assets need only be actually present at the time of the establishment and registration of the foundation. It must be dedicated to the foundation before its registration in the commercial register. The asset management and investment of the assets is completely free. The law does not stipulate any requirements in this respect. As already mentioned, about two-thirds of the foundation's assets are invested in participations, 20% in real estate and 10% in other assets. The law does not provide for any permanent minimum assets. There are no basic assets (Grundstockvermögen) that may not be touched. There are no obligations that the capital must be maintained. The assets may be sold and may also be distributed among the beneficiaries. Thus, in the Austrian foundation, not only may the income be distributed to the beneficiaries, but so too may the substance assets (Substanzvermögen) of the private foundation. Thus, there is not only a foundation for use (Gebrauchsstiftung), but also a foundation for consumption (Verbrauchsstiftung).[29] In the foundation's declaration, i.e. both in the foundation deed and in the supplementary foundation deed, the founder can lay down guidelines for the management of the assets and therefore make specifications to the board of directors. Frequently, certain

29 Kalss in Kalss/Nowotny/Schauer, Österreichisches Gesellschaftsrecht[2] Rz 7/28; Reiter, Die Aufgaben des Stiftungsprüfers im Zusammenhang mit unzulässigen Substanzauszahlungen an Begünstigte, ZFS (2014), 152.

parts of the assets are excluded from the disposition of the board of directors. Thus, the founder can stipulate certain parts of the assets, for example real estate, and some participations or so-called core assets (Kernvermögen) can be distributed or disposed of, while other assets must not be distributed. If the foundation does not contain any regulations, the board of directors may also set its own guidelines.[30] The assets are subject to internal control. According to the provisions of the Austrian Commercial Code (UGB), the board of directors is responsible for the foundation's accounting and for preparing a balance sheet. If the private foundation has subsidiaries, consolidated financial statements (konsolidierter Abschluss) must also be prepared with the subsidiaries. This has a disciplinary function, even if the additional information content is not very great. These financial statements (the balance sheet) prepared by the board of directors must be audited by an auditor (Stiftungsprüfer) appointed by the court. The foundation only has a right to propose the appointment of the foundation auditor, i.e. an accountant. The foundation auditor audits the annual financial statements and prepares a report to the private foundation, i.e. to the board of directors. Neither the annual financial statements nor the audit report are filed to the commercial register; the annual financial statements only have to be filed to the tax authorities. However, it is not published and cannot be inspected. The annual financial statements and other accounting documents are accessible to all other bodies and members of bodies of the private foundation. The beneficiaries also have a right to inspect the annual financial statements and to receive a copy pursuant to section 30 PSG. The founder only has such a right if it is granted by the foundation's declaration. They are not entitled to this by law. An external office, who is neither the commercial register court (Firmenbuchgericht) nor any other foundation office, controls the management, the status of the assets and their use.

6. THE FOUNDER

Pursuant to section 3(1) PSG, one person may establish a foundation or several individuals or legal entities may be founders of a private foundation. The founder is the person designated as such in the foundation's declaration (Stiftungserklärung). It is not absolutely necessary that all co-founders contribute to the foundation's assets. Thus, not every founder has to make

30 Kalss/Müller in Gruber/Kalss/Müller/Schauer, Erbrecht und Vermögensnachfolge^2 (2018) §26 Rz 198 ff.

a minimum contribution to the foundation.[31] Often, a foundation has a main founder (Hauptstifter) who contributes the substantial assets to the foundation, while other founders only dedicate a symbolic amount to the foundation. Minors may become founders. The founder or founders must be named in the foundation deed (Stiftungsurkunde) in accordance with section 9 (1) and (5) PSG. The status of founder cannot be acquired subsequently – for example, by a subsequent dedication of assets or by a subsequent amendment of the foundation's declaration.[32] As such, the status of founder cannot be subsequently renounced. The historical fact of having established a foundation and therefore of being a founder can no longer be eliminated. However, a founder can subsequently waive the rights to which they are entitled in the context of an amendment to the foundation's declaration. They must declare this to the foundation and this must be executed by means of a declaration of amendment (Änderungserklärung) and a notarial act entered into the commercial register (Firmenbuch).[33]

The PSG grants only a few rights to a founder. The founder has only marginal rights when dissolving the private foundation. However, the law offers the founder the possibility of retaining comprehensive rights and influence by means of explicit provisions in the foundation's declaration.[34] The founder's most important rights of influence, which they can stipulate in the foundation deed, are the right to amend the foundation's declaration, to revoke the foundation's declaration, to appoint and dismiss board members, and to have information rights. A founder can therefore retain a comprehensive right to participate in and shape the foundation, as well as a far-reaching permanent right to shape the foundation similar to that of an owner.

The right of amendment (Änderungsrecht) and the right of revocation (Widerrufsrecht) are highly personal and cannot be transferred to another person. Therefore, the right ends when it is granted to a natural person as founder. Continuation and perpetuation is only possible if the right of amendment is granted to a company or other legal entity.[35] The founder

---

31 Explanations of the materials on the law: 1132 Supplements to the stenographic minutes of the Austrian Parliament (Nationalrat) 18th GP 21; Kalss/Müller in Gruber/Kalss/Müller/Schauer, Erbrecht und Vermögensnachfolge² §26 Rz 42.

32 OGH 1 Ob 166/04z; Arnold, PSG³ §3 Rz 13; Kalss/Müller in Gruber/Kalss/Müller/Schauer, Erbrecht und Vermögensnachfolge² §26 Rz 44.

33 OGH 6 Ob 78/06y; Arnold, PSG³ §3 Rz 15.

34 Kalss/Müller in Gruber/Kalss/Müller/Schauer, Erbrecht und Vermögensnachfolge² §26 Rz 46; C Nowotny, Stifterrechte – Möglichkeiten und Grenzen, JBl 2003, 779.

35 Kalss/Müller in Gruber/Kalss/Müller/Schauer, Erbrecht und Vermögensnachfolge² §26 Rz 51.

can completely change the purpose and the complete charter,[36] e.g. first to promote vegetarianism and then to promote meat consumption. There has never been any discussion of whether this entity is a foundation, although the founder can change the foundation totally. The foundation was shaped in this manner by the law and therefore opens up this broad scope of ongoing influence of the founder.

The founder may also be a member of a body. They may also be a member of the board of directors; however, section 15(2) PSG then prohibits them from receiving benefits, thus making them a beneficiary at the same time. Being a founder and being a member of a governing body are not mutually exclusive, but it is not permissible to be a member of the board of directors and a beneficiary of the private foundation at the same time.

If the founder has the right to appoint and dismiss members of the board of directors, they also have a material position as a body based on this competence.[37] Therefore, they also have the control rights associated with membership of a body, in particular the right to inspect the foundation documents and the right to file an application with the court in the event of dismissal proceedings.[38]

A founder can therefore continue to interfere with the foundation by granting the right of amendment and revocation. They actually have an extended right of disposal, which is close to a right of ownership. The founder's right to change the foundation is not limited in content,[39] i.e. they can completely change the purpose of the foundation, change the beneficiaries, and change the object and the asset structure. A total of 90% of all founders reserve the right of amendment. However, according to a recent survey, the right of amendment is often missing for the second and third generation of founders, because these persons were not yet founders or were not granted it as founders.

The founder has no right of instructions in the private foundation, but they may stipulate individual founder missions (einzelne Stifteraufträge) in the foundation deed or supplementary deed.[40]

---

36 OGH 1 Ob 214/09s (Point 1.9.1).

37 OGH 6 Ob 141/20h.

38 Zentrum für Stiftungsrecht, Resümeprotokoll des Fachgesprächs mit Firmenbuchrichtern, GesRZ 6/2021.

39 OGH 1 Ob 214/09s, GesRZ (2011), 53.

40 Briem, Gestaltungsmöglichkeiten in der Privatstiftung, in Kalss, Aktuelle Fragen des Privatstiftungsgesetzes (2014) 61, 92; Kalss in Kalss/Nowotny/Schauer, Österreichisches Gesellschaftsrecht[2] Rz 7/76.

7. BENEFICIARIES

Beneficiaries are the addressees of the foundation. Pursuant to section 5 PSG, a beneficiary is anyone who, according to the law or the foundation deed, has a right to a donation or an expectancy thereof and is therefore entitled to exercise the beneficiary rights.[41] The beneficiary is to be designated as such in accordance with section 5 PSG. By law, beneficiaries have only very minor rights, and they only have the right to receive information and to inspect the foundation deeds as well as the annual financial statements and the accounting documents. They have no further rights of control. By law, the beneficiaries are therefore only the beneficial owners of the foundation. However, they have no participation rights and no rights to shape the foundation.

Ex lege, a beneficiary may request the private foundation to provide information on the fulfilment of the foundation's purpose and to inspect the annual financial statements, as well as the management report, the audit report, the books of account, the foundation deed and the supplementary foundation deed. The beneficiary rights may also be exercised after the expiry of the beneficiary rights. However, the right then only relates to the period of the beneficiary status.

However, the founder can grant the beneficiary certain rights in the foundation's declaration over and above the statutory provisions.[42] Thus, the beneficiary can be granted economic rights (rights of donation) and rights of influence. In practice, the beneficiaries are often members of the advisory board and have the right to nominate the members of the management board and the advisory board. Often these rights come into force after the death of the founder or the members of the first generation of founders.

The property right could be structured in such a way that not only is an expectation of a donation and of a certain benefit granted, but so too is an enforceable claim. However, this is rare, and an enforceable claim is mainly used, for example, to secure care and utility services or retirement claims.

Possible rights are, for example, control rights that go beyond the legal requirements, such as the initiation of a special audit or participation in an advisory board, or rights of influence on the board of directors, such as

---

41 Kalss in Kalss/Nowotny/Schauer, Österreichisches Gesellschaftsrecht[2] Rz 7/110; Kalss, Die einmalige Zuwendung, ZFS (2015), 139.

42 Kalss/Zollner, Mitwirkungs- und Kontrollrechte der Begünstigten – Gestaltungsmöglichkeiten des Stifters, GesRZ (2008), 126 ff.

appointment and dismissal rights.[43] It is not permissible for a beneficiary to be a member of the board of directors. Section 15(2) PSG excludes beneficiaries from this office. However, not only the beneficiary himself/herself is excluded, but also all his/her relatives in a straight line up to the third degree of the collateral line. Not excluded is the affinity, e.g. the daughter-in-law or the mother-in-law or also the brother-in-law. Also excluded is the spouse. According to section 23(2) PSG, the beneficiaries may not constitute more than half of the members of the supervisory board.

8. GOVERNANCE OF THE FOUNDATION

8.1. OVERVIEW

The foundation must have at least two bodies, namely the board of directors and the foundation auditor. Pursuant to section 14 PSG, it is permissible for the founder to establish further bodies in the foundation deed to control or advise the board of directors. The foundation bodies must in any case be determined in the foundation deed, otherwise they do not qualify as bodies.[44] According to the latest opinion of the Supreme Court, the appointment and dismissal of the board of directors establishes the status of a body.[45] In this context, what matters in the case of an institution is not the formal designation, but the decisive and enforceable influence, the decision-making process, and the management and supervision of the private foundation. If a body does not have the status of an executive body (Organ), it forms a committee (Gremium), which can also be standardized in the supplementary foundation deed or on the basis of a resolution of the board of directors. Committees also have an advisory and control function and can perform important tasks for the private foundation. However, they do not have a function as a body (Organ) and cannot, for example, exercise certain control rights and application rights in court. However, internally the significance and competences of bodies and legal committees are quite the same and play an important role in the foundation governance.

---

43 Kalss/Zollner, GesRZ (2008), 131 ff; Kalss in Kalss/Nowotny/Schauer, Österreichisches Gesellschaftsrecht² Rz 7/111.

44 OGH 6 Ob 305/01y; OGH 6 Ob 95/15m; Kalss/Müller in Gruber/Kalss/Müller/Schauer, Erbrecht und Vermögensnachfolge² §26 Rz 176.

45 OGH 6 Ob 141/20h; anderer Ansicht noch OGH 6 Ob 291/02s.

8.2. THE BOARD OF DIRECTORS

Pursuant to section 15 PSG, the board of directors must consist of at least three persons. Only individuals can be members of the board of directors. The number of three directors serves the purpose of mutual control. In its case law, the Supreme Court has strongly secured the position of the board of directors and has established it as a strong independent body. Thus, according to the case law, a member of the board of directors must be appointed for at least three years, without a legal basis. A shorter term of appointment is only permissible if there is an objective reason for it (an age limit). The Supreme Court started this chain of decisions ten years ago without convincing arguments.[46]

A member of the board of directors may only be dismissed for an important reason. This provision can only be derived indirectly from the law. In addition, the Supreme Court prohibits the board of directors from being subjected to an excessively narrow framework of transactions requiring approval vis-à-vis other bodies.[47]

The board of directors must exercise the diligence of a prudent manager. The specific level of diligence must therefore be determined in a way that is appropriate to the sector, size and situation of the foundation.[48] The board of directors is subject to the business judgement rule, i.e. it has entrepreneurial discretion (judgement) in its business decisions.[49] Although this is not expressly regulated in the PSG, the Supreme Court has used general principles of law for justification.

The beneficiaries and the close relatives of the beneficiaries, all relatives in the direct line, as well as up to the third degree of the collateral line are excluded from the office of the board of directors.

8.3. THE AUDITOR OF THE FOUNDATION: THE OBLIGATORY CONTROL BODY

The foundation auditor (Stiftungsprüfer) is a permanently appointed controlling body of the private foundation. The law expressly standardizes

---

46 OGH 6 Ob 211/20b; OGH 6 Ob 195/10k; OGH 6 Ob 140/14b.

47 OGH RIS Justiz RS 0115030; OGH 230/13m.

48 Csoklich, Rechte und Pflichten des Stiftungsvorstands, RdW (1999), 254; Kalss/Müller in Gruber/Kalss/Müller/Schauer, Erbrecht und Vermögensnachfolge^2 §26 Rz 198.

49 OGH 6 Ob 160/15w.

their position as a body. The foundation auditor must be appointed by the court. The foundation has only a right of nomination. The foundation auditor may be appointed for a limited or unlimited period. The one-year appointment period as for corporations does not apply in this case.

The auditor of the foundation has to check the legality of the annual financial statements and the accounting. However, their duties go further – namely, they also have the obligation to verify compliance with the purpose of the private foundation by the board of directors and is obliged to provide information to the beneficiary. They are entitled to inspect the audit report. However, the foundation auditor has no obligation to make public any irregularities or, in any case, to notify the commercial register.

8.4. OTHER BODIES

The founder(s) may establish other supervisory bodies in addition to the foundation auditor. In this respect, the founder is free to decide whether this is an advisory board (Beirat), a board of trustees (Kuratorium) or the beneficiaries' meeting (Begünstigtenversammlung). The other bodies may be granted control rights such as information rights, hearing rights and the right to comment. However, the Supreme Court has largely limited the right to consent and genuine control, and it allows only selected measures and matters to be subject to consent.[50] It is at least permissible that the right to appoint or dismiss members of the board of directors is assigned to a supervisory body. The Supreme Court has significantly weakened the other control bodies pursuant to section 14 PSG as a whole through its jurisdiction and thus has also shaken the governance of the private foundation, updating a control deficit resulting from the lack of owners and only making it a problem by generally structuring the board of directors so strongly. In addition, it has extended its far-reaching case law on the incompatibility of the supervisory board to other supervisory bodies, so that beneficiaries on the advisory board may exercise even fewer rights. This is disadvantageous because the beneficiaries are the beneficial owners of the private foundation and it is actually they who have a real interest in the functioning of the private foundation.

---

50 OGH 6 Ob 95/15m, GesRZ (2015), 338.

The Supreme Court has therefore massively weakened the private foundation as a whole by its very strict view, which is hardly anchored in the text of the law or in the telos of the regulation. The legislator has already required a mandatory third-party management of three non-family members. The Supreme Court extends this restrictive stance to the advisory board and thus the most important controlling body. This largely pushes the family back from management and control. In any case, this is dysfunctional for the long-term functioning of the foundation's business and thus for active entrepreneurial ownership.[51] This strong position of the board of directors sometimes leads to beneficiaries who are represented less in the foundation and in the foundation's bodies seeking help from the court and very often demanding the dismissal of the foundation's board members. The court then has to conduct non-contentious proceedings (außerstreitiges Verfahren). This shifts part of the control to the judicial level. In order to forestall this, it is necessary that a foundation's declaration is carefully prepared from the outset and that there is appropriate influence of the family members in the foundation and the corporate holdings held by the foundation.

9. OUTLOOK

The Austrian foundation is a story of success. The main characters are the open purpose, the liberal legal framework and the strong continuing influence of the founder. The Supreme Court has limited the legal framework to a certain extent. The founder is well advised to shape a strong and well-functioning governance within the foundation. In this way, the Austrian Foundation will play an important role in the Austrian economy.

The Austrian private foundation is an important organizational form for companies, especially family businesses. It has the role of the core shareholder of the holding company and the anchor shareholder.

Since private foundation law is open, it is necessary to carefully prepare the foundation deeds and the interaction of the governing bodies from the outset, otherwise the adverse case law of the Supreme Court will take effect, which has an anti-business and anti-family view of the foundation, especially since it wants to keep beneficiaries and thus the typical successor generation of the founders out of the foundation.

---

51 Kalss/Probst, Familienunternehmen (2013) Rz 7/158 ff.

In terms of legal policy, it is therefore absolutely necessary to strengthen the position of the family in the governing bodies, especially in the advisory board, and to improve the position of the supervisory body as a whole, namely to grant rights of approval and far-reaching other possibilities of influence in addition to the rights of appointment and dismissal. It also makes sense to make the right of amendment more flexible. Only in this way can the success story of the Austrian foundation be continued in the coming decades.

SWISS ENTERPRISE FOUNDATIONS

Overview and Current Challenges

Dominique JAKOB*

* The author wishes to thank his assistant Laura Studhalter for her valuable assistance in drafting this chapter.

ABSTRACT

This chapter aims to give an overview of the law and practice of Swiss enterprise foundations and the current challenges in Switzerland. It will try to embed the special form of enterprise foundations into the framework of Swiss foundation law, and will then focus on the specific topics and challenges Swiss enterprise foundations face, such as: the admissibility of self-maintaining foundations; the scope of state supervision; how to deal with reduced flexibility; how to deal with the unfriendly tax environment for charitable (tax-exempt) foundations holding companies and the unclear situation for mission-based investments, impact investments and entrepreneurial grant-making schemes (by investments in companies). Subsequently, the general need for good 'foundation governance' and, in a family business context, for 'family governance', is discussed as a crucial success factor for enterprise foundations. As a final point, the chapter will provide an outlook into the future.

1. INTRODUCTION

The Swiss foundation law was introduced in the Swiss Civil Code (CC)[1] in 1912 and follows a 'classical' foundation model. According to this notion, a foundation is a legal person that is established by dedicating assets for a specific purpose. After coming into force, the foundation is characterised by the principle of separation and solidification: the founder and the foundation are two separate and independent legal persons, and the original will of the founder is perpetuated and shall guide the foundation for its entire existence. The Swiss foundation is not a corporation (with members like associations or shareholders like stock companies), but is an establishment with an ownerless purpose fund for the benefit of the beneficiaries.[2]

---

1 Civil Code of the Swiss Confederation of 10 December 1907, as amended, AS 24 233.

2 For a general overview of Swiss foundation law, see D. Jakob and G. von Schnurbein, *Charitable Foundations, A Practical Guide: Build and Lead Charitable Foundations in Switzerland*, Credit Suisse Group AG (ed), Zürich 2021; D. Jakob and G. Studen, 'Foundation Law in Switzerland: Overview and Current Developments in Civil and Tax Law' in C. Prele (ed), *Developments in Foundation Law in Europe*, Berlin 2014, pp. 283–310; D. Jakob, commenting on arts. 80–89a CC, in A. Büchler and D. Jakob (eds), Kurzkommentar ZGB, Schweizerisches Zivilgesetzbuch, 2nd ed., Basel 2017; for a comparative overview, see D. Jakob, '§30 Internationale Stiftungen' in A. Richter (ed), *Stiftungsrecht Handbuch*, München 2019, pp. 911–983 with special regard to Switzerland, Austria, the Principality of Liechtenstein and Germany.

Of course, the foundation as a legal person needs organs to act. However, it is crucial to understand that these organs are, in principle, not allowed to create their own actual will, but must execute the (original) will of the founder. But how can one ensure that only the will of the founder is fulfilled, and that the organs do not replace the will of the founder with their own actual will? Upon a closer look, the foundation is running into a so-called 'principal-agent problem' because the persons who act are not the persons who own the assets, and the problem is even multiplied as there are no shareholders or members that could control the agent. This is the reason why the historic legislator already decided in 1912 that the foundation (as the only private law entity in Swiss law) needs to be under the supervision of a state authority, the supervisory authority, which has to protect the foundation and has to see that the foundation's organs always fulfil the will of the founder and do not harm the foundation's assets.[3] The competent authority in Switzerland depends on whether the foundation is active at a municipal, cantonal or federal level.[4]

On the other hand, Swiss foundation law is characterized by a great freedom of the founder. Under Swiss foundation law, a foundation can be established for any purpose that is not contrary to law or morality, among which are also business and enterprise-related purposes.[5] Furthermore, the founder is entitled to create the foundation's organisation more or less freely and can decide on the asset structure of the foundation. From that follows – which is important in this context – that a foundation with a business or enterprise-related purpose is a 'classical' foundation and not a 'special' legal foundation form (which the law provides in the case of family, ecclesiastical or pension fund foundations, for which special provisions are applicable). There is, at least in principle, no special law for enterprise foundations, but the normal legal rules for foundations do apply.[6] Hence, enterprise foundations are normal or classical private purpose foundations under Swiss law without any specific provisions.[7]

---

3 D. Jakob, 'Ein Stiftungsbegriff für die Schweiz', ZSR 2013 II 185, pp. 209 et seq. and pp. 315–317; D. Jakob, commenting art. 84 CC, in A. Büchler and D. Jakob (eds), above n. 2.

4 See art. 84 CC.

5 See decision of the Federal Supreme Court of Switzerland BGE 127 III 337.

6 Attention must be paid to the accounting rules in arts. 957 et seq. of the Federal Act on the Amendment of the Swiss Civil Code, Part Five, The Code of Obligations (CO) of 30 March 1911, as amended, SR 220, which are effective for all legal forms and for foundations in particular according to the reference in art. 83a CC. Depending on the size of the foundation, different regulatory accounting requirements have to be met.

7 In December 2021 a reform of Swiss foundation law was adopted (see the text of final vote BBl 2021 2992). However, this reform is not aimed at enterprise foundations

In this sense, tax-related questions regarding enterprise foundations are also assessed based on the Swiss tax law generally applicable to all legal entities. Tax law aspects are critically important for prudent and effective asset planning. Therefore, a brief overview of the basic principles of Swiss tax exemption shall be given in the following discussion: enterprise foundations with a purely economic purpose are considered equal to other legal entities with regard to tax law aspects and therefore do not benefit from special tax privileges. On the other hand, enterprise foundations with an exclusively charitable purpose can be exempt from taxation for profits that are exclusively and irrevocably committed to these charitable purposes.[8] The same applies to cantonal taxes on profit and capital.[9] Pursuant to Article 56 lit. g DBG, the acquisition and holding of significant capital stakes in companies are considered to be charitable where the interest in maintaining the company is subordinate to the charitable purpose and no management activities are carried out. Considering limited tax law regulations on charitable status, the practices of the cantonal tax authorities – which are generally guided by the Circular No. 12 issued by the Federal Tax Authority from 1994[10] – are critically important.[11]

2. TYPES OF ENTERPRISE FOUNDATIONS

2.1. BUSINESS OPERATING AND HOLDING FOUNDATIONS

According to this wide-meshed framework of Swiss foundation law, in business reality various forms of business-linked or enterprise foundations have developed. The first distinction can be made between (direct) business operating and (indirect) holding foundations. A business operating foundation operates an economic business itself to fulfil its purpose, which is, for example, the case when a foundation with the purpose of taking care

specifically. In its final form, the revision contains (only) three provisions: a regulation of the supervisory complaint in art. 84 para. 3 CC; a flexibilization of minor statute amendments in art. 86b CC; and an extension of the founder's right in art. 86a CC from (only) the amendment of the purpose to (also) the amendment of the organisation of the foundation.

8 Art. 56 lit. g Direct Federal Taxation Act (DBG) of 14 December 1990, as amended, AS 1991 1184.

9 Art. 23 para. 1 lit. f Federal Act on the Harmonization of Direct Cantonal Taxation and Direct Community Taxation (StHG) of 14 December 1990, as amended, AS 1991 1256.

10 Circular No. 12 of 8 July 1994, available at: http://www.estv.admin.ch.

11 The tax-exemption criteria in general and for holding foundations specifically will be discussed further in section 3.3.1 below.

of the elderly runs its own foster home. One other common example would be a hospital run by a foundation.

However, the majority of business-linked foundations are holding foundations, which hold the shares of an operational business. The reasons for this setup can be numerous: if, for example, the shares in the business are held by the foundation as an ownerless entity, these shares do not fall into someone's estate in the case of death. From a business point of view, such a construct can perpetuate the business independently from individuals, can channel succession matters and can protect the business against hostile takeovers. In a family context, it can support the family while keeping it away from actually running the business. Of course, a structure like this ought to be backed up by means of an effective form of 'family governance'.[12]

2.2. DISTINCTION ACCORDING TO THE PURPOSE OF THE FOUNDATION

It is not quite clear in the Swiss doctrine what will constitute an enterprise foundation,[13] the pure fact that a (somehow substantial part of a) business is held, the possibility of exerting influence on the business, or a purpose that is related to the business. In any case, in business reality we can distinguish different types of enterprise or business foundations according to the foundation's purpose.

2.2.1. Pure Business Foundations

A foundation with the sole purpose of holding a business could be described as a 'pure business foundation'.[14] In this context, two remarks seem to be of crucial importance.

First, for quite a while it was disputed among Swiss scholars if a foundation with an economic purpose was permissible.[15] In 2001 the

12 See D. Jakob, 'The Role of Foundations in Family Governance', *Trusts and Trustees*, Vol. 26, No. 1, February 2020, pp. 6 et seq.

13 For an overview of the controversy, see H. Grüninger, preliminary remarks on art. 80–89a CC, in T. Geiser and C. Fountoulakis (eds), *Basler Kommentar Zivilgesetzbuch I, Art. 1–456 ZGB,* 6th ed., Basel 2018, marginal nos. 15 et seq.

14 D. Jakob, above n. 3, pp. 188, 273–276; D. Bottge, 'Shareholder Foundations (Holding Foundations) in Switzerland', Expert Focus 3/2019, p. 180.

15 Against admissibility, see H.M. Riemer, 'Systematischer Teil' in *Berner Kommentar, Die Stiftungen*, Bern 1975, marginal nos. 82, 392 et seq.; R. Bär, 'Aktuelle Fragen des

Federal Supreme Court of Switzerland decided this dispute and held that foundations with a (partial) economic purpose are admissible.[16] The Court correctly argued according to the general principles of Swiss foundation law and upheld the neutrality of the legal concept towards all purposes and the freedom of the founder. For foundations in particular, which do not strive for tax exemption – where economic purposes, of course, would harm the charitable tax-exempt status of the foundation[17] – this was a welcome decision.

Second, pure business foundations face the potential issue of so-called self-maintaining purposes. According to the general principles of foundation law, a foundation with the only purpose of holding its own assets would not be permissible because it lacks an outward-directed purpose and, thus, constitutes a *perpetuum mobile*.[18] Against this background, one could argue that a pure business foundation is a self-maintaining foundation because the business could be seen as the only self-perpetuated asset (thus leaving aside all the additional outbound effects such a foundation purpose may have). And in fact, some scholars require that a foundation (at least additionally) pursues other outward purposes.[19] However, the discussion has never been conducted as intensively in Switzerland[20] as it has been in Germany.[21] A reason for this might be that Switzerland always had

Aktienrechts', ZSR 85/1966 II, pp. 532 et seq.; M. Pedrazzini and N. Oberholzer, *Grundriss des Personenrechts*, 4th ed., Bern 1993, p. 255. In favour of admissibility, see H. Grüninger, *Die Unternehmensstiftung in der Schweiz: Zulässigkeit – Eignung – Besteuerung*, Basel 1984, pp. 39 et seq.; P. Liver, 'Rezension zu Riemers Kommentar zum Stiftungsrecht, ZBJV 112/1976, p. 317; P. Nobel, *Anstalt und Unternehmen*, Diessenhofen 1978, p. 582; R. Portmann, *Wege zur Perpetuierung der Aktiengesellschaft*, Bern 1983, pp. 57 et seq.; J.N. Druey, 'Die Rechtsgültigkeit von Unternehmensstiftungen', SZW 1992, p. 174.

16 Decision of the Federal Supreme Court of Switzerland BGE 127 III 337.

17 Circular No. 12, pp. 2 et seq.

18 Cf. D. Jakob, preliminary remarks on arts. 80–89a CC, in A. Büchler and D. Jakob (eds), above n. 2; D. Jakob, above n. 3, pp. 272 et seq.

19 Cf. L. Brugger, *Die gemischte Stiftung – Die Stiftung zur Verfolgung unterschiedlicher Zwecke im Lichte des schweizerischen ZGB und des österreichischen PSG*, Zürich 2019, pp. 28 et seq. for more details.

20 In the above-mentioned BGE 127 III 337 decision, the Federal Supreme Court of Switzerland left the question of the admissibility of self-maintaining foundations open.

21 D. Jakob, *Schutz der Stiftung, Die Stiftung und ihre Rechtsverhältnisse im Widerstreit der Interessen*, Tübingen 2006, pp. 51–53 with further references to D. Reuter, preliminary remarks on §80 BGB in *Münchener Kommentar, Bürgerliches Gesetzbuch, Band 1, Allgemeiner Teil*, 4th ed., München 2005, marginal no. 42, 50; P. Rawert, 'Der Stiftungsbegriff und seine Merkmale – Stiftungszweck, Stiftungsvermögen, Stiftungsorganisation' in K. Hopt and D. Reuter (eds), *Stiftungsrecht in Europa*, Köln

pure business holding foundations, such as the Victorinox Foundation.[22] In practice, it could nevertheless be advisable for founders to install an independent secondary purpose alongside the pure business holding purpose, even if it is solely to avoid discussions and recognition problems with courts or authorities abroad.[23]

2.2.2. *Pure Charitable Foundations (Holding a Business)*

The next possible type would be a pure charitable foundation, i.e., a foundation with the sole purpose to pursue a charitable goal. Accordingly, the business is (or the shares of the business are) only an asset or the only asset of the foundation which is used to fulfil the charitable purpose.[24] In fact, many of the largest Swiss foundations are such pure charitable (business) foundations such as the Jacobs Foundation or the Kühne Foundation holding the Kühne and Nagel Group. Transferring the business to a pure charitable foundation has an important side effect and advantage: the transfer of the business does not levy any gift or inheritance tax if the recipient of the asset itself is tax-free for charitable purposes.[25] Furthermore, a philanthropic vehicle can play a rather important role in a family context as a shared philanthropic activity. It can, for example, serve as a platform where family members of all generations can work together, learn from each other, and share values and experiences.[26] Moreover, it can create a separate management level where family members can learn to take responsibility before taking a leadership role at the business level.[27]

2.2.3. *The Double Foundation Model*

If the founder wishes to profit from a tax-free transfer of assets while at the same time retaining control over the enterprise, it could be considered

---

2001, pp. 117 et seq.; P. Rawert, 'Stiftung und Unternehmen' in H. Kötz, P. Rawert, K. Schmidt and R. Walz, *Non-profit Law Yearbook 2003*, Köln 2004, p. 15.

22 See for further examples of Swiss enterprise foundations H. Grüninger, 'Unternehmensstiftung' in P.V. Kunz, F.S. Jörg and O. Arter, *Entwicklungen im Gesellschaftsrecht V*, Bern 2010, pp. 21 et seq.

23 D. Jakob, above n. 3, pp. 274 et seq.

24 T. Wüstemann, 'Familienpartizipation und gemeinnützige Stiftungen – rechtliche Herausforderungen und Chancen im nationalen und internationalen Kontext' in D. Jakob (ed), *Stiftung und Familie*, Basel 2015, p. 25.

25 See details in section 3.3.1 below.

26 See details in section 3.4 below.

27 D. Jakob, above n. 12.

to create a so-called double foundation model.[28] In this scenario, there are two shareholders – a family foundation or family holding and a charitable foundation – whereby the latter holds the majority of the share capital in the enterprise (which it has normally received as a tax-free donation). The 'trick' is that the share capital and the voting rights are distributed disproportionately between the two shareholders: immensely simplified, one shareholder – the tax-exempt charitable foundation[29] – holds perhaps 90% of the share capital; however, these shares carry only 10% of the voting rights in order to accumulate the actual control in the non-tax-exempt family entity that holds only 10% of the shares but 90% of the voting rights. The rather smart idea behind a vehicle like this is the tax-free transfer of an enterprise while retaining family control. One downside is that public opinion on such a setup might be negative because the construct appears to contain an abusive element: Why should the transfer of the enterprise be tax-free when the family remains in control of the assets going to the charitable foundation? By retaining control of the business through voting rights, family members in charge of the family foundation can control the dividends going up to the two shareholders. In the end, a structure like this might save the family a larger sum of money in the form of taxes than the charitable foundation ends up investing in the charitable purpose over the years. For this reason, the admissibility of this model under foundation and tax law has caused controversy.[30] This model has been intensively discussed in Germany, where there are quite a few well-known family businesses held in such a structure (with the Bertelsmann Foundation being the most prominent example), but should in principle also be possible in Switzerland.[31]

2.2.4. *Mixed Foundations*

The next model would be a mixed foundation – a foundation that pursues more than one purpose, such as a holding, a charitable and a family

[28] D. Jakob, above n. 3, pp. 185, 276–281; R. Hüttemann, 'Die gemischte Stiftung' in D. Jakob (ed), *Universum Stiftung*, Basel 2017, p. 29, 45; D. Jakob, *Schutz der Stiftung*, Tübingen 2006, pp. 78 et seq.

[29] Whether this construction is still possible regarding the recent judgment of the Federal Supreme Court, BGE 147 II 287 (see section 3.3.1 below) remains to be seen. However, it seems clear that the court did not waste any thought on the consequences of its (rather surprising) judgment to special situations such as the present one.

[30] See D. Jakob, p. 276 with further references.

[31] D. Jakob, above n. 12. Whether this is still the case after the BGE 147 II 287 decision (discussed in section 3.3.1.2 below) remains to be seen.

purpose all in one vehicle.[32] In fact, this structure is quite well known in Switzerland and includes some important family businesses such as the Ernst Göhner Foundation. It can be an efficient structure to use in order to hold the enterprise and to pursue other interests at the same time. This is especially common in Switzerland, where partial tax exemption is, at least in principle, also admissible.[33] However, from a governance point of view, the problem with this structure is that if purposes are mixed in one entity, there is quite a high risk that the interests of the involved persons start drifting apart, especially over the generations.

Typically, in a family context, the authority of the founder remains present within the first generation of family members and is universally respected, whereas in the second or third generation, this authority might dwindle, and the interests start falling apart. Some members of the governing bodies might want to place greater emphasis on the business aspect, while others might wish to focus on the charity; family members, on the other hand, might want to put the emphasis on the wellbeing of the family. In a case like this, conflict resolution can be difficult as it is not easy to restructure a foundation and to provide for the exit of one part. This begs the following question: is the only proper solution from a family governance perspective to build two independent structures instead of a mixed foundation? While this might be an alternative, of course, one could also pay special attention to a prudent drafting of the foundation statutes. Unlike the 1950s, when some famous examples of mixed foundations in Switzerland were established, nowadays we have a more modern understanding of foundations, and it is possible to create a vehicle that is more flexible and thus more suitable in this respect. For instance, one could provide for fair exit measures for one of the interested parties or for family members who wish to follow their own path; also, one could establish a robust conflict resolution mechanism in advance.[34]

2.2.5. *No Enterprise Foundation: Corporate Foundations*

Finally, if a *company* establishes a foundation – for example, to fulfil its corporate social responsibility (or, in a family context, a charitable foundation is set up by and next to a family business holding) – Swiss

---

32 R. Hüttemann, 'Die gemischte Stiftung' in D. Jakob (ed), above n. 28, pp. 29, 30–31, 47; F. Zihler, 'Zulässigkeit von Holdingstiftungen aus der Sicht der Handelsregisterbehörden', Reprax 2/2018, 69, pp. 74–75.

33 Cf. Circular No. 12, p. 6.

34 D. Jakob, above n. 12.

practice speaks of a 'corporate foundation', which is a different structure from an enterprise foundation.[35] Such a charitable foundation would have no holding function whatsoever and therefore does not constitute an enterprise foundation in the given sense.

2.2.6. *Interim Result*

These example structures show that there is not 'the' enterprise foundation under Swiss law and that businesses can be connected to foundations on various levels and for various motives and purposes. The examples also demonstrate the importance of drafting the statutes and setting up these structures in a way that leaves room for adaptability in a world that evolves quickly, and that keeps in mind that there is an intrinsic conflict between the rigid perpetuation on the one hand and the need for certain flexibility on the other hand. Against this background, the emphasis should now be put on specific challenges that enterprise foundations can typically face.

3. CURRENT CHALLENGES

3.1. STATE SUPERVISION AND ASSET MANAGEMENT

As can be seen above, Swiss enterprise foundations are no special legal structures and are regulated by the general provisions of Swiss foundation law. Therefore, the rules of state supervision apply and follow the normal regime of supervision regarding classical foundations.[36]

While state supervision is sometimes seen as a problem for enterprise foundations, it can be regarded as an advantage or a disadvantage depending on the perspective of the founder who favours more or less external control over his or her foundation. However, in contrast to what is sometimes thought, the supervisory authority will, in principle, not interfere with the business activities or business decisions of the board – especially when it comes to holding foundations.

---

35 Cf. T. Sprecher, *Stiftungsrecht in a nutshell*, Zürich 2017, p. 152; T. Sprecher, P. Egger and G. von Schnurbein, 'Der Swiss Foundation Code' in P. Egger and G. von Schnurbein (eds), *Foundation Governance*, Vol. 11, Basel 2015, p. 140; T. Gehringer, 'Corporate Foundations as Hybrid Organizations: A Systematic Review of Literature', VOLUNTAS 32/2021, pp. 257–275.

36 See art. 84 para. 2 CC.

Of course, the assets of the foundation must be used according to the purpose of the foundation. This can lead to a stricter controlling mechanism for business *operating* foundations regarding business decisions, which are in this structure made at the foundation level.[37] In this regard, *holding* foundations are less problematic as the business decisions are made at the level of the held corporation, and thus usually beyond state supervision.[38]

The bigger problem in fact is that the supervisory authority will have a quite strict control regarding the asset management of the foundation. Also in general, the topic of asset management of foundations can be a difficult subject in practice. The Swiss Civil Code does not contain any provisions on asset management. Solutions must therefore be derived from the general principles of foundation law. As a starting point, the founder's intention takes priority in asset management as well.[39] When setting up a foundation, each founder is free, in the foundation articles, to both define individual regulations on the investment of assets and to stipulate how the foundation assets must be used to achieve the relevant purpose.[40] If the foundation articles do not contain any specifications regarding the investment of assets or leave room for discretion, the foundation board must generally act in accordance with the principles of diligent asset management. According to a quite elderly jurisprudence, these principles include the elements of asset maintenance, security, risk diversification, profitability and liquidity.[41] Based on these principles, while the foundation board should avoid speculative investments, assigning 'gilt-edged status' to investments is not advisable. In addition, according to the Federal Supreme Court, the investment principles laid down in the Ordinance on Occupational Retirement, Survivors' and Disability Pension Plans[42] for staff pension funds can be used by boards of trustees of classical foundations as a 'guide'.[43] Since the suitability of these principles of jurisprudence for

37 See A. Meier-Hayoz, P. Forstmoser and R. Sethe, *Schweizerisches Gesellschaftsrecht*, 12th ed., Bern 2018, §23 marginal no. 27.

38 Ibid.

39 See ibid., p. 824; F. Zihler, 'Zulässigkeit von Holdingstiftungen aus der Sicht der Handelsregisterbehörden', Reprax 2/2018, pp. 69 et seq.

40 See art. 84 para. 2 CC.

41 Decisions of the Federal Supreme Court of Switzerland BGE 124 III 99; 108 II 352, E. 5.a.; for a foundation under federal state supervision, see also VEB 30 (1961) no. 45 p. 78; H. Grüninger, commenting on art. 84 CC, marginal no. 14.

42 Arts. 49 et seq. in the regulation on occupational retirement, survivors' and disability pension plans (BVV 2), SR 831.441.1.

43 See decisions of the Federal Supreme Court of Switzerland BGE 108 II 352 and 124 III 97.

many, particularly enterprise foundations, is limited, the statutes ideally define a concrete strategic position for the foundation with regard to its assets. However, the day-to-day balancing of investment security against generating returns generally remains at the individual discretion of the foundation board, and these decisions must be made according to the board's best judgement in its proper exercise of discretion. The supervisory authority can only check this exercise of discretion for any error of law and cannot interfere with the result of a lawful exercise of discretion, whether the authority entirely agrees with the decision or not.[44] For instance, if a board decides in its proper exercise of discretion that the special purpose relation of an investment (a so-called mission-based investment) should prevail over the classic criteria (such as diversification), the supervisory authority should respect this decision. However, supervisory authorities sometimes have to be reminded of this rule. It becomes evident that regarding the asset management, every individual foundation is different; what is possible for one foundation may not be permitted for another. However, one must be aware that in this field lurk potential discussions with the supervisory authority.

Another problem in the context of foundation assets can be faced when the foundation wants to separate from or restructure its assets. The question of if a foundation is allowed, for example, to sell the shares it holds, must in principle also be answered in accordance with the asset management criteria described above.[45] This leads to the next topic, which is whether and to what extent a foundation is a suitable structure in a business environment.

3.2. ENTERPRENEURIAL SUITABILITY OF THE FOUNDATION STRUCTURE

3.2.1. *Inflexibility*

The legal framework of foundations is sometimes seen as too inflexible to adapt to the dynamic business developments in an entrepreneurial

44 D. Jakob, commenting on art. 83 CC, marginal nos. 12 et seq. and commenting on art. 84 CC, marginal no. 5 in A. Büchler and D. Jakob (eds), above n. 2; D. Jakob, above n. 12, p. 316 et seq.

45 See n. 42.

environment.[46] This fundamental critique could be evaluated in two aspects: first, this reservation is mainly made with regard to Articles 85 et seq. CC, which constitute difficult conditions for changes in the purpose or the organisation of the foundation. However, this argument ignores a number of practical planning elements. It is possible to formulate a wide foundation purpose that is accompanied by examples or even another (secondary) purpose. Moreover, Swiss foundation law allows the reservation of a statutory founder's right to modify the purpose of the foundation.[47] Besides, it is always advisable to outsource the organisational details to separate regulations because they can be modified more easily.[48] This shows that Swiss foundation law in fact provides instruments to deal with the need of flexibility in a changing (business) environment,[49] provided that the foundation statutes and regulations are drafted appropriately. Competent legal advice may also consider possible combinations with other legal or hybrid structures to achieve the desired flexibility to maintain the entrepreneurial freedom.[50]

On the other hand, the robust structure of a foundation can be seen as an advantage. In fact, most of the time, the foundation is especially chosen because of its durability and independence, protection against hostile takeovers and ability to facilitate succession planning. Of course, the inevitable degree of rigidity can lead to difficulties, especially if drastic business decisions need to be taken or if restructuring of the business needs to take place by selling the assets or the shares of the foundation. Here, the solution depends on the type of foundation (see section 2.2 above) and the asset purpose relation: is the purpose of the foundation to hold the

---

46 A. Meier-Hayoz, P. Forstmoser, R. Sethe, above n. 37, §23 marginal no. 25; H. Grüninger, 'Unternehmensstiftung', in P. Kunz, F. Jörg and O. Arter (eds), above n. 22, pp. 34 et seq.

47 See art. 86a CC.

48 H. Hausheer and R. Aebi-Müller, *Das Personenrecht des Schweizerischen Zivilgesetzbuches*, 5th ed., Bern 2020, marginal no. 1297, 1324; H. Grüninger, 'Unternehmensstiftung', in P. Kunz, F. Jörg and O. Arter (eds), above n. 22, p. 35; decision of the Federal Supreme Court of Switzerland, BGE 76 I 77.

49 H. Grüninger, Unternehmensstiftung', in P. Kunz, F. Jörg and O. Arter (eds), above n. 22, p. 34; A. Meier-Hayoz, P. Forstmoser and R. Sethe, above n. 37, §23 marginal no 25.

50 A. Meier-Hayoz, P. Forstmoser and R. Sethe, above n. 37, §23 marginal no. 25; M. Uhl, *Kooperation im Stiftungsrecht*, Basel 2016, pp. 16 et seq.; H. Peter, 'Profit and non-profit purposes: can legal entities serve two masters at once?', EF 03/2019, pp. 163–165; V. Pfammatter, 'Hybrid entities in Switzerland: can Swiss entities pursue for- and non-profit purposes at the same time?', EF 03/2019, pp. 175–179.

shares or are the shares only an asset to fulfil a separate purpose? In any case, it usually requires some creativity and legal advice in order to restructure a (held) business in line with the rules of the (holding) foundation. That is the important message: simply the fact that a restructuring would make sense from a business point of view does not mean that it is automatically admissible and allowed under foundation law.

3.2.2. Absence of Shareholders

As is well known, foundations do not have shareholders or any kind of members, because the foundation consists of self-contained assets dedicated to a specific purpose. Therefore, another objection to foundation structures in a business context is the absence of directly interested shareholders to exert pressure on the profitability of the business, which is a decisive aspect of corporations.[51] However, this argument is countered by a number of studies that argue that foundations are the better owners of businesses than profit-driven shareholders.[52] This discussion cannot be conducted here, but it shall be emphasised that there is a multitude of – also in an economic sense – very successful enterprise foundations in Switzerland and other German-speaking countries.[53]

3.3. UNFRIENDLY TAX ENVIRONMENT

3.3.1. Holding Foundations

The next challenge is that in Switzerland there is a more and more unfriendly tax environment for charitable tax-exempt foundations that are

---

51 See A. Meier-Hayoz, P. Forstmoser and R. Sethe, above n. 37, §23 marginal no. 25; H. Grüninger, 'Unternehmensstiftung', in P. Kunz, F. Jörg and O. Arter (eds), above n. 22, p. 41.

52 Cf. S. Thomsen, *The Danish Industrial Foundations*, Copenhagen 2017, pp. 25 et seq., 38; H. Hansmann and S. Thomsen, *The Governance of Foundation-Owned Firms,* Copenhagen 2018, pp. 2 et seq.; S. Thomsen, T. Poulsen, C. Borsting and J. Kuhn, 'Industrial foundations as long-term owners', Wiley Corp. Govern Int Rev. 2018/26, pp. 180–196; M. Habersack, P. Horvath et al., *Stiftungsunternehmen in Deutschland, Gesetzliche Grundlagen, unternehmerische Motive, Reformvorschläge,* München 2021, pp. 19 et seq.

53 See A. Meier-Hayoz, P. Forstmoser and R. Sethe, above n. 37, §23 marginal no. 38; H. Grüninger, above n. 13, preliminary remarks on art. 80–89a marginal no. 17 et seq.; H. Grüninger, 'Unternehmensstiftung', in P. Kunz, F. Jörg and O. Arter (eds), above n. 22, pp. 21 et seq., 41; H. Grüninger, *Die Unternehmensstiftung in der*

holding a business. One must recall that the pure charitable foundation is a major foundation model with a large number of important examples.[54] In order to understand why and to what extent holding significant shares of a company is compatible with or detrimental to tax exemption, a brief look shall be taken at the requirements of tax exemption in general.

3.3.1.1. General Requirements of Tax Exemption

In the first place, a tax exemption requires a 'tax-exemption-worthy' purpose of the foundation. Legal entities are tax-exempt if they pursue specific, charitable purposes. The criteria require two aspects: an activity of a general interest and an altruistic action.[55] To be subsumed under a general interest, which is evaluated from a Swiss perspective, the activity has to take place in the charitable, humanitarian, health, ecological, cultural, educational or scientific sectors.[56] However, not every effort to support individual sections of the population in an economic or social way counts as an effort in the service of the general public; in fact, the pursued purpose has to be seen as worthy of support from a general Swiss social perspective.[57] In addition, the group of possibly eligible beneficiaries has to be open.[58]

The requirement of altruism means that the foundation must pursue neither the interests of the legal entity itself nor those of persons

---

Schweiz, Zulässigkeit – Eignung – Besteuerung, Basel 1984, pp. 28 et seq.; T. Sprecher and U. von Salis-Lütolf, *Die schweizerische Stiftung*, Zürich 1999, no. 265; M. Feick, *Stiftung als Nachfolgeinstrument*, München 2015, pp. 362 et seq.; S. Scherer, *Münchener Anwaltshandbuch Erbrecht*, 5th ed., München 2018, §38 marginal no. 24.

54 See section 2.2.2 above.

55 See Circular No. 12, pp. 2 et seq.; decisions of the Federal Supreme Court of Switzerland BGer 2C_385/2020 25 June 2020, E. 4.2.1; BGer 2C_147/2019 20 August 2019, E. 4.4; BGer 2C_484/2015 10 August 2015, E. 5.3; BGer 2C_251/2012 17 August 2012, E. 2.1.

56 See Circular No. 12, p. 3; and for the criteria in more depth, see M. Greter and A. Greter, commenting on art. 56 DBG in M. Zweifel and M Beusch (eds), *Kommentar zum Schweizerischen Steuerrecht, Bundesgesetz über die direkte Bundessteuer*, 3rd ed., Basel 2017, marginal no. 29; M. Greter and A. Greter, commenting on art. 23 StHG in M. Zweifel and M. Beusch (eds), *Kommentar zum schweizerischen Steuerrecht, Bundesgesetz über die Harmonisierung der direkten Steuern der Kantone und Gemeinden*, 3rd ed., Basel 2017, marginal no. 27a; T. Koller, 'Stiftungen und Steuern' in H.M. Riemer (ed), *Die Stiftung in der juristischen und wirtschaftlichen Praxis*, Zürich 2001, pp. 66 et seq.

57 Decision of the Federal Supreme Court of Switzerland BGE 114 Ib 277, E. 2b.

58 Circular No. 12, p. 3; see further M. Greter and A. Greter, commenting on art. 56 DBG, above n. 56, marginal no. 30; M. Greter and A. Greter, commenting on art. 23 StHG, above n. 56, marginal no. 27b.

behind it.[59] Altruistic action means sacrifices,[60] not self-helping purposes or commercial interests – business or profit purposes are not charitable purposes.[61] However, not every gainful activity of a foundation is incompatible with tax exemption; it can be regarded charitable if it is a meant to fulfil a charitable purpose and is subordinate under that purpose.[62]

3.3.1.2. Specific Tax Exemption Criteria for Holding Foundations

Against this background, it can be seen that foundations pursuing business purposes do not qualify for tax exemption in Switzerland. However, the crucial question is what happens if foundations with charitable purposes hold for profit, business-making companies.[63] Here, Circular No. 12 and practice have developed specific criteria.[64]

In order to be compatible with these criteria, it is necessary that the interest in the business is subordinate to the purpose of the foundation. Therefore, the foundation must not have a dominant influence on the business, and a clear separation of the management of the foundation and the company is required (while one connecting person is allowed). As a consequence, the possibility of interference with the business management should be avoided, which would possibly also be the case if another legal entity was holding the majority of the voting rights.[65] As evidence of the fact that the interest in the held business is subordinate to the (charitable) foundation purpose, the authorities have formulated the further requirement of a regular and substantial funding of the foundation by the business[66] and that the foundation must actually be using this funding for its charitable purposes.

However, against this (already quite difficult) background, the Federal Supreme Court of Switzerland dealt with the requirement of subordination

59 Circular No. 12, p. 3; see further M. Greter and A. Greter, commenting on art. 56 DBG, above n. 56, marginal no. 31 et seq.; M. Greter and A. Greter, commenting on art. 23 StHG, above n. 56, marginal nos. 27c et seq.; see also decisions of the Federal Supreme Court of Switzerland BGer 2C_166/2020 10 May 2021, E. 6.1; BGer 2C_251/2012 and 2C_252/2012 17 August 2012, E. 2.1.

60 For more details, see M. Reich, 'Gemeinnützigkeit als Steuerbefreiungsgrund', ASA 58/1989, pp. 471 et seq.

61 Art. 56 lit. g DBG; art. 23 para. 1 lit. f StHG; Circular No. 12, p. 3.

62 Circular No. 12, pp. 3 et seq.

63 See art. 56 lit. g DBG; art. 23 para. 1 lit. g StHG.

64 See Circular No. 12 of 8 July 1994, available at: http://www.estv.admin.ch.

65 Circular No. 12, p. 4.

66 Ibid.

in its latest decision of 2021.[67] Here, a non-tax-exempt foundation had transferred its commercial catering business to a 100% held subsidiary company and then applied for tax exemption because of its charitable purpose. In its conclusion, the Court interpreted the requirement of subordination in a new way and no longer referred to the requirement of a regular and substantial alimentation of the foundation by the business. Rather, it surprisingly held that an adequate asset investment diversification was decisive. Having transferred the business of the foundation to *one* underlaying company, which is the *only* asset, would make the foundation dependent on that company and the interest in the latter would not be subordinate to the charitable foundation purpose.[68] As a result, the Court seems to require investments in various companies or assets – and not only in one – which might be in line with the general *civil law* principles of asset management (especially the principle of risk diversification), but not with the established *tax* practice and the structure of many charitable Swiss holding foundations.

The described tax criteria for holding foundations are not only vague and difficult to handle in practice; there are also several critical aspects to be pointed out: the tax authorities seem to deny that the investment in one prosperous business can be more reasonable and profitable for a charitable foundation than a more diversified investment in a normal portfolio – however, if such an asset management is deemed admissible from a foundation law perspective (according to the above-mentioned principles),[69] the tax authority should exercise restraint when evaluating the tax exemption and accept the structure. The tax authority and the Court also disregarded the fact that the subsidiary company must pay taxes in an orderly fashion – hence, the assets are already taxed and therefore the foundation does not take any advantage of the tax-free business activity when using the profits for the charitable purpose. Finally, they neglect a clear distinction between the asset management and the purpose of a foundation. That been said, with the new jurisprudence of the Swiss Federal Court, if it is not an outlier decision, there might be a new risk of losing tax exemption or never even getting the exemption if a charitable foundation holds significant shares in only one company.[70]

---

67 Decision of the Federal Supreme Court of Switzerland BGE 147 II 287.

68 Ibid., E. 8.6.

69 See section 3.3.1.1 above.

70 Covering the whole topic in detail, see A. Opel, 'Steuerbefreiung von Holdingstiftungen', IFF Forum für Steuerrecht 4/2021, pp. 341–357.

3.3.2. *Impact Investments*

The next problem is the unclear situation in the Swiss tax environment for mission-based investments, impact investments and entrepreneurial grant-making schemes by investments in companies. If a foundation invests in companies (mostly start-ups or social businesses) and receives shares in return, the situation also results in a special kind of enterprise foundation (mostly with the intention of taking an active ownership role to bring the company forward). The conventional understanding regarding philanthropic foundations used to be that the activities of a foundation are largely limited to the management of the foundation's assets and the distribution of the *income* to the benefit of its purpose. However, the calls for a more impact-oriented approach are growing louder. The question of whether and when purpose- or impact-related investments are 'permitted' for a certain foundation is therefore a common issue. From a tax perspective, the criteria for tax exemption must be met so that a tax-exempt foundation does not lose its tax exemption. As it is still a quite new phenomenon, the challenge is that the permissibility under foundation and tax law is assessed by authorities on a case-by-case basis. Furthermore, because the Swiss authorities have only recently started to engage more closely with the concept of impact investments, the process of categorizing and developing legal admissibility requirements is still ongoing. Cantonal tax authorities in particular are reluctant when it comes to deciding on tax exemption.

Because foundations traditionally distribute funds *à fonds perdu* and are not meant to act as entrepreneurs (at least from the conventional perspective of the tax authorities), profits from such activities (such as the successful disposal of shares in a start-up)[71] could be regarded as profit-making, which would go against the criteria for charitable status (see section 3.4 below). It is therefore important to demonstrate that such models do not aim to generate profit, but rather must be assessed based on their effectiveness at fulfilling the foundation purpose; furthermore, any income from the entrepreneurial approach is only the by-product of the exceptionally effective fulfilment of the purpose.

The crucial question is actually the following: under what conditions can charitable foundations use entrepreneurial funding models without losing their tax exemption, and how can the fiscal authority prevent foundations from abusing their charitable status? Therefore, criteria are

---

[71] Cf. T. Sprecher, above n. 35, p. 112.

currently to be defined that can help to differentiate between genuine entrepreneurial funding models and disguised profit-making activities that would (legitimately) be excluded from tax exemption.[72]

3.4. GOVERNANCE

As a final remark, it should be noted that in order to make an enterprise foundation work, there is a strong need for a good foundation governance (and in a family or family business context, also for family governance).

As foundations are increasingly expected to operate as effectively as possible and should improve in terms of accountability and transparency, effective governance practices are crucial for a foundation that wants to achieve impact and creditability at the same time. Nowadays, founders and foundations should strive for a system to protect the foundation and its purpose fulfilment, as well as for checks and balances and precise standards of actions that lead to an effective foundation governance as a legal and actual regulatory framework.[73]

This is especially true for enterprise foundations as the interaction with the business might lead to conflicts of interests that should be avoided and require measures to ensure that diverging interests can be harmonised.

Since Swiss enterprise foundations often result from a generation transition in a family context, a sensitive look at family governance is also crucial if the foundation should not only work successfully but should also play a part in the wellbeing of a family. The main questions to ask are as follows: how can we take advantage of the additional management level? And how do we integrate family values into legal tools? Here, the role of a shared philanthropic activity is a significant one as it can build a bridge between family values and the business activities.[74] At the same time, it shows that the secret of successful enterprise foundations is a truly interdisciplinary matter.

---

72 For the suggestions of such criteria by the present author, see D. Jakob and G. von Schnurbein, above n. 2, p. 50; see T. Sprecher, 'Zur steuerlichen Behandlung von neuen Förder- und Finanzierungsmodellen' in B. Eckhart, D. Jakob and G. von Schnurbein (eds), *Der Schweizer Stiftungsreport 2013*, Zürich 2013, pp. 19 et seq.

73 D. Jakob, above n. 12, pp. 314 et seq.; see also T. Sprecher, P. Egger and G. von Schnurbein, *Swiss Foundation Code 2021, Principles and Recommendations for the Establishment and Management of Grant-Making Foundations*, Bern 2021.

74 Cf. D. Jakob, above n. 12.

4. CONCLUSION

As a conclusion, it can be observed that Swiss foundation law provides a liberal environment for different kinds of enterprise foundations. Combined with the freedom of the founder, many structures and solutions are possible. It is therefore not surprising that enterprise or business foundations have a long tradition and many famous examples in Switzerland. On the other hand, there is a general trend towards regulation and stricter authorities, especially regarding the tax exemption for charitable foundations holding or interacting with businesses. Also, a sensitive foundation and family governance is crucial if an enterprise foundation should work successfully over the generations. If one wants to make a prediction, it seems unlikely that the Swiss legislator will specifically address enterprise foundations in the near future. However, it should be noted that the current revision of the Swiss inheritance law will reduce the forced shares of heirs as of 2023 and will thus (among other provisions) facilitate the transfer of businesses in a forced heirship context.[75] This may further promote an increase of enterprise foundations in Switzerland in the future.

[75] See BBl 2020 9923.

ENTERPRISE FOUNDATIONS IN SWEDEN

Katarina Olsson

ABSTRACT

This chapter discusses enterprise foundations in Sweden. Although foundations have a long history and a strong tradition in Sweden, there has been little focus on foundations that either conduct business in their own name or own shares in a company. There is a lack of a common understanding of the notion of 'enterprise foundation' and there is no legal definition of it either. Notably, there is also an almost complete absence of a political, legal or economic discussion which results in a situation where enterprise foundations seem to exist more or less unnoticed as a separate category in the foundation world. Greater transparency and a more conscious discussion are needed in order to shed light on this interesting legal entity.

1. INTRODUCTION AND HISTORICAL CONSIDERATIONS

1.1. BACKGROUND

There are almost 20,000 foundations according to the Swedish official registry on foundations.[1] About 1,800 foundations are registered as enterprise foundations. However, the number of enterprise foundations is not necessarily accurate. There are probably more enterprise foundations than the registry information suggests. Many enterprise foundations in Sweden are registered according to their purpose, as charitable foundations, even in cases where the foundation has a strong connection to an enterprise.

The concept of 'enterprise foundation' in Sweden is not straightforward. The two words 'enterprise' and 'foundation' are inherently complicated and require special attention in a legal discussion.[2] An enterprise (*näringsverksamhet*) has one meaning in Swedish private law and a slightly different meaning in tax law. To further contribute to the complexity, there is no legal definition of an enterprise foundation in Sweden. It is probably not uncommon that a foundation that is presented and described as a charitable foundation is actually a controlling owner of a business entity. Enterprises in themselves are usually profit-driven, but when it comes to ownership, the foundation can provide a legal form that allows for the charitable distribution of wealth.

One problem when discussing foundations is that it is difficult to organize and classify foundations into a unified system. Therefore, it is not easy to discuss enterprise foundations. Each author has to present his or her description or definition of the investigated foundations.

We know fairly little about enterprise foundations in Sweden and there seems to be no political or societal interest in discussing these foundations today. Legal writings[3] on the issue are scarce and case law on private law issues is almost non-existent.[4]

---

1 The registry at the County Administration Boards is available at: https://stiftelser.lansstyrelsen.se.

2 *Stiftelse* is the Swedish word used for an entity covered by the Foundation Act (Stiftelselagen 1994:1220). It is not obvious that the word *stiftelse* is to be translated into 'foundation' in English; however this is the terminology often chosen for a text in English.

3 There are only two doctoral dissertations in Sweden that deal exclusively with foundations: H. Hessler, *Om stiftelser*, Norstedts Juridik, Stockholm 1952

Enterprise foundations can live a rather quiet life, without attracting attention from the legislator, the judiciary or the academic environment. Myths, lack of transparency and hidden motives have often been at the forefront in the Swedish discussion on enterprise foundations.[5]

Notably for Sweden, relatively few influential family business groups have used foundations to exercise far-reaching control over Swedish industry.[6] The fact that, for example, the Wallenberg family business group is controlled by the fifth generation of family members through foundations and the Ax:son Johnson family business group is controlled by the fourth generation indicates that enterprise foundations may be effective in creating and sustaining large family business groups.[7]

Since there is not much legal research or political discussion on foundations in Sweden, one might conclude that to some extent the foundations are rather poorly understood as actors in the Swedish business life and society in general. However, lately economists have turned their attention on the enterprise foundations.[8]

(foundations in general); and K. Olsson, *Näringsdrivande stiftelser*, Nerenius & Santérus Förlag, Stockholm 1996 (enterprise foundations). There is no comprehensive academic study on Swedish foundations in English. A number of smaller books of a handbook nature, all of them in Swedish, mainly discuss practical issues on foundations. For example, see K. Fagerberg, J. Lindman, B. Löfgren Lewin and P. Aamisepp, *Stiftelsehandboken*, Norstedts Juridik, Stockholm 2019.

4 When it comes to tax law there is an extensive case law, see M. Berglund, *Beskattning av stiftelser*, IUSTUS, Uppsala 2021.

5 For a discussion on the motives behind the creation of a foundation, which is not always made clear in its purpose, see K. Olsson, above n. 3, pp. 199–210.

6 D. Johansson, M. Stenkula and N. Wykman, 'The Taxation of Industrial Foundations in Sweden (1862–2018)', *Nordic Tax Journal* 2020: 1, 1–14, 4–5 give a short presentation on family business groups and connected industrial foundations. M. Henrekson, D. Johansson and M. Stenkula, 'The rise and decline of industrial foundations as controlling owners of Swedish listed firms: the role of tax incentives', *Scandinavian Economic History Review* 2020: 68(2), 170–191 discuss potential explanations as to why Sweden has seen a decline in the creation of enterprise foundations. The authors point to the importance of tax incentives for the use of enterprise foundations as control vehicles for listed firms.

7 D. Johansson et al., above n. 6, p. 5. M. Henrekson et al. above n. 6, p. 174 mention other foundations that are used as controlling vehicles: Dunkerstiftelserna: https://dunkerstiftelserna.se, Söderbergstiftelserna: https://ragnar.soderbergs.org and https://www.torstensoderbergsstiftelse.se, and Kjell och Märtha Beijers stiftelse: https://www.beijerstiftelsen.se/about. See also D. Johansson, M. Stenkula and N. Wykman, *The Rise of Private Foundations as Owners of Swedish Industry: The Role of Tax Incentives 1862–2018*, IFN Working Paper No. 1245, Research Institute of Industrial Economics, Stockholm.

8 For recent information, see M. Henrekson et al. above n. 6; D. Johansson et al. above n. 6; F. Wijkström and S. Einarsson, 'Comparing Swedish Foundations: A Carefully Negotiated Space of Existence', *American Behavioral Scientist* 2018: 62(13), 1889–1918.

1.2. HISTORICAL REMARKS

Foundations often come with an interesting history that will help provide the reasons for setting up the foundation, the founder's ambitions and wishes, but also information that might help in interpreting and applying the provisions in the charter.

Sweden has a long history of foundations. The oldest foundations date back to the 16th century,[9] when people donated to religious purposes and for taking care of the poor. In the 18th century, foundations were set up to support education. Higher education and scientific research became more important purposes in the late 19th century. Enterprise foundations are a phenomenon of the 20th century.

Foundations are closely linked to the economic and societal development in any country. In order to fully understand how the foundations function and are regulated in Sweden, it is vital to understand not only the legal situation but also the societal implications and the political aims.[10]

The emergence of a strong welfare state in Sweden in many ways changed how and why foundations were set up. Due to the Swedish welfare system, foundations led a rather quiet existence way into the 20th century. Through the tax system, the state financed education, research, social benefits and economic support for those in need. The foundations provided supplementary grants. According to Wijkström and Einarsson, 'the foundation world is still deeply embedded in the social contract and strong Social-Democratic regime of the 20th century'. The authors refer to this position as a carefully negotiated space of existence.[11]

Sweden, like many other countries in Europe, was a rather poor agricultural country until the start of the Industrial Revolution in the mid-19th century. As Johansson et al. observe, entrepreneurs at that time started successful family businesses controlling large parts of

---

9 See, for example, Stiftelsen Danviks Hospital, which was created in 1551, https://www.danvikshem.se/historia/grundades-ar-1551. For a comprehensive historical background, see F. Wijkström and S. Einarsson, *Foundations in Sweden: Their Scope, Roles and Visions*, Economic Research Institute at the Stockholm School of Economics, 2005, available at: https://www.researchgate.net/publication/273775439_Foundations_in_Sweden_Their_Scope_Roles_and_Visions.

10 For a short background, see F. Wijkström and S. Einarsson, above n. 9; and S. Einarsson and F. Wijkström, *The EUFORI Study, European Foundations for Research and Innovation, Country Report Sweden*, report for the European Commission, 2015, section 1.1: http://euforistudy.eu/wp-content/uploads/2015/07/Sweden.pdf.

11 F. Wijkström and S. Einarsson, above n. 8, p. 1889.

Swedish industry.[12] This of course attracted attention from policy makers and analysts, but it was not until the 1960s that a systematic examination of their influence was conducted. According to the inquiry on concentration, family and foundations controlled many of the spheres of ownership in the Swedish industry.[13]

Henrekson et al. argue that enterprise foundations became a vehicle for corporate control of large listed firms in Sweden in the period between the two World Wars. Wealthy individuals replaced these foundations in the 1990s either through direct ownership or holding companies.[14]

In the 1960s the discussion arose about the permissibility of both concentration of power and foundation ownership. From a political perspective, foundations are not always regarded as beneficial to society. In different public inquiries and reports, one can observe a hostile and suspicious attitude towards private initiatives through foundations. In the debate, arguments can be found that foundations are used for criminal purposes, money laundering or hiding assets in order to benefit the founder.[15] Einarsson and Wijkström attribute this criticism to the character of foundations 'as inflexible pools of capital without easily identified proxies for their owners'.[16]

1.3. THE FOUNDATION WORLD IN SWEDEN TODAY

Foundations today represent a significant part of the Swedish non-profit sector. The foundations form a heterogeneous group that cannot be defined or described in a uniform way. There are very small foundations in the sense that they have very limited capital – maybe only €1,000. But there are also large foundations with capital of millions of euros and with complicated structures when it comes to purposes and activities. The vast

12 D. Johansson, M. Stenkula and N. Wykan, above n. 6.

13 Government inquiry on concentration, *Koncentrationsutredningen, Ägande och inflytande i det privata näringslivet* (SOU 1968:7).

14 M. Henrekson et al. above n. 6. In the article the authors examine why enterprise foundations became vehicles for control over large companies at the Stockholm Stock Exchange and why the importance of the legal form of enterprise foundations has declined in recent decades. They focus on tax incentives for establishing enterprise foundations as control vehicles.

15 See Government Bill, Prop. 2004/05:50 *Åtgärder mot missbruk at stiftelser* (Measures against abuse of foundations).

16 S. Einarsson and F. Wijkström, above n. 10, section 1.1. See also F. Wijkström and S. Einarsson, above n. 8.

majority of foundations have a charitable purpose. They are grant making, and many of them lead a rather quiet existence, although they perform important tasks that benefit a lot of people.

The enterprise foundations can be categorized as grant-making foundations, although they conduct business in their own organization or own shares in a business corporation. Such foundations can be controlling vehicles with great influence and power. Although there are some very large enterprise foundations, it must not be forgotten that many of the enterprise foundations are small and there is no family involved or no controlling motive.

Foundations are important in several sectors of Swedish society, especially in funding research and education. External funding is often vital in order for excellent research to be conducted.[17]

In the historical context, it is also important to point out the dissolution of the wage-earner funds (*löntagarfonderna*) and the creation of the so-called wage-earner fund foundations (*löntagarfondsstiftelserna*). These huge foundations are not considered as enterprise foundations, but their giving of grants to research is often combined with conditions of cooperation with businesses.[18] It is also important not to forget savings-banks foundations (*sparbanksstiftelser*) that own many Swedish savings banks.

Looking at the foundation sector today, it can be concluded that it is a healthy and prosperous legal entity. As the public welfare sector is struggling to finance, for example, education and research, healthcare and care for the elderly, the financing from foundations is becoming more and more important. The criticism against the foundation format is seldom heard, and enterprise foundations as a form for conducting or owning

---

17 F. Wijkström and S. Einarsson, above n. 8, p. 1911, conclude that the Swedish foundation sector is complementary rather than a substitute to public financing. However, there is one exception. Funding of scientific research perhaps has a more important function as a substitute. Many of the foundations funding scientific research are owners of businesses, and thus enterprise foundations according to the terminology used in this book.

18 See e.g. KK-stiftelsen: https://www.kks.se/om-oss/in-english. The foundation funds activities conducted in collaboration with academic staff and business sector partners. The aim is to build internationally competitive, integrated research and education environments. Eleven foundations were set up with a total capital of €2 billion, all derived from the wage-earner funds. Over the years, political discussions have suggested the dissolution of these foundation and transfer of the money back to the state. The foundation form has proved to be a guarantee of stability and long-term management.

business activities are not discussed in Swedish society or in a political or legal context.

However, new developments can be observed. Rich and young entrepreneurs sometimes create foundations and want the foundation to be an extension of their entrepreneurial experiences. Such a wish can take the form of, for example, social or impact investment rules for investing the foundation's capital.

According to the research of Wijkström and Einarsson, 1,400 foundations were created between 2002 and 2012.[19] Compared to the total number of almost 20,000 foundations, this is a rather high rate of new establishment. Foundations of all categories are growing, in terms of numbers as well as assets. Unfortunately, it is not possible to extract any reliable estimate on how many of the new foundations that can be categorized as enterprise foundations. The official registries in Sweden are simply not consistent and accurate when it comes to this rather undefined legal entity.

1.4. SOME WORDS ABOUT TERMINOLOGY

The term 'enterprise foundation' does not have an unambiguous meaning in Swedish law, nor does it expressly refer to a clearly defined type of foundation. The enterprise foundation (*näringsdrivande stiftelse*) concept does not, as mentioned above, have a legal definition or legal effect.

In the preparatory work for the Foundation Act, the foundations were divided into two groups: grant-making foundations (*avkastningsstift elser*) and activity-based foundations (*verksamhetsstift elser*). The notion *verksamhetsstiftelse* refer to foundations which 'as a rule fulfil their purpose by carrying on business activities'.[20] This terminology does not recur in the Foundation Act. The fact that a foundation is described as carrying out a business does not entail any legal effects of a private law nature – except that the foundation is obliged to follow certain rules that apply to all organizations that conduct business – but is more a description of foundations with a specific type of purpose and/or activity.

The enterprise foundation (*näringsdrivande stiftelse*) concept does not appear in the Foundation Act, but Chapter 7 refers to 'foundations that

19 F. Wijkström and S. Einarsson, above n. 8, p. 1894.
20 Government Bill, Prop. 1993/94:9, pp. 40 et seq.

carry out business activities' and regulates situations of liquidation and dissolution.[21]

Foundations connected to a business in the sense discussed in this book appear in many forms in Sweden: industrial foundations,[22] operation foundations[23] and more rarely enterprise foundations. As far as it has been possible to ascertain, the terminology and language have not given rise to any major problems, either in legal or other respects.

The Swedish private law definition of an enterprise (*näringsidkare*) is someone who professionally runs activities of an economic nature with independence and duration. No profit motive with the business is required in order to be qualified as an enterprise. The business must be of an economic nature, i.e. refer to the sale of goods or services that have an economic value. Professionally conducted activities place demands on a certain scope, regularity and duration. The fact that the activity intends to promote a non-profit or charitable purpose does not constitute an obstacle to considering it as a business activity in an enterprise foundation.

The term 'business activity' (*näringsverksamhet*) is often used in everyday speech as a description of the company, the enterprise. The entity that runs the business is organised as a natural or legal person – a company, an association or a foundation.

In Sweden there is also sometimes a difference between the private law and the tax law notion of business activity (*näringsverksamhet*), which might complicate the discussion. In the tax legislation, the concept of business activity refers to independently conducted profit-making activity. The difference between the private law and the tax law meaning of the concept of 'business activity' is mainly that in private law there is no requirement for profit. This means that the concept of private law is somewhat broader than the concept of tax law. The private law definition thus also includes typically non-profit activities that take place without interest in an economic exchange. The foundation can, for example, run a café at cost price or provide care to the beneficiaries for a heavily subsidized fee. Sometimes the foundations also receive state or municipal grants, which may be the case for a foundation that runs a nursing home, a theatre, a museum or a daycare centre.

---

21 The preparatory works refer to *näringsdrivande stiftelse*, e.g. Government Bill, Prop. 1993/94:9, p. 48.

22 See e.g. M. Henrekson et al., above n. 6; and D. Johansson et al., above n. 6.

23 S. Einarsson and F. Wijkström, above n. 10, section 1.1.

In summary, the term 'business activity' (*näringsverksamhet*) has no clearly defined meaning and it can sometimes be doubtful whether a foundation conducts such activities that are to be regarded as business activities.

1.5. THE NOTION OF THE ENTERPRISE FOUNDATION

In the eyes of the public in general, a foundation distributes grants for a non-profit or charitable purpose. The foundation's wealth consists of assets that can easily be transformed into cash for distribution to the beneficiaries. Swedish tax rules give a very clear incentive for distributing profits and dividends to the beneficiaries (see section 3 below).

Business operations, on the one hand, typically require flexibility and some risk taking. The foundation, on the other hand, is expected to be unchangeable and eternal. Business activity may at first glance seem incompatible with the foundation and its lasting purpose. To some viewers, it might seem somewhat strange that a foundation can own a company or conduct a business in its own name.

In many enterprise foundations, it is not possible to see from its charter whether the foundation runs or owns a business. This is a crucial difference compared to the companies and associations where the business activity is evident from the documents in connection with their formation, and in some cases also directly from the legal rules. There is a presumption in the law for business activities in limited companies and economic associations. Such presumptions are not linked to foundations.

The relationship between the foundation and the business can be constructed in different ways depending on a variety of causes and factors. Business activities within a foundation may arise in accordance with the founder's instructions in the charter or by decision of the board of the foundation. The design of the purpose provision determines whether the business activity is an aim for the fulfilment of a purpose, will function as a profit generator or in some other way will be part of the asset management. The difference in the way of looking at it is that the business activity is either a purpose in itself or a means for the fulfilment of the purpose. It must follow from the central function of the purpose provision in the charter of the foundation that the connection with the business is regarded as being in line with the purpose. A business activity that cannot be included under the purpose is not acceptable.

It is a striking feature that enterprise foundations often operate at the outer limits of what is normally accepted within the concept of a foundation, in terms of either their purpose or activity. Enterprise foundations often also operate on the outer fringes of the 'business' concept. This may, for example, be the case for a foundation that runs a non-profit-oriented business with no real profit motive, where the foundation only strives to cover its costs.

Running a certain business does not have to be the sole purpose of the foundation. The foundation may have ancillary, superior or subordinate purposes of a different nature. The assets may also consist of property other than that attributable to the business. There is then often a close connection between other purposes in the foundation and the business activities.

The question of foundations that own shares and therefore could be identified as enterprise foundations have scarcely been discussed in legal terms in Sweden. Sweden is therefore in a completely different situation compared to, for example, Denmark.

The 'enterprise foundation' notion generally refers to a foundation that conducts business activities in its own name or that in its capacity as owner or member has a controlling influence and an interest in a business activity outside the foundation. Based on the business operations' relationship to the foundation, there are two forms of business foundations in Swedish law: direct enterprise foundations and indirect enterprise foundations.

It could be discussed whether foundations solely in their capacity as owners are to be classified as enterprise foundations. The role of ownership alone cannot generally lead to the foundation being regarded as an enterprise foundation. But additional factors that bind the foundation to a business can lead to it being justified to talk about indirect enterprise.

1.6. DIRECT AND INDIRECT ENTERPRISE FOUNDATIONS

For pedagogical reasons, it might be interesting to further discuss the two different types of enterprise foundations: direct enterprise foundations and indirect enterprise foundations.[24]

Direct enterprise foundations include foundations that run a business in their own name in accordance with an express order from the founder

---

[24] Writing my dissertation on enterprise foundations in the early 1990s (K. Olsson, *Näringsdrivande stiftelser*), I decided to use the more extended notion and include both direct and indirect enterprise foundations. This has not been criticised or commented on, but it is important to stress that there are no legal effects connected to the terminology itself.

in the charter. The business is the foundation's purpose or object of activity and follows directly from the founder's appointment. From the foundation's point of view, the business is thus originally an external decision that the board has to comply with.

A distinctive feature of several foundations in the group is a close and natural connection between the foundation's purposes and the business activities. In its purest form, the business is the foundation's purpose – the foundation shall, for example, run a vegetarian restaurant or a bookstore for children's books. Foundations without an external purpose (called Selbstzweckstiftung according to the German terminology) are allowed in Sweden, and unlike other jurisdictions like Denmark, there has been no discussion on the permissibility of this kind of purpose.

In these foundations, there is an identity between wealth and business. Since the purpose directly indicates the business activity, these foundations seldom present any problems from a foundation law point of view with regard to the business activity and its compatibility with the purpose. The business can also be the foundation's object of activity – in the examples above, the charter can prescribe that the foundation must spread knowledge about the lacto-vegetarian diet and for this purpose run a vegetarian restaurant, or that the foundation must contribute to the dissemination of good literature for children and run a bookstore.

Sometimes it is not even possible to distinguish between purpose and business objects. This is the case if the foundation's purpose is to 'run a bookstore for children's books' or 'publish a journal in law', without any further information in the charter about the specific focus or purpose of the activity.

Indirect enterprise foundations include foundations where the founder has admittedly not prescribed that the foundation shall conduct business activities, but where the board has made the assessment that the foundation's purpose is best met by the foundation conducting business activities. In the examples above, the operation of the vegetarian restaurant and the bookstore in this group of foundations would not appear in the charter. The business activity shall function as a contribution to or a way of fulfilling the purpose and is then the foundation's object of activity, even if it is not expressed in the charter.[25] The business follows from an internal

---

25 A somewhat odd feature in Swedish foundation law literature is the description of a foundation's purpose as consisting of three parts. The first part, the aim (*syftet*), describes what the founder wants to achieve through the purpose. This part is necessary in all foundations. The second part is the type of activity that is to be conducted in order to fulfil the aim, the object of activity (*verksamhetsföremålet*).

decision by the board of the foundation. The foundation's purpose does not have to have any connection to the business, and the business does not have to have direct support in the charter. However, the purpose and the founder's additional regulations in the charter must not constitute an obstacle for the foundation to conduct business activities.

Many foundations invest their assets in shares of various companies. Some of them might be characterized as indirect enterprise foundations. The share investment can be a way of managing the foundation's capital in order to meet the foundation's purpose with the return on the shares. The shareholding is then a pure investment issue and a means to achieve the purpose. As far as the purpose is concerned, it usually does not matter what type of business is conducted in the company where the founder or the board has chosen to invest all or part of the foundation's assets.

However, the share investment can also be based on the fact that the founder or the board has an interest in the company and the business that the company conducts. Of course, such an interest does not exclude an interest in a return on the shares. On closer inspection, it may turn out that the main reason why the foundation was formed is that the foundation should strive for control and influence over the business.

Another example includes foundations where the founder or board has chosen the connection to a business activity, because the business activity as such is of interest. Foundations that own shares are therefore not included in the group as a way of obtaining a return on capital. In this connection, one can also discuss so-called impact investment, social investment or purpose-based investment, but that is quite another story.

A very large proportion of the number of foundations in Sweden seldom have any decisive influence over the company or any interest in the business. The return on shares, for distribution to the beneficiaries of the charitable purpose, is the primary interest. It is also characteristic that these foundations often have shareholdings in listed companies.

Foundations that indirectly run business activities are sometimes referred to as holding foundations according to the corresponding terminology in company law. A holding foundation would then be a foundation whose purpose is to own and manage shares and participations in subsidiaries of the foundation. Through different voting values of the shares, the foundation can be assured of influence over the company even

The third part is the designated beneficiaries stating who is going to benefit from the purpose (*destinatärskretsen*). The two latter parts are not necessary in the purpose regulation of the charter. This way of dividing the purpose is not reflected in any legislation on foundations.

if it only owns a rather small part of the shares. The circumstances of the individual case may determine the influence of the foundation over the business.[26]

The supervision authority (County Administration Boards) does not seem to have any clear view on whether foundations with a business ownership should be regarded as enterprise foundations. Moreover, the tax authorities have their own definitions for tax purposes. Of course, this inconsistency complicates the picture and the legal discussion.[27]

1.7. THE ADMISSIBILITY OF ENTERPRISE FOUNDATIONS

One of the issues that has been debated, mainly in connection with the preparatory work for the Foundation Act of 1994, is whether the foundation should be used as an organizational form for all conceivable activities and then especially business activities, regardless of the wording of the purpose provision in the charter.

The story of enterprise foundations in Sweden is quite a remarkable one. In the early 1960s it was revealed that many of the large companies in Sweden were owned and controlled by a small number of families, in many cases including foundation structures. During the 1960s and 1970s, there were strong voices advocating against allowing enterprise foundations. But in the end, the preparatory works to the current Foundation Act concluded that there should not be a ban against enterprise foundations acting in their own name.[28] However, the indirect enterprise foundations were not mentioned. The reason is probably because they were, and still are, not regarded as enterprise foundations according to the law or the authorities. But in an academic discussion, and for comparative reasons, these foundations of course are of interest.

Why are foundations used for business reasons? There are many motives and explanations. One important motive is to secure the future of the company. All shares are irrevocably transferred to the foundation and through a well-formulated and future-oriented charter, the founder's

---

26 The Foundation Act has a definition and regulation of 'a group of business entities' in Chapter 1, section 5 that resembles definitions in company law. It should be noted that there is only one place for a foundation in an organization chart of a foundation company group and that is at the very top of the organization. The reason for this is simple. A foundation does not have any owners. Nonetheless, statements sometimes imply that a foundation is 'owned' by a family or a company.

27 This section is mainly based on the results in my dissertation: K. Olsson, above n. 3.

28 Government Bill, Prop. 1993/94:9, p. 60.

will is secured. Another reason can be lack of family members or no suitable family members for succession as the owners and managers of the company. Sometimes one can see an ideological reason, such as a political view, cultural values or religious values. The tax favours that follow from a non-profit purpose is another motive. Often the charter combines the interest of running and developing the company, and a charitable purpose of some kind.

Ownership and influence in the business world were addressed in several public inquiries and reports during the period from 1960 to 1990. Some of these inquiries observed the strong ownership by foundations in many areas of the Swedish private business sector. Most of the identified foundations had small shareholdings, but there were also foundations with very large shareholdings.[29] Although several of these investigations are more than 50 years old, there is reason to believe that the ownership situation is not different today, although some of the families are exchanged by new families.[30]

Up to the Foundation Act in the mid-1990s, foundations as owners of large companies or groups of companies had long attracted interest, mainly from a political point of view. The interest was strengthened by the possibility of keeping the foundation out of the supervisory system, at least until the introduction of the Foundation Act. In the eyes of the public, the foundations are still often surrounded by secrecy and mystery, which has helped to further spin myths about charismatic persons such as Ingvar Kamprad, Alfred Nobel, the Wallenberg family and the Rausing brothers and their life's work.

The arguments put forward in the debate up to the turn of the century against business in the form of a foundation have almost exclusively been of a socio-political or legal policy nature. The debate has been characterized by a reasoning about the suitability and need for the foundation form based on such factors as transparency, control, societal benefit and concentration of power.

The arguments for a ban on business activities in the form of foundations were based, among other things, on the perception that the

---

29 The Concentration Inquiry's report (*Koncentrationsutredningen*) (SOU 1968:7), of certain major ownership groups in Swedish business and industry included, among others, the following families or ownership groups associated with foundations: the Wallenberg family, Industrivärden-Svenska Handelsbanken, the Ax:son Johnson family, the Dunker group, the Ericsson family, the Åhlén family, the Kempe family and the Söderberg family.

30 For a closer analysis of the different inquiries, see K. Olsson, above n. 3, pp. 195 et seq.

foundation is abused and that business activities entail a risk that the foundation's purposes are jeopardized. The foundation form can be used as a means of concentrating the ownership of the business community to a few people or interest groups. Critics also point to the risk of tax evasion and avoidance, for example by using the foundation as a party to various financial transactions and corporate structures.

Other arguments that are put forward in the discussion against allowing business activities in the form of a foundation include that there are already different forms of associations that are suitable and intended for business activities. The foundation is strongly fixated on the unchanging purpose, which does not provide sufficient flexibility for changing economic situations or changed market conditions. There is a risk that the resources are not used correctly from the point of view of business operations. The great emphasis on the will of the founders can also have an inhibiting effect on business activities. The foundation is best suited for more passive asset management. Enterprise foundations with non-profit purposes have, through tax privileges, a competitive advantage over other forms of business organizations. The tax privileges give the foundation a better financing opportunity. In cases where the foundation has a purpose other than being a trader, there may be a tension between the purpose of the business and the foundation's 'non-financial' purpose. The risk is that the business is not conducted sufficiently efficient because the profit is to go to the beneficiaries of the foundation or that the interest in the business takes over and too little consideration is given to the foundation's purposes.

With regard to the importance of business for the society as a whole, it has been argued that a business must not be used for purposes that are too self-centred. The legal system should only support what society as a whole benefits from, i.e. non-profit foundations.

To conclude, Swedish law does not generally reject the idea that the foundation's purpose is to run a business or that the foundation's assets consist of a business or shares in a business. The question of a restriction or a ban on the right to conduct business in the form of a foundation has been discussed in various contexts from the 1960s up to the turn of the century. In the preparatory works to the Foundation Act in the 1980s and 1990s, the discussion was settled. Enterprise foundations are allowed in Sweden. There are not any restrictions in foundation law for certain purposes or certain commercial activities. There is no discussion today on the admissibility of enterprise foundations.[31]

---

31 For a more detailed discussion of the admissibility of enterprise foundations, see K. Olsson, above n. 3, pp. 234–291.

2. THE LEGAL FRAMEWORK FOR ENTERPRISE FOUNDATIONS

Since the late 19th century, there have been discussions about regulating foundations in Sweden. It took almost 100 years to reach the goal of comprehensive foundation legislation. The reason for this reluctance to regulate was a fear that future donors would object to too many compulsory rules on how to set up and administer foundations, and therefore would diminish the will to donate.[32]

The main private law regulation of foundations today is the Foundation Act of 1994 (Stiftelselagen 1994:1220), which came into force on 1 January 1996. This is the first general private law legislation on foundations in Sweden.[33]

Many rules in the Foundation Act are default rules. This indicates that the founder's will is of great importance when creating the foundation and later for the board when interpreting the charter of the foundation. A political reason behind the construction of the act was the wish from the legislator to enhance the will to donate to charitable purposes.[34] The rules on taxation of foundations are also generous to those who want to donate to a charitable purpose in the form of a foundation (see section 3).

The Foundation Act and the preparatory works[35] mention four types of foundations in Chapter 1, section 1: general foundations (*stiftelser i allmänhet*), fundraising foundations (*insamlingsstiftelser*), collective agreement foundations (*kollektivavtalsstiftelser*) and pension and employee foundations (*pensions- och personalstiftelser*). The latter type is used to guarantee employers' pension obligations and personnel benefits to employees.[36]

Most enterprise foundations belong to the general foundations group. This also indicates that enterprise foundations are not considered a separate form of foundations according to the legislation. Yet, somewhat

---

32 The earlier legislation, the Supervisory Act of 1929 (*lag (1929:116) om tillsyn över stiftelser*) had primarily supervisory focus and contained few private law rules.

33 The Foundation Act is supplemented by an Introductory Act (*lag (1994:1221) om införande av stiftelselagen*) regulating the relationship between existing foundations as of 1996 and the Foundation Act. None of the acts has an official translation into English.

34 Government Bill, Prop. 1993/94:9, p. 303.

35 Government Bill, Prop. 1993/94:9, p. 104.

36 Pension and employee foundations are regulated by a special act on safeguarding of pension commitments (*lag (1967:531) om tryggande av pensionsutfästelse m.m.*).

surprisingly, in the official registry on foundations, enterprising foundation is a group of its own.[37]

According to Chapter 1, section 2 of the Foundation Act, a foundation is established when one or more founders donate certain property for independent administration on a permanent basis in order to serve a specific purpose. The property has to be separated from the founder's property and transferred into the hands of someone who can represent the foundation at the time of creation. This is usually one or several members of the board. The charter of the foundation (*stiftelseförordnandet*) must be in writing and signed by the founder or founders, but it can consist of several documents. Often the charter is in the form of a will or a gift, supplemented by statutes (*stadgar*). The charter carries the legal consequence that the legal person foundation is created. A Swedish foundation can never have owners or members. The foundation is 'owned by its purpose' and it is the strong lock between purpose and property that identifies the foundation.[38]

There is no requirement for state approval to set up a foundation. Registration is required with the County Administration Boards (*länsstyrelsen*) and the registry is public.[39] The registration only has an informative and transparency function.

The word *stiftelse* has to be included in the name of the foundation. This means that as of 1996, the legal term *stiftelse* is reserved for foundations only.

There are no minimum capital requirements, but it must be possible to achieve the purpose in the foreseeable future. A foundation must be durable in the sense that it must exist for a reasonable period of time.[40] There is no eternal requirement and a spend-down foundation is accepted if it is stipulated in the charter.

In order to fulfil the purpose, the foundation must have same sort of management or administration. As a global unique feature, the Foundation Act regulates two organizational forms for managing the foundation. Either the foundation has a separate board consisting of

37 In the official registry on foundations by the County Administration Boards, there are six types of foundations: other foundations (*annan stiftelse*), fundraising foundations (*insamlingsstiftelse*), enterprise foundations (*näringsdrivande stiftelse*), collective agreement foundations (*kollektivavtalsstiftelse*) pension foundations (*pensionsstiftelse*) and employee foundations (*personalstiftelse*).

38 The foundation is sometimes described as a self-owning entity (*självägande enhet*).

39 Information on all registered foundations is available at: https://stiftelser.lansstyrelsen.se.

40 Government Bill, Prop. 1993/94:9, pp. 52 and 108.

natural persons as board members, which is called own administration or autonomous administration (*egen förvaltning*), or the foundation is managed by another legal person, which is called attached administration (*anknuten förvaltning*).[41] In the latter form of administration, it is the decision-making body of an existing legal person that carries the legal responsibility for administering the foundation. It can, for example, be a university, a state institution, a company or a church. Many foundations in Sweden have attached administration. This is often a cost-efficient way of administration, since many Swedish foundations are rather small. An enterprise foundation can have attached administration, but it is probably rather unusual. According to the registry on foundations, about 10,600 out of nearly 20,000 foundations (which is more than 50% of the total number) have attached administration.

As a general rule, and if not otherwise stated in the charter, only return on assets can be distributed. The assets can generally not be distributed unless the founder permits it in the charter. According to the default rules in the Foundation Act, asset management must be acceptable (*godtagbar*). If the founder has regulated the asset management in the charter, it is considered acceptable and has to be followed by the board or the administering body.

If the foundation has an autonomous administration, the governing board must not consist of the founder only. Otherwise, there are no requirements as to the number of board members. It is often the case that the founder is a member of the board during his or her lifetime. All foundations are also required to have an external audit.

State approval is required for all changes of the foundation's purpose. The founder has the right to regulate changes of provisions other than the purpose. These kind of changing provisions are often included in the charter.

A Swedish foundation may operate abroad if the charter does not forbid this. Sweden also allows foreign foundations to operate in Sweden. There are no restrictions when it comes to foreign funding, and a Swedish foundation can receive donations from abroad. In the individual case, it is of course a question of what the charter allows.

Enterprise foundations that operate a business must be registered before the business begins operating (Chapter 10, sections 6–10 of the

[41] In Chapter 2 of the Foundation Act, there are certain provisions that are common for both types of administration, but also separate subchapters for each of the two types of administration.

Foundation Act). All Swedish foundations are under the supervision of the County Administration Board according to Chapter 9 of the Foundation Act. However, the founder can exempt the foundation from supervision. The effect of this exemption is that the foundation is under very limited supervision. Foundations that carry out business activities cannot be exempt and are always under full supervision even if the founder has stipulated an exemption in the charter (Chapter 9, section 10 of the Foundation Act).

There are separate rules in the Foundation Act that targets enterprise foundations in three chapters. As mentioned above, the registration of enterprise foundations is regulated in Chapter 10. Chapter 7 regulates foundations that carry out business activities and end up being liquidated or dissolved. Chapter 8 regulates issues concerning the 'business name' of the foundation. These rules have little effect on the everyday life of an enterprise foundation and are of a public law character to protect third parties.

3. TAX TREATMENT

Tax rules[42] that apply to legal persons in the Income Tax Act (Inkomstskattelagen 1999:1229) also apply to foundations.[43] As a rule, foundations pay tax on all income and capital gains. A foundation that does not have a non-profit or charitable purpose is fully taxed. Yet, as will be shown below, many foundations receive tax exemptions due to their charitable purpose and activities. A tax-exempt foundation pays tax only on income derived from real property or business activities, but in most cases no tax on dividends from the share holdings. Many enterprise foundations have charitable purposes that allow tax exemption for dividends and capital gains. There is no inheritance tax, gift tax or wealth tax in Sweden.

The tax rules have great practical significance for the design of the foundation's purposes. Therefore, in practice, these rules impose restrictions on the design of the purpose, especially for non-profit and

---

42 I would like to express my gratitude to Lynda Ondrasek Olofsson at Unum Tax for helping me understand the mysteries of the tax rules.

43 For an in-depth analysis of the current rules for taxation of foundations, see M. Berglund, above n. 4, which covers relevant legal sources on tax rules concerning all types of foundations.

charitable foundations.[44] Since most foundations invest in financial instruments of some kind, the exemption from capital income tax is of the highest importance for the foundation, because more money can be distributed according to the purpose.

Since 1942, the basic structure of the legal framework for the taxation of foundations has been more or less the same, offering tax relief for charitable purposes. The rationale behind the fact that a foundation with a charitable purpose is tax-exempt is probably some sort of gratitude from the state. Tax-exempt foundations contribute to activities that otherwise have to be financed by the state through taxes.[45] Also, the state and the regional and local authorities are tax-exempt, and it would be unreasonable to tax foundations that perform tasks that are considered to be charitable.

A foundation must satisfy three requirements to qualify as a tax-exempt foundation (according to Chapter 7, sections 3–6 of the Income Tax Act): the purpose requirement (*ändamålskravet*), the activity requirement (*verksamhetskravet*) and the completion requirement (*fullföljdskravet*). Sometimes a fourth requirement is mentioned – the recipient requirement (*destinatärskravet*) – which means that the foundation's purpose must not be limited to certain families or specific persons. All requirements must be fulfilled in order to receive favourable tax treatment.

According to the purpose requirement, the foundation must have a charitable, public benefit (*allmännyttigt*) purpose that in one way or another benefits the public good. The tax-exempt purposes are enumerated in Chapter 7, section 4 of the Income Tax Act. These are sports, culture, religion, child and youth care, social assistance, healthcare, environmental protection, politics, Sweden's defence and emergency preparedness in cooperation with authorities, education and scientific research. An abundance of case law sets the limits for the different tax-exempt purposes.

As of 2014, the tax-exempt purposes have been somewhat expanded. Furthermore, the enumeration in Chapter 7, section 4 ends with the words 'another equivalent activity'. This might open the way to a more generous application of the tax-exempt area. However, as yet, there is little case law

---

44 For a somewhat more detailed description, see K. Olsson, 'Tax Treatment of NGOs in the Nordic Countries' in P. Bater, F. Hondius and P. Kessler Lieber (eds), *The Tax Treatment of NGOs: Legal, Ethical and Fiscal Frameworks for Promoting NGOs and Their Activities*, Kluwer Law International, The Hague 2004, pp. 153–171.

45 For a general understanding of the political rationale behind taxation, see: https://www.government.se/government-policy/taxes-and-tariffs.

on the interpretation of what type of activity that could be considered as 'equivalent' to the enumerated purposes.

The activity requirement states that the activities of the foundation must be mainly (*huvudsakligen*) to promote charitable purposes. In practice, this means that 90–95% of the foundation's activities must serve to satisfy the non-profit charitable purpose. This condition may be calculated in the form of, for example, promotion through resources such as money, time or labour. The requirement for activity means that there is little room to act outside of the charitable purpose and still keep the tax-exempt status.

The completion requirement states that a foundation's income must to a reasonable extent be used to promote the charitable and tax-exempt purpose. Case law has defined 'reasonable' as 80% of the net return. The taxable income shall not be included, nor shall the costs incurred to procure this income. With this requirement, it is not possible for a foundation to, more than to a limited extent, accumulate tax-exempt income over time.[46] This can be a negative effect for enterprise foundations, since there in no possibility of permanently accumulating wealth in the foundation.

A difficulty when interpreting the private law rules and tax rules applicable to foundations is that there are some differences in terminology. This sometimes makes it difficult to classify or define certain types or operations and actions conducted by the foundations.

An enterprise foundation, where the foundation itself operates a business, is taxed like any other business entity. The corporate income tax rate as of 2022 is 20.6%, which has been slightly lowered in the last couple of years.

A foundation that owns an enterprise as a holding foundation can receive dividends tax-free from the business. Dividends are tax-exempt if they are business-related, according to the so-called rules of participation exemption (*näringsbetingade andelar*).[47] This exemption applies to dividends received from a company and to capital gains derived from the sale of shares, provided that the shares qualify as business-related. Unlisted shares

---

46 For further information, see the website of the Swedish Tax Agency (Skatteverket): https://www.skatteverket.se/servicelankar/otherlanguages/inenglish/businessesandemployers/nonprofitassociations.4.569165a01749e7ae7891106.html.

47 Auditing firms often have information in English on current rules on their websites. See, for example, Deloitte, International Tax, Sweden Highlights 2022: https://www2.deloitte.com/content/dam/Deloitte/global/Documents/Tax/dttl-tax-swedenhighlights-2022.pdf.

that are fixed business assets are always considered as business-related assets. Listed shares that are fixed business assets are considered to be business-related if the participation comprises at least 10% of the company's voting rights or is considered to be necessary in terms of conducting the company's business.[48]

According to Johansson et al, it has been argued that the Swedish tax system has favoured control over business entities through enterprise foundations. This is said to have inhibited entrepreneurship and economic growth. It is held that the favourable tax rules might be one tool for family business groups using enterprise foundations to employ in order to exercise far-reaching control over Swedish industry.[49]

Henrekson et al. point out that tax incentives were important for the use of foundations as a control vehicle of listed firms. But the fact that many of these enterprise foundations have to use 80% of their net returns on their charitable purpose also means that the foundation is drained of resources. This can be equivalent to a large tax.[50] If, for example, the foundation-controlled company will need new capital, it might be difficult for the foundation to participate.

Henrekson et al. build their study on examinations of the Swedish tax system with the conclusion that since the 1980s, there are no motives for setting up an enterprise foundation that can be found in the tax system or rules on taxation. Entrepreneurs tend to control their companies by direct ownership today. This might also explain why there is no discussion on enterprise foundations in Sweden today.

There is no system of tax credit or tax deduction for donors[51] to enterprise foundations.[52] An individual who receives a grant from a tax-exempt foundation is also exempt from paying tax on the grant, provided that some conditions are met.[53]

---

48 Deloitte, above n. 47, p. 2.

49 D. Johansson et al., above n. 6. The purpose of their study was to describe the evolution of tax rules for industrial foundations in Sweden between 1862 and 2018 and to calculate the marginal effective tax rate (METR) on capital income.

50 M. Henrekson et al., above n. 6.

51 A very limited tax deduction for private persons is permitted for gifts; see: https://skatteverket.se/privat/skatter/arbeteochinkomst/skattereduktioner/skattereduktionforgavor.4.5fc8c94513259a4ba1d800064144.html.

52 When it comes to corporate donors, some donations can be deducted as business expenses.

53 For a more elaborate nutshell summary including several European countries, see Dafne, Donors and Foundations Networks in Europe, and EFC, European Foundation Centre, *Comparative Highlights of Foundation Laws: The Operating Environment for Foundations in Europe*, Brussels 2021.

4. REFORM AND OUTLOOK

The author fears that the reader's confusion might have increased while reading through this chapter instead of giving a clear and comprehensive crash course in rules for Swedish enterprise foundations. The first problem is of course that there is no definition of 'enterprise foundations' in Swedish legislation. Therefore, it is difficult to identify the legal entity. Foundations as owners of business are not even discussed as a form of enterprise foundations in Sweden.

According to the preparatory works to the Foundation Act, foundations are allowed to conduct business in their own name. There are very few legal rules targeting enterprise foundations and case law on the issue is absent. There seems to be no political, legal, economic or social encouragement today for setting up enterprise foundations, although advisors active in the consultancy market try to persuade people to set up foundations and let the foundation be the dominant shareholder.

However, foundations run businesses and foundations own businesses in Sweden, regardless of what we call these foundations. Although the legislation is deficient, the political discussion is absent and the foundations involved in enterprises often 'fly under the radar', there are still questions and problems to address.

As seen in this chapter, there are many motives for setting up an enterprise foundation. It gives an entrepreneur the possibility to keep companies under the control of a family for many generations, with a very low level of taxation due to its charitable purpose. Through the foundation, it is possible to keep assets, capital, voting rights and other control mechanisms in one owner's hand. Through generations, the company will avoid inheritance division. Last, but not least, the social status of the family might benefit from the foundation's funding of charitable activities.

However, there are also disadvantages to setting up an enterprise foundation as a control vehicle. The entrepreneur irrevocably loses ownership of the assets. Capital and dividends must be used for this purpose. An aspect that is often overlooked is the fact that the founder can move himself or herself and his or her assets to another jurisdiction. This is not easily done for a foundation.

When focusing on the large enterprise foundations with economic, political and social influence and importance as owners, employers and producers, there is a risk to forget the smaller ones. Many smaller enterprise foundations run business-oriented activities, perhaps because the foundation format is a good way for cooperating with others without ownership. Maybe the founder wants to label the foundation with a particular ideological idea. These foundations run, for example, schools, nursing homes, museums, newspapers, bookshops and daycare centres. They are also part of the enterprise foundation family.

The Foundation Act is now 28 years old. There have been some minor changes over the years, but no general revision of the legislation. Instead, changes have been more patchwork without attempting a comprehensive approach. The two authorities in the foundation world, the County Administration Boards and the Legal, Financial and Administrative Services Agency, have called for an investigation into a revision of the Foundation Act, but so far, the Ministry of Justice has not taken any action in this respect.[54]

Looking at the statistics, Sweden has a strong and growing foundation sector.[55] Neither foundations in general nor enterprise foundations seem to present any major problems when it comes to management, financing, purpose activity or any other aspect. Once in a while, arguments that foundations are used for criminal activities, like money laundering and fraud, are heard, but the reasoning and empirical evidence for these has always been rather weak.

However, it is definitely time for a revision of the Foundation Act. Swedish society has changed and the conditions for philanthropy as well as conducting business have developed in the 28 years that have passed. This is not a Swedish phenomenon; it happens all over the world.

Enterprise foundations have two parts: the business side and the foundation side. The two interests do not always coincide. Regardless of the type of business the foundation conducts or owns, it is the foundation issues that are of relevance in this chapter. Rules and legislation on foundations target the business side of the foundation to a very limited extent.

The first item on a wish list would be a definition of enterprise foundations and clear answers on some regulatory issues. Perhaps Sweden is not yet ready for a separate piece of legislation on enterprise foundations

---

54 The documents are publicly available: *Länsstyrelserna* 2019-07-23 Dnr 206-22738-2019 and *Kammarkollegiet* 2019-06-14 Dnr 1.1-5600-19.

55 F. Wijkström and S. Einarsson, above n. 8, p. 1909. The authors discuss enterprises set up and controlled by foundations in the sense that different forms of control and power mechanisms can be used to secure influence and control from a group of organizations, a certain family, a value-based community or a public sector body. Somewhat surprisingly the authors state (at p. 1900) that foundations 'set up and controlled by corporations, were not as many'. The authors convincingly explain that this is an illustration of control and power mechanisms.

as is the case in Denmark. However, some adequate rules are better than no rules. Second, private law and tax law have to share a common view of legal aspects and definitions of enterprise foundations.

The foundations have considerable economic power, but there is no registry on the fortune of the foundations. The County Administration Boards register asset information from the foundations' annual reports, but this is not done on a regular or complete basis. This is of course not acceptable.

Foundations are involved in the redefinition of the role and scope of the welfare state of today.[56] Yet, as noted by Wijkström, there is no critical and informed public debate on foundations and their role in contemporary Sweden. I definitely share this view, even some 20 years after Wijkström first noted this fact.

It is a striking feature that several foundations in Sweden are controlling owners of large firms and company groups. It is even more striking that there is no debate on this. Somehow, as also observed by Wijkström and Einarsson,[57] philanthropy is underanalysed in Sweden because the issues fall under the radar and simply continue to be unnoticed. These large enterprise foundations are often hidden behind the charitable umbrella. Of course, this does not imply any negative aspects, but living in a very transparent society, it is somewhat surprising that decade after decade, these foundations seem to live in the shadows. Research is needed, but so too is a political discussion on the values of foundations running and/or owning enterprises. For a fruitful discussion, it is necessary to lift the veil from the enterprise foundations and look behind the curtains.

So, what can be done to increase the establishment of new enterprise foundations? As a lawyer, it would be easiest to call for separate legislation of enterprise foundations, as exists in Denmark. But this is probably fruitless since there seem to be no voices advocating for more or different legislation in Sweden. Also, I do not think that the current legislation is an obstacle for the will to donate or set up new enterprise foundations. As shown above, foundations with a charitable purpose already receive favourable tax treatment and the taxation of business activities is neutral.

Information is needed so that the foundations can do even more good. Knowledge is power and on the wish list is definitely an increased degree of transparency when it comes to the two foundation authorities.

---

56 F. Wijkström, 'Foundations in Sweden', in M. Bennet and R. Clay (eds), *Foundations in Europe*, Directory of Social Change, London, 2001, p. 245.

57 F. Wijkström and S. Einarsson, above n. 8.

Creating a best practice, like the Danish example of Recommendations on Foundation Governance, would probably strengthen the management and create greater self-confidence in the boards.[58] National and international umbrella organizations can also strengthen the impact of the foundation sector.[59]

Foundations have to talk to each other, learn from each other and talk to the rest of the world. In that respect, international contacts are vital. There is a lot to learn from other countries. A catalytic approach to grant giving and partnerships with other foundations or organizations can increase the efficiency of grant giving.

Looking into the crystal ball, the author sees a prosperous future for foundations in general, simply because of the need for charitable purposes as substitutes or complements to state measures. But the author also sees a future for enterprise foundations as long-term sustainable owners of enterprises. One way to start on the road ahead is to increase communication and transparency and to learn from each other. Another way is to persuade the legislator to take more interest in foundations in general and enterprise foundations specifically.

58 https://godfondsledelse.dk/english.

59 According to F. Wijkström and S. Einarsson, above n. 8, p. 1905, the creation of a type of umbrella organization has probably contributed to a less negative attitude towards foundations.

DENMARK

Enterprise Foundations

Rasmus Kristian FELDTHUSEN

ABSTRACT

Denmark has recognised foundations being owners and having a controlling interest in companies since at least 1876. In 1985, Denmark enacted special legislation on enterprise foundations with the Danish Enterprise Foundation Law. Simultaneously legislation was enacted for all non-enterprise foundations, and Denmark has since had two separate pieces of legislation on foundations to thereby suit the different needs and requirements of these two types of foundations. Today the importance of enterprise foundations and their companies to the Danish economy cannot be understated and Danish legislation serves as an example of how to introduce enterprise foundations into a legal system.

1. HISTORICAL BACKGROUND

Enterprise foundations began their existence in Denmark with lawyers, utilizing the freedom of contract, drafting bylaws and transferring assets to 'funds' or foundations, and in the 18th century, also transferring shares in companies, with Carlsbergfondet in 1876 as probably the first actual enterprise foundation. After Carlsbergfondet, many followed – for example, Novo Nordisk Foundation and Egmont H. Petersens Fond.

It was not until 1985 that Denmark enacted legislation on foundations in the shape of two separate laws on foundations, one on enterprise foundations[1] and one on non-enterprise foundations.[2] The reason Denmark chose to have two laws on foundations was that a number of special considerations apply to enterprise foundations, which were deemed to justify a deviation from a number of the general rules and principles. The Committee noted:

> The starting point for the committee's deliberations has been that for enterprise foundations, a reasonable equality should be sought between the rules that must apply to these foundations and the rules that apply to commercial activities that are conducted in other entities. The considerations which have motivated the implementation or consideration of rules on such other forms of business apply to a considerable extent to the enterprise foundations. This applies thus – especially in the case of foundations that directly carry on business activities – securing creditors, co-contractors and employees. In the Committee's view, the aim should be to ensure that the rules applicable to the pursuit of a commercial activity are independent of the form in which the activity is conducted. The rules of law should thus, as a starting point, be 'neutral' in relation to the various forms of business.[3]

---

1 Law on Enterprise Foundations (Erhvervsfondsloven) consolidated as of 28 December 2021.

2 Law on Non-Enterprise Foundations (Lov om ikke-erhvervsdrivende fonde) consolidated as of 28 December 2021.

3 'Betænkning om fonde afgivet af det af justitsministeren den 14. juli 1978 nedsatte udvalg' nr. 970 [1982], 31.

In 1986 a separate law on foundation taxation was enacted entailing that foundations – as a point of departure – are taxed the same way as companies (see below section 8).[4]

2. DATA ON THE PREVALENCE AND IMPORTANCE OF ENTERPRISE FOUNDATIONS IN DENMARK

There are approximately 1,400 enterprise foundations in Denmark. The size distribution of enterprise foundations is large, with only a small number of very big foundations. The largest of the Danish enterprise foundations control, through a majority of voting rights, a very large proportion of the dominant companies in Denmark, such as Carlsberg, Danfoss, Mærsk, Novo, Grundfos, J. Lauritzen, Lundbeck and Rambøll.

In 2020 enterprise foundations paid out DKK 13.3 billion in (mainly) charitable distributions.[5]

The foundation-controlled companies make up 16% of all companies in the private sector with 500+ employee-years and 7% of the companies in the private sector with 250–499 employee-years.[6]

Professor Steen Thomsen has calculated that enterprise foundations account for 5–10% of the economic activity in Denmark, more than 70% of stock market capitalization and roughly 50% of the total Danish research and development.[7]

Although the number of foundation-controlled companies is limited, they still represent 12% of the turnover in the private sector. This corresponds to a turnover of DKK 527 billion. The majority of the turnover comes from the companies within the transportation sector (DKK 191 billion) and the manufacture of medicinal products, etc. (DKK 122 billion). These two groups make up 60% of the foundation-controlled companies' total turnover. In the manufacture of medicinal products, etc., the foundation

4 R.K. Feldthusen, 'The Danish Law on Foundations' (2016) 22(1) *Trusts & Trustees* 146 et seq.; S. Thomsen, *The Danish Industrial Foundations*, DJØF Publishing (2017); S. Thomsen and N. Kavadis, 'Enterprise Foundations. A Review. Law, Taxation, Governance and Performance' (2022) *Annals of Corporate Governance*, 227 et seq.

5 Danmarks Statistik and Fondenes Videnscenter, 'Fondenes bevillinger i 2020', November 2020: https://fondenesvidenscenter.dk/app/uploads/Fondenes-Videnscenter-faktaark-over-Fondenes-bevillinger-i-2020_final-1.pdf.

6 Fondenes Videnscenter, 'Fondes erhvervsaktivitet i Danmark', 24 November 2021: https://fondenesvidenscenter.dk/app/uploads/Fondes-erhvervsaktivitet-i-Danmark_final.pdf.

7 S. Thomsen, above n. 4, p. 125.

controlled-companies also make up 77% of the total turnover in the industry, while the same figure for transportation is 42%.[8]

Foundation-controlled companies contribute a value added growth of approximately DKK 158 billion in Denmark. The vast majority of the value added comes from the manufacture of medicinal products, etc. (approximately DKK 61 billion) and transportation (approximately DKK 33 billion). These two groups make up approximately 60% of the foundations' total value added. In the manufacture of medicinal products, etc., the companies also account for 77% of the total value added in the industry, while the same figure for transportation is 29%.[9]

Foundation-controlled companies account for 23% of total Danish exports of almost DKK 1.470 billion, which corresponds to DKK 337 billion. The vast majority of exports come from the transportation industry (approximately DKK 184 billion) and the manufacture of medicinal products, etc. (approximately DKK 93 billion). In total, these two industries account for 82% of the foundation-controlled companies' exports and almost 19% of Danish exports.[10]

Together, the enterprise foundations and the foundation-controlled companies spend almost DKK 24 billion on research and development, which corresponds to approximately 1% of GDP. The amount has been calculated by adding the foundations' grants for scientific purposes in 2019 to almost DKK 8 billion (minus the appropriations for companies of DKK 118 million), together with the foundation-controlled companies' financing of their own research and development in Denmark of DKK 16 billion.[11]

It should be noted that there are also a number of significant non-enterprise foundations in Denmark having sizeable ownership interests in Danish companies, often in conjunction with family ownership – for example, Rockwool Fonden, Ole Kirks Fond and Villum Fonden og Velux Fonden.

3. KEY FEATURES

An enterprise foundation is an independent and self-governing entity without owners and residual claimants that own and control one or

8 Fondenes Videnscenter, above n. 5.
9 Ibid.
10 Ibid.
11 Ibid.

more companies. An enterprise foundation is typically established for an indefinite period and may thus be regarded as a strong 'commitment device'.[12] Without the sometimes more short-term interests of (controlling) shareholders, the enterprise foundation can focus on its task to maintain the survival of the business and balance the interests of all stakeholders.

Traditional ownership structures may create continuity problems in the event of any separation or buy-out of family members, since each and every family member is subject to the main forces of life, such as love, conflict and death.[13] This is by no means not to say that families are not able to also (through multiple generations) run and develop large and successful companies.

An enterprise foundation model may foster social responsibility and ethical behaviour by the business that is owned by the foundation, since it is lacking an impatient controlling shareholder. It could be argued that the business of an enterprise foundation is therefore ideally suited to qualify as an impact or purpose organization. This adds to the legitimacy of the business and the alignment of the stakeholders, thereby increasing the reputation and expression of the business.[14]

The key features of an enterprise foundation are thus continuity, stewardship, commitment and purpose, often combined with philanthropic distributions of the surplus of the business.

4. OWNERSHIP STRUCTURES

As stated above, enterprise foundations may either carry on their business within the foundation or – as is most often the case in large enterprise foundations – through a majority ownership in a subsidiary. The foundation may elect to insert a holding company between itself and its subsidiary. Enterprise foundations generally retain a voting majority even where the operating company is listed on the stock exchange.

---

12 On commitment in business, see C. Mayer, *Firm Commitment: Why the Corporation is Failing Us and How to Restore Trust in it*, Oxford University Press, Oxford (2017); and S. Thomsen et al, 'Industrial Foundations as Long-Term Owners' (2018) *Corporate Governance: An International Review* 180 et seq.

13 I. Koele and R.K. Feldthusen, 'Shareholder Foundations of Enterprises: The North European Style of Securing Family Businesses for the Long Term – Rising up to the Global Challenge' (2020) 26(7) *Trusts & Trustees* 654 et seq.

14 Ibid.

Below are the different main structures of enterprise foundations regarding their business activity.

Here the operating business takes place inside the foundation.

Figure 1. Structure #1

Source: Produced by the author.

Here the operating business takes place in a subsidiary, with the foundation in turn receiving dividends which it can use for distributions pursuant to its purpose.

Figure 2. Structure #2

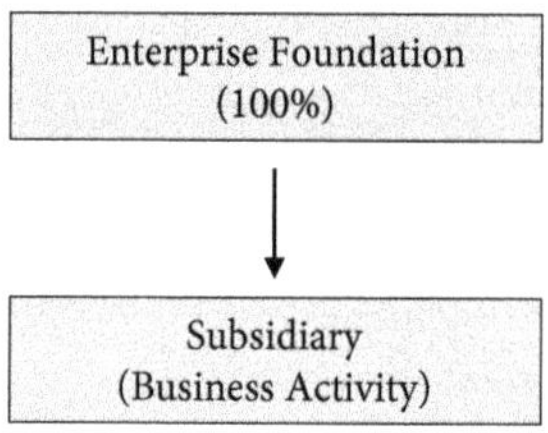

Source: Produced by the author.

This is the same as structure #2, with the exception that there are now minority shareholders also having an ownership stake in the operating company. As will be explained below, it might instead be the foundation which has a minority stake in the share capital, but instead has a majority vote in the company.

Figure 3. Structure #3

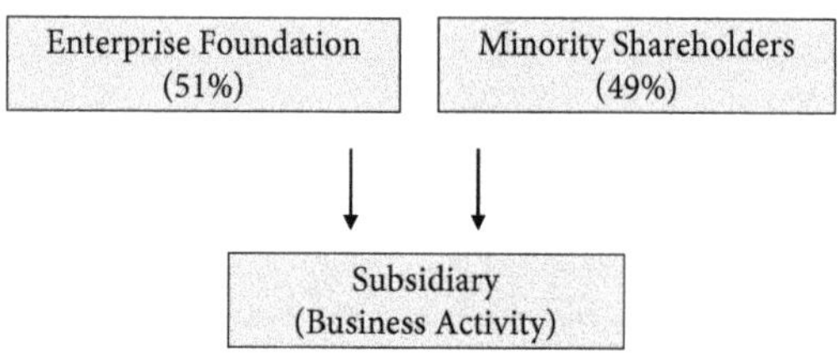

Source: Produced by the author.

Employing holding companies have become more common in large enterprise foundations. There are several reasons for this, but tax is often a factor if the enterprise foundation owns less than 76% of the share capital of the operating company (see section 8 below). Employing a holding company may also serve strategic purposes.

Figure 4. Structure #4

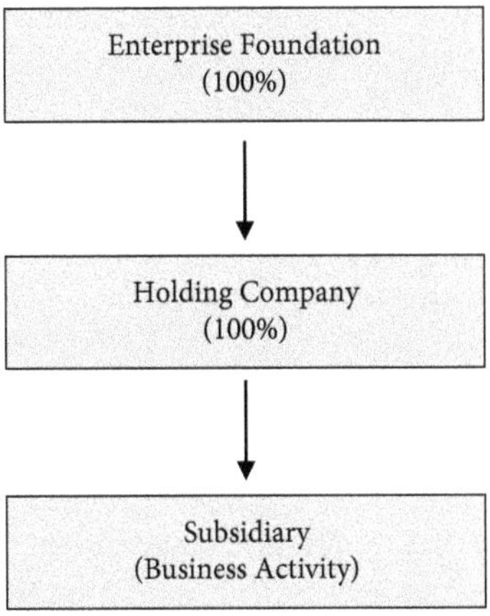

Source: Produced by the author.

The above structures are of course simply generalizations as each foundation group structure is individual and often involves more than one subsidiary, joint venture, etc.

5. SPECIAL DANISH LEGISLATION ON ENTERPRISE FOUNDATIONS

5.1. THE DEFINITION OF 'FOUNDATION'

A foundation is created by a donation (gift or will).

A Danish foundation, whether it is an enterprise or a non-enterprise foundation, is characterised mainly by the following criteria:

a. An irrevocable transfer of property from the founder to the foundation.
b. One or more purposes, being charitable, family and/or commercial.

c. The power to make dispositions of the assets in the foundation rests in a board of directors.
d. The foundation can acquire rights and incur liabilities in its own name (separate legal personality).
e. No natural or legal person outside the foundation has any property rights to the assets in the foundation, which implies that the foundation owns the assets in its own right (self-owned and independent).
f. At least one-third of the members of the board of directors must be independent of the settlor (this does not apply to foundations established before 1985).

Furthermore, the foundation must from the outset be able to exist for at least ten years. The purpose, governance rules, etc. of the foundation are set out in a foundation charter.

5.2. REQUIREMENTS

The above characteristics apply to foundations in general. In order for a foundation to be an enterprise foundation, it must also fulfil the requirement of carrying out a business activity, either in its own right or through one or more subsidiaries owned or controlled by the foundation (cf. section 2 of the Law on Enterprise Foundations):

> Paragraph 1. Pursuant to this Act a foundation is considered being commercial if the foundation:
>
> 1. Trades goods or intellectual property rights, copyright, provides services or the like, for which it normally receives payment,
> 2. Carries out activities involving the sale or lease of real estate, or
> 3. Has a connection to a limited liability company mentioned in the Companies Act section 7.[15]

It is a requirement to establish an enterprise foundation that at least DKK 300,000 (approximately €40,000) is donated, either in cash or in kind, to the foundation.

[15] If the business activity and/or the business assets are limited, the foundation is not considered an enterprise foundation.

When registering a newly established enterprise foundation, the Danish Business Authority conducts a legality check of the bylaws, and it is a condition that this test is passed in order for there to be a valid enterprise foundation.

5.3. CAPITAL STRUCTURE

As mentioned above, the capital requirement to establish an enterprise foundation is at least DKK 300,000 (approximately €40,000). Enterprise foundations use the same capital structure as Danish limited liability companies (*anpartsselskaber*) and joint stock companies (*aktieselskaber*) with a division between base capital and free reserves.

The minimum capital requirement relates to the base capital (*grundkapital*) and if the founder wants to establish the foundation with additional funds, the founder has the choice between adding these to the base capital and/or to the free reserves. An enterprise foundation may only make distributions from its free reserves.

Once the enterprise foundation is established, the base capital does not have to be in a special account separate from the foundation's other assets. In the annual report, the base capital is shown as a separate accounting item under equity. The base capital must be stated as an exact DKK amount and cannot be specified as an interval. The base capital also cannot be stated as the assets, e.g., shares in a specific company that the enterprise foundation has received in connection with the establishment of the fund.

The capital structure of a non-enterprise foundation is fundamentally different as its base capital consists of the assets it received when established or which have replaced these, and any capital gains received on these. A non-enterprise foundation does not as such have 'free reserves' but is expected to use the bulk of its net income for distributions.

A founder may specify in the bylaws that owning the shares of a company is a purpose in itself (see below). In this case, the board of directors is not allowed to divest itself of the shares in the company.

5.4. PURPOSE

Danish law allows a foundation to have any purpose as long as it is not illegal or *contra bono mores*. A foundation may have several purposes – for example, a charitable purpose, a family purpose and a business purpose (for the latter, see below).

Danish law not only allows an enterprise foundation to either carry out a business or have majority control of a business, but also allows the founder to stipulate that the foundation will have a 'business purpose', i.e., that running or owning the business is a purpose of the foundation. This is the case with many of the large Danish enterprise foundations:

Novo Nordisk Foundation:

> [T]o provide a stable basis for the commercial and research activities of the companies in the Novo Group (Novo Nordisk A/S and Novozymes A/S).

Lundbeck Fonden:

> [T]to secure and expand the LUNDBECK GROUP's business.

Bitten og Mads Clausen's Fond:

> The purpose of the foundation is primarily through its holding of shares in DANFOSS A/S – within the provisions of these bylaws – to strengthen this company for the benefit of all who are connected to the company.

According to the preparatory works of the 1982 report on the first Enterprise Foundation Act, an enterprise foundation may have, as its only purpose, a business purpose. The report states as follows:

> The Committee must emphasize that the purpose of a foundation can be to only pursue business interests, such as to maintain and expand a business enterprise which the foundation either runs itself or in which the foundation owns a significant shareholding. Such foundations exist in practice and the committee's proposal does not change the current law on that point.[16]

The report goes on to state:

> However, the consideration of pursuing the purpose of the foundation and the consolidation of the foundation coincide where the purpose is solely to run the business.[17]

---

16 'Betænkning om fonde afgivet af det af justitsministeren den 14. juli 1978 nedsatte udvalg' nr. 970 (1982), 98. See also the preparatory remarks to the legislative draft Folketingstidende 1983/84 (2. Saml.), tillæg A, sp. 2846.

17 'Betænkning om fonde afgivet af det af justitsministeren den 14. juli 1978 nedsatte udvalg' nr. 970 (1982), 115. See also p. 31 and p. 115.

In 2012 a committee charged with drafting a revised act on enterprise foundations reaffirmed the position on an enterprise foundation being allowed to only have a business purpose:

> The Committee emphasizes that there is nothing that prevents an enterprise foundation from having only a business purpose and not having an external distribution purpose.[18]

Despite the clear statements in the preparatory works, there is still not a consensus in Danish legal theory on whether an enterprise foundation can have a business purpose as its sole purpose. The arguments put forward by the opponents to the above statements are, however, mainly *de lege ferenda* in nature – see, for example, Lennart Lynge Andersen:

> More questionable – with regard to enterprise foundations – is it if the purpose is stated as highlighted in the motives (p. 98), e.g. 'The purpose of the foundation is to own and operate N.N.A/S', and the foundations's use of its profits – which must be stated in the articles of association – is concentrated on the limited company in question. Regarding these cases, the motives of the Enterprise Foundation Act are divisive with themselves. The background for the foundation reform and the Enterprise Foundation Act's rules on articles of association and profit use argue that one does not accept a scheme according to which all funds that a foundation receives from a subsidiary can only be used in a continued cycle back to the subsidiary – but opposite here stands the opinion stated in the Foundation Report and the submission of the Minister of Industry. There is no doubt that such foundations existed prior to the fund legislation in 1984 and have existed since 1984.[19]

There is no requirement as to an enterprise foundation making minimum distributions. A minimum requirement for distributions may threaten the interests of the business. This is because foundations by definition do not have owners, and thus only have the revenue stream from the business enterprise and possibly a securities portfolio as a source of financing for the foundation's investments in the business, including for development

---

18 Erhvervsfondsudvalget, 'Erhvervsfondsudvalgets rapport om fremtidens regulering af erhvervsdrivende fonde' (2012), 72.

19 L.L. Andersen, *Fonde og Foreninger I – Fondslovene med kommentarer*, Gjellerup, (2003) 5th. revised ed., 126. Regarding this discussion, see also E. Werlauff, 'Erhvervsdrivende fonde' (1987) *Juristen* 96 et seq.; J.H. Mikkelsen, 'En replik vedrørende erhvervsdrivende fonde' (1987) *Juristen* 147 et seq.

activities. The Law Committee drafting the report on the proposal for the new law on enterprise foundations thus stated:

> The importance of the enterprise foundations for the Danish economy via the business activity is far greater than via their distributions. Thus, it is important that the legislation does not impede the business activity of the enterprise foundations.
>
> The consideration for the business makes it generally appropriate or even necessary for the foundation to build up reserves which make it possible to participate in later capital increases in the company in connection with mergers or acquisitions, financial crises, major investments and so on. This will be hampered by minimum requirements for distributions.
>
> The business activities of enterprise foundations are quite different and therefore provide widely differing returns depending on industry, competitive position, economic development, tax conditions and so on. It would not make sense to set fixed requirements for distributions across these differences. What is relevant for a foundation's distribution activity is the actual return compared to the company's and the foundation's current situation, while the determination of a return requirement, which must form the basis for a possible minimum distribution, will in any case be based on historical averages. (...)
>
> In relation to other forms of ownership, foundation ownership is characterised by being long-term, i.e., that the exact requirement for profits in the short term is not exactly the same as in other forms of ownership. This longevity can be challenged by minimum requirements for distributions.[20]

If an enterprise foundation has large free reserves, the state supervisor may enquire about this. If there is no justifiable reason for this, the state supervisor may recommend to the board to consider increasing the foundation's distributions.

Interpretation of the bylaws and purpose of an enterprise foundation is done solely on the basis of the bylaws and objectively. It is thus important that all of the founder's wishes and intentions are clearly expressed in the articles of the foundation's bylaws.

---

20 Erhvervsfondsudvalget, 'Erhvervsfondsudvalgets rapport om fremtidens regulering af erhvervsdrivende fonde' (2012), 261. My translation.

5.5. HARD AND SOFT LAW GOVERNANCE RULES

The Danish Law on Enterprise Foundations includes governance rules (hard law) which are complemented by recommendations on governance (soft law). The soft law governance rules are discussed in section 7 below.

The main governance rules are that a board of directors must comprise of at least three natural persons. The board of directors may employ an executive tasked with the daily management of the foundation, but otherwise this function also belongs to the board of directors. At least one-third of the board of directors must be independent of the founder of the foundation.[21] The board of directors is tasked with only being allowed to pursue the purposes and interests of the foundation.

A majority of the board of directors may not be employed as executives in the foundation, and an executive may not also be chairman or vice-chairman of the board. This prohibition is to avoid an unwanted concentration of power in that person. The provision is supplemented by a provision barring a chairman of the board from performing duties for the foundation that are not part of the position as chairman, i.e., a 'working chairman'. However, a chairman of the board may, where there is a special need for this, perform tasks which the person in question is requested to perform by and for the board.

The management or an equivalent body in the foundation, and members of the management or an equivalent body of the foundation's subsidiaries and of a company which is not a subsidiary, but in which the foundation and its subsidiary exercise a significant influence on the company's operational and financial management, may not appoint members to the board of the foundation. This provision is to avoid bottom-up appointment to the board of the foundation. In other words, is must be the head (the foundation) that wags the tail (of the subsidiary), not the other way round.

The chairman or vice-chairman of the board of directors may not be an executive of a subsidiary or of a company that is not a subsidiary, but in which the foundation and its subsidiary exercise a significant influence on the company's operational and financial management, unless the Business Authority (the state supervisor on enterprise foundations) provides permission. This provision is to ensure a degree of separation

---

21 Originally the requirement was just one independent person. This requirement was adopted from tax law before there was any legislation on foundations in order to ensure that there was an independent ownership other than that of the founder's economy.

and independence between the foundation and the management of the subsidiary.

The founder, his or her spouse or permanent cohabitant or persons linked to the said persons by consanguinity or in-laws in the right ascending or descending line or the collateral line as close as siblings, cannot constitute the majority of the board without the consent of the foundation authority.

If an enterprise foundation has been established by a company,[22] a person who directly or indirectly owns more than half of the ownership shares or voting shares in the company may not, without the consent of the Business Authority, constitute the majority of the board together with the people so closely linked to a founder, the founder's spouse/permanent cohabitant or family, just as the latter persons cannot, without the consent of the Business Authority, constitute the majority of the board. In the same way, the majority of a founding company's management may not, without the consent of the Business Authority, constitute the majority of the board of directors together with persons who have the above-mentioned specified affiliation with the relevant management members. This provision is to avoid a founder circumventing the prohibition described above by instead establishing the foundation by means of a company.

The members of the board are duty-bound to only pursue the interests and purposes of the foundation.

A member of the board of directors or an executive may not take part in the consideration of questions concerning agreements between the enterprise foundation and the person concerned or actions against the person him- or herself, or about agreements between the foundation and third parties or actions against third parties if the person concerned has a significant interest in them which may be contrary to those of the foundation.

Members of the board of directors or executives may not make such dispositions as to obviously provide the aforementioned or others with an undue advantage at the foundation's expense. Improper board decisions that violate the law or the bylaws are invalid.

---

22 The general assembly of a company may by vote decide to donate to a charitable purpose, for example, an enterprise foundation with a charitable purpose. Depending on the value of the donation, this can be done by either a simple majority or a supermajority in the company, in some cases with an obligation on the majority shareholders to redeem a minority of the value of their shares should they demand that.

Agreements between the foundation and one or more members of the board of directors or executives are only valid if they are drafted in a way that can be documented later unless they are agreements on usual terms as part of a current account.

The Business Authority has the power to dismiss one or more members of the board of directors if the Business Authority deems it necessary. Nobody else can have a power to dismiss a member of a board of directors.[23] A member may, of course, always resign from the board.

Board members are chosen by means of either co-optation or appointment by third parties, or a combination of both.[24] Third parties can, for example, be an organization, a public authority, or a private person.

Board members must fulfil certain requirements to be appointed and during their tenure at the board. A member of the board of directors must resign from the board if the person in question is bankrupt, due to long-term illness or other impairment, has proven to be unable to hold the position as a member of the board of directors, commits an act that makes them unworthy to continue to be a member of the board of directors or should generally be considered as being unsuitable to perform the tasks of a board member.

As a non-profit organization, the enterprise foundation is barred from distributing its net earnings to anyone exercising control over it. Professor Henry Hansmann has described this prohibition on distribution of profits as the 'nondistribution constraint':[25]

> A nonprofit organization is, in essence, an organization that is barred from distributing its net earnings, if any, to individuals who exercise control over it, such as members, officers, directors, or trustees. By 'net earnings' I mean here pure profits-that is, earnings in excess of the amount needed to pay for services rendered to the organization; in general, a nonprofit is free to pay reasonable compensation to any person for labor or capital that he provides, whether or not that person exercises some control over the organization. It should be noted that a nonprofit organization is not barred from earning a profit. Many nonprofits in fact consistently show an annual accounting surplus. It is only the distribution of the profits that is prohibited. Net earnings, if any, must be retained and devoted in their entirety to financing further production of the services that the organization was formed to provide. Since a good deal of the

23 The Business Authority may also dismiss the entire board of directors.

24 If the appointment of a board member does not take place according with the foundation's bylaws, the appointment is done by the Business Authority.

25 H. Hansmann, 'The Role of Non-profit Enterprises' (1980) 89(5) *Yale Law Journal* 835 et seq.

> discussion that follows will focus upon this prohibition on the distribution of profits, it will be helpful to have a term for it; I shall call it the 'nondistribution constraint'.
>
> Most non-profits of any significance are incorporated. For these organizations, the nondistribution constraint is imposed, either explicitly or implicitly, as a condition under which the organization receives its corporate charter. Thus, a non-profit corporation is distinguished from a for-profit (or 'business') corporation primarily by the absence of stock or other indicia of ownership that give their owners a simultaneous share in both profits and control.[26]

In his definition of a non-profit, Professor Hansmann emphasises whether the organization's net profit can be paid out to people who manage it. The fact that a non-profit creates – and aims to create – profit does (subject to legislation that stipulates otherwise) not matter as to whether an organization is a non-profit: 'the nondistribution constraint … is the defining characteristic of non-profit organizations'.[27]

According to section 49 of the Law on Enterprise Foundations, remuneration to members of the board of directors and executives may not exceed what is considered customary according to the nature of the position and the scope of work, and what may be considered justifiable in relation to the business fund and in parent funds in the group's financial position.

According to section 87 Law on Enterprise Foundations, founders, members of the board of directors and executives, auditors or persons holding a senior position in the foundation may not be granted any benefits from the foundation. The aforementioned are only allowed to receive a remuneration which may not exceed what is considered usual according to the nature of the position and the extent of the work involved. The same applies to a person who is connected to one of the persons mentioned by marriage or permanent cohabitation, and the minor children of such persons.

Both of these provisions are expressions of 'the nondistribution constraint' according to which the net profit – regardless of how this may be created – must only be used for the furtherance of the foundation's purpose.

Steen Thomsen comments on this as follows:

> The separation transforms the foundation into a non-profit entity, which, as emphasized by Hansmann …, may make profits but cannot distribute those

26 Ibid, 838.
27 Ibid, 842.

profits to the organization's members, directors, officers, or other persons who exercise control of the organization.[28]

5.6. CO-DETERMINATION

The Danish Companies Law has rules on co-determination, by granting employees a right to elect company or group representatives to the board of directors of the foundation. These rules apply correspondingly for enterprise foundations and their subsidiaries with some modifications. The rationale behind applying these rules also to enterprise foundations is that electing to conduct business by means of an enterprise foundation should not deprive employees of their right to co-determination. Additionally, applying this requirement also to enterprise foundations ensures a level playing field with companies.

The right to co-determination applies both where the persons are employed in the foundation itself (foundation representation) and where they are employed in the enterprise foundation's subsidiaries (group representation).

The enterprise foundation, respectively the group, must in the last three years have employed an average of at least 35 employees.

The employees may elect a number of members to the enterprise foundation's board of directors corresponding to half of the other board members rounded up, but always have a right to elect at least two members, or three members in case of there also being group representation. The board members appointed by the bylaws of the enterprise foundation must always constitute the majority of the members on the board of the foundation.

There are, of course, situations where an enterprise foundation differs from that of a company and where it is prudent to modify the rules of co-determination. The first modification is where the enterprise foundation has a purpose which provides for distributions to e.g. charity. Board members, who are elected by the employees, may accordingly only participate in the consideration of questions that do not concern the business enterprise, if this is stipulated in the bylaws of the enterprise foundation. The second modification deals with the election of new board members not being elected by the employees. If the bylaws state that one or more of the

28 S. Thomsen, *The Danish Industrial Foundations*, DJØF Publishing (2017), 15.

non-employee representative board members are elected by way of co-option, the board members elected by the employees do not participate in this appointment, unless otherwise specified in the bylaws of the enterprise foundation.

5.7. THE RULE AGAINST PERPETUITIES

As of 1 January 1985, when the two Danish foundations laws entered into effect, they included a rule against perpetuities. According to this rule, bylaws which confer on members of a particular family or families a right to preferential distribution shall not have legal effect according to their content to the extent that the preferential right extends beyond those living at the time of incorporation and to one unborn generation.[29] A rule of perpetuities already existed in the Danish Inheritance Act in relation to fideicommissa[30] as a consequence of the prohibition in the Danish Constitution against family fideicommissa.[31] It was thus natural that this rule would also be made applicable to foundations once legislation was drafted.

The rule against perpetuities does not prevent distributions to family members on an equal footing with others who are also covered by the foundation's purpose.

The rule against perpetuities only applies to foundations established on or after 1 January 1985. This was to not infringe upon the legitimate rights of already-established foundations and their beneficiaries. Hence, there are

---

29 To avoid a circumvention of the rule against perpetuities, this applies *mutatis mutandis* to bylaws which confer on members of a particular family or families preferential rights to hold a particular position or otherwise, including in the form of remuneration, to receive financial benefits from the foundation or from an undertaking over which the foundation has a controlling influence. However, this does not apply to positions as a member of the board of directors.

30 As opposed to a foundation, a fideicommissum is not a legal person and is not governed by a board of directors. Instead, a fideicommissum relies on the conditions stipulated by the testator on the order of succession. For a comprehensive analysis of fideicommissa in Denmark, see R.K. Feldthusen, *Succession*, DJØF Publishing (2001).

31 See section 87 of the Danish Inheritance Law: 'Inheritance [which is not subject to forced heirship rules] may be inserted by will in a succession order [fideicommissum], so that the inheritance goes to an heir or legatee in the first place and then one or more other heirs or legatees in the second or later places. In the case of a will, inheritance or bequest may not be attributed to several unborn persons in succession upon the testator's death.'

older foundations which today are distributing to later generations of the founder.

For all practical purposes, foundations for the benefit of the founder's family are not established any longer as the tax implications are disincentivizing (see further section 8 below).

6. ROLE OF THE STATE SUPERVISION

Even before Denmark enacted its two foundation laws in 1985, it was possible for foundations to request the receipt of a royal confirmation. By doing so, the foundation would become subject to public supervision by the governmental ministry with the closest connection to the purpose of the foundation, i.e., if the foundation had as its purpose to support culture, then it would be the Ministry of Culture having the supervisory function.

From 1985, the supervision of foundations was assigned to the Danish Business Authority (enterprise foundations) and the National Board of Civil Affairs (non-enterprise foundations).

The Business Authority exercises legal supervision to ensure that the board of directors adhere to the law and the bylaws of the foundation. The Business Authority does not have the competence to question the board of directors' decisions, which are not in contravention with these legal requirements.

The Business Authority may issue orders on specific matters in relation to the foundation, for example, reduce the board remuneration if it is considered unreasonable, order the board of directors to take the necessary steps to reduce or increase distribution according to the purpose(s) of the foundation, etc.

Several of the provisions in the Danish Enterprise Foundation Act are subject to a fine – for example, for violating the rule against a majority of the members of the board of directors being employed as directors of the foundation and the rule against a director also being the chairman or deputy chairman of the board of directors.

The Business Authority may decide on a special audit (*granskning*) of a foundation, its management or its annual reports. One or more special auditors are appointed at the expense of the foundation and may require all information relevant to the audit.

The Business Authority may remove one or more members of the board of directors. As the removal of board members is a far-reaching intervention, this power is only to be used in situations where a need has clearly manifested itself to dismiss the board member in question and replace this person with a more competent and responsible board member.

The Business Authority is authorised to initiate a lawsuit holding the board of directors, accountants, special auditors, appraisers and/or third parties liable for damages.

If the board is contemplating extraordinary decisions that may entail a risk that the bylaws may not be complied with or that the foundation will not be able to continue to exist, it must obtain the consent by the Business Authority in advance. It should be noted that this approach cannot be used to achieve a result that is in contravention with the purpose and bylaws of the foundation. In this case, the board of directors must follow the procedure of amendment of the purpose, which can only be allowed if pursuing the purpose is no longer possible or clearly unsuitable.

A foundation must apply to the Business Authority if it wants to make amendments to its bylaws and/or purpose. The criterion for allowing a change of the bylaws is that the existing provision is not suitable. If the amendment instead concerns the purpose or other material provisions (for example, concerning the dissolution of the foundation), the criterion is that it is otherwise either impossible or unsuitably qualified for the foundation to continue without the requested amendment.

The requirements for allowing a foundation to amend its purpose may, on the face of it, seem rigid with regard to the foundation's business purposes, as changes in the market, competitors, etc. require a flexible and expedited process for amendments. The Business Authority has over the years however proven to understand the needs and wishes of foundations of having their business purposes amended in order for the foundations to stay competitive. Often a need to amend a foundation's business purpose is to raise capital to the company and that means relaxing the foundation's ownership stake, typically from 100% to a lower ownership stake, even below 50%, but then with a requirement to maintain a controlling influence through a majority of votes. Over time, several large Danish enterprise foundations – with the approval of the Business Authority – have amended their business purposes in order to retain a majority of votes (preferential voting shares), but have diluted their ownership:

- Carlsberg Foundation: 75% of the votes and 29% of the share capital in Carlsberg A/S.[32]

[32] In 2000, the Carlsberg Foundation's board of directors was granted permission to in the future – in connection with a share issue and/or merger – change the purpose of

- Novo Nordisk Foundation (through Novo Holdings A/S): 75% of the votes and 28% of the share capital in Novo Nordisk A/S, and 71% of the votes and 25% of the share capital in Novozymes A/S.
- A.P. Møller Foundation (through A.P. Møller Holding A/S): 51.45% of the votes and 41.51% of the share capital in A.P. Møller – Mærsk A/S.

The existence of a pragmatic business-oriented state supervisor and the possibility of splitting up shares between share capital and votes have been paramount in ensuring that the foundation-controlled companies have had access to raise more capital.

Any decision made by the Business Authority may be appealed to an administrative complaints board which publishes its decisions, although these are anonymized. Public access is given to decisions made by the Business Authority and documents pertaining to this.

7. RULES ON DISCLOSURE AND TRANSPARENCY

As enterprise foundations are separate legal entities running a business or controlling an operating company, the disclosure requirements have generally been the same as for other Danish limited liability companies, i.e., public annual accounts and registration in a central public business registry.

With the new legislation on enterprise foundations in 2015 came additional requirements as to disclosure and transparency. It is now a requirement that all transactions with related parties, whether at market value or not, are disclosed in the enterprise foundation's annual accounts. The legislation uses the definition of 'related parties' in the International Accounting Standards (IAS 24). If, for example, a member of the board of directors renders services to the foundation at market value, it must be disclosed in the annual accounts.

The foundation must disclose the total remuneration of the board of directors and management in two separate categories in its annual accounts.[33]

---

the foundation from having a controlling interest in the Carlsberg Brewery to instead having a 'significant influence', in order to ensure the preservation of 'Carlsberg' as a widespread and recognised beer brand and continue beer production in Denmark.

33 If the information about remuneration will lead to the display of amounts for a single member of a management category, the amounts may instead be stated together for

The foundation must establish and publish its distribution policy. The requirement is intended to improve public insight into the distributions of enterprise foundations. As part of the policy, the foundation must state which main categories to which the board of directors have made distributions during the financial year. The distribution policy must contain any strategy prepared, as well as guidelines and goals that the board of directors follows when making distributions. The distribution policy cannot just be a copy of the foundation's bylaws but must be an elaboration of how the foundation specifically realizes its purpose though its distributions.

Large enterprise foundations must also comply with the Financial Statement Act's provisions on reporting on social responsibility and on the fulfilment of setting a target figure for the share of the underrepresented gender on the board of directors.

In 2014 a Committee on Foundation Governance was established. Its purpose was to issue a set of recommendations on which the enterprise foundations were obligated by law to report, but on a comply-or-explain principle. It is thus voluntary for an enterprise foundation to follow the recommendations, but it must report whether it does or not, and in the latter case the explanation on why it does not follow and how the foundation has instead designed its governance.

Failure to comply with a recommendation is not considered a breach of rules, but merely implies that the board of directors has specifically and for the reasons it has explained chosen a different approach.

The state supervisor can order the board of directors to account for its response to the recommendations when the foundation:

- Fails to address one or more recommendations,
- fails to explain a deviation,
- provides an explanation for a deviation that is apparently unjustified or without meaning or
- explains a deviation but does not explain what it decided to do instead.

The reporting on the recommendations is made public either through the foundation's annual report and/or its website. The requirement to report applies to all approximately 1,400 enterprise foundations.

---

the two categories or omitted if only one category receives remuneration, a pension or a special incentive programme.

There are currently 17 recommendations divided into the following categories:[34]

1. Transparency and communication
2. Tasks and responsibilities of the board of directors
   a. Overall tasks and responsibilities
   b. Chairman and vice-chairman of the board of directors
   c. Composition and organization of the board of directors
   d. Independence
   e. Appointment period
   f. Evaluation of the performance of the board of directors and executive board
3. Remuneration of management

The recommendations are meant to reflect best practice and thus go above and beyond the hard law requirements in the Danish Law on Enterprise Foundations, which can be illustrated with the two recommendations on independence and remuneration:

> **Independence**
>
> 2.4.1 It is recommended that an appropriate proportion of the board of directors are independent.
>
> If the board of directors (excluding employee representatives) is composed of:
>
> - up to four members, at least one member should be independent,
> - between five and eight members, at least two members should be independent, or
> - nine to eleven members, at least three members should be independent, and so on.
>
> To be considered independent, this person may not, for example:
>
> - be or within the past three years have been member of the executive board or a senior employee in the foundation or an essential subsidiary or associated company to the foundation,
> - within the past five years have received larger emoluments, including distributions or other benefits from the foundation/group or a subsidiary

[34] The recommendations can be found at: https://godfondsledelse.dk/english.

or associated company to the foundation in other capacity than as member of the board of directors or executive board of the foundation,
- within the past year have had a significant business relationship (e.g. personal or indirectly as partner or employee, shareholder, customer, supplier or member of the executive management of companies with corresponding connection) with the foundation/group or a subsidiary or associate of the foundation,
- be or within the past three years have been employed or partner at the external auditor,
- have been a member of the board of directors or executive board of the foundation for more than 12 years,
- be a close relative or in another way be very close to persons who are not considered as independent,
- be the founder or a significant donor if the purpose of the foundation is to grant support to this person's family or others who are especially close to this person, or
- be a member of the management of an organization, another foundation or similar, which receives or repeatedly within the past five years have received significant donations from the foundation.

In addition to the above, there is also a recommendation on providing information on each member of the board of directors on the following:

- the name and position of the member,
- the age and gender of the member,
- date of original appointment to the board, whether the member has been re-elected, and expiry of the current election period,
- any special competences possessed by the member,
- other managerial positions held by the member, including positions on executive boards, boards of directors and supervisory boards and board committees in Danish and foreign foundations, enterprises and institutions, as well as other demanding organization tasks,
- whether the member owns shares, options, warrants and similar in the foundation's subsidiaries and/or associates,
- whether the member has been appointed by authorities/providers of grants etc., and
- whether the member is considered independent.

The board of directors should at suitable intervals consider whether the composition of the board and the competences of its members individually and collectively reflect the requirements imposed by the purpose of the foundation, including commercial and distribution purposes, strategy, financial position, and other circumstances. The consideration should also include the ability and willingness of the members of the board of directors to impartially carry out the purpose of the foundation:

> **Remuneration of management**
>
> 3.1.1 It is recommended that the members of the board of directors of enterprise foundations be remunerated with a fixed remuneration and that members of a potential executive board be remunerated with a fixed remuneration, possibly combined with a bonus which should not be dependent upon accounting results. The remuneration should reflect the work and responsibilities consequential to the position.

The position of a board member of a foundation entails a special obligation to ensure that the board of directors' decisions on remuneration are made solely for the fulfilment of the foundation's purpose and interests, and thus solely correspond to the responsibilities and work effort associated with the duties of board member.

The Business Authority is tasked with enforcing the obligation to comply or explain, but whether a foundation complies or instead explains is equally as good.

8. TAXATION

On 1 January 1987 a separate law on taxation of foundations entered into force. As a point of departure, foundations, whether enterprise foundations or non-enterprise foundations, are taxed in the same way as corporations. This means that foundations are taxed at the same tax rate as companies (currently 22%), and on the same types of income, capital gains etc., as companies.

However, foundations enjoy greater access to deducting costs and may furthermore deduct charitable distributions from their income. A foundation may also set aside income for later charitable distributions with a deduction if the aforementioned is used for actual distribution within a maximum of five years.

The rationale behind the tax legislation is thus that foundations, which make charitable distributions, should be able to reduce their taxes by the amount of the distributions. However, the reality is that foundations, or rather their subsidiaries, still pay taxes on their income.

Foundations are not able to be jointly taxed with their subsidiaries. If the foundation owns at least 10% of the share capital, it receives dividends from its subsidiary tax-free. However, any charitable distributions must first be offset against tax-free dividends from its subsidiary.

It is, however, recognised that a foundation may transfer the income of a subsidiary to the foundation, before the income is taxed in the subsidiary, if the foundation uses this income for charitable distributions. Thereby the foundation can achieve a full deduction of the income in the subsidiary in its charitable distributions, effectively avoiding paying any tax. However, this only applies to subsidiaries in which the foundation owns at least 75% of the share capital and only if the subsidiary is owned directly by the foundation, and thus not through other companies, such as a holding company.

Establishing a foundation with a charitable purpose does not incur any taxes, whether it is by way of a gift or will. If a business purpose is added, it is still tax-free if it is by way of gift, but if it is instead in a will, it incurs an inheritance tax of 36.25%.[35] Foundations with a family purpose (as one of their purposes) incur a tax of 20% if the transfer is by way of a gift and 36.25% in inheritance tax if the transfer is by way of a will.

A transfer of tax-relevant assets to a foundation will trigger capital gains which have to be paid by the donor of the estate of the deceased donor. However, it is possible to either a) transfer the tax burden onto the foundation or b) altogether avoid paying capital gains on transferring shares in a company to a foundation pursuant to special tax rules implemented to encourage the establishment of more enterprise foundations in Denmark.

Model b) is a very favourable way of transferring the shares of a company without the founder incurring any taxes whatsoever. It is, however, a prerequisite, that the shares to be transferred are owned – in practice 100% – by another company (a holding company).

9. FINAL REMARKS

The Danish model in relation to enterprise foundations has proven to be successful and has supported large Danish companies to grow even larger over the years.

35 This is not logical and is a consequence of Danish tax rules not having been harmonised.

In a way, the story of enterprise foundations is like the story of the bee. According to traditional laws of aviation, there is no way that a bee should be able to fly, as its wings are too small to get its body off from the ground. However, on further inspection, the secret of bee flight, the researchers say, is the unconventional combination of short, choppy wing strokes, a rapid rotation of the wing as it flops over and reverses direction, and a very fast wing-beat frequency.[36] Correspondingly, according to traditional economic theory, enterprise foundations should be inefficient and outcompeted by their for-profit competitors, as companies are motivated by profit maximization of their owners, and as enterprise foundations have no owners and boards members no personal profit motive.[37]

However, the case of Denmark serves as empirical evidence that enterprise foundations actually can fly and prosper, and thus are a viable instrument to combine long-termism, purpose, business and philanthropy.

---

36 D.L. Altshuler, W.B. Dickson, J.T. Vance, S.P. Roberts and M.H. Dickinson, 'Short-Amplitude High-Frequency Wing Strokes Determine the Aerodynamics of Honeybee Flight' (2005) 102(50) *PNAS* 18213; and Calltech, 'Deciphering the Mystery of Bee Flight': https://www.caltech.edu/about/news/deciphering-mystery-bee-flight-1075.

37 S. Thomsen, *The Danish Industrial Foundations,* DJØF Publishing, (2017), 25 *et seq.*

INDUSTRIAL FOUNDATIONS UNDER ITALIAN LAW

Eugenio Barcellona

ABSTRACT

Enterprise foundations are a legal institute that, in the past, has not found widespread application in Italy. This chapter analyses the reasons for this phenomenon and the subsequent evolution of enterprise foundations in Italy. After addressing the cultural and political reasons for which foundations have largely been neglected (section 1), the original provisions of the Italian Civil Code will be analysed (section 2). Then, section 3 will cover the doctrinal developments of the 1960s that reinstated the legitimacy of foundations. Subsequently, the three most important pieces of legislation on the matter will be examined: the 1990s laws on banking foundations (section 4), the 2000 law on recognition of legal personality and on the requirements of the foundation's 'purpose' (section 5) and the 2017 Code for the Third Sector (section 6). The chapter will conclude with a reflection on the current state of enterprise foundations and the directions towards which their further evolution should aim.

1. INTRODUCTION

In Italy, 'industrial foundations' or 'enterprise foundations' – i.e. profit-driven companies held by private law foundations – are a rather rare phenomenon. The reasons for this minor significance are essentially twofold.

The first reason is cultural: it is mainly rooted in the Catholic and Marxist influence that shaped Italian culture. 'Industrial foundations' thrive in those jurisdictions where, to use Max Weber's words,[1] 'the spirit of capitalism' blossoming out of 'Protestant ethics' is deeply rooted:[2] under the Protestant perspective, not only does the pursuit of profit on earth not violate any religious writ, but on the contrary signifies an ascetic and vocational tendency towards productive work. Profit is not merely an

1 W. Weber, 'Die Protestantische Ethik und der Geist des Kapitalismus', in *Archiv für Sozialwissenschaft und Soziapolitik*, [1904–1905] nn. 20–21 (translated into Italian: *L'etica protestante e lo spirito del capitalismo*, Sansoni, Florence 1970, passim).

2 P. Rescigno, 'Le "non profit organizations" come formazioni sociali', in G. Ponzanelli (ed.), *Gli enti 'non profit' in Italia*, Cedam, Padua 1994, p. 263.

instrument of accumulation of wealth to live an opulent life, but rather clear and objective evidence of the success of the entrepreneur's creative endeavour. It is no coincidence that Walter Rathenau's well-known theory of *Unternehmen an sich*[3] originated in a predominantly Protestant context. More than just a money-making machine, an enterprise is an 'institution' that, through profit, ultimately contributes to the wellbeing of the entire community.

Such an institutional view of enterprises never really took root in Italy. The Catholic ethic, unlike the Protestant one, always looked askance at those who handled the 'devil's excrement' (a Catholic expression to describe money).[4] From a very different perspective, Marxism helped to portray the entrepreneur as the 'evil' exploiter of the proletariat. Last but not least, a highly non-meritocratic structure of crony capitalism made the equation 'profit = deserved success' hardly credible.

The second reason for the limited diffusion of 'enterprise foundations' is directly linked to the specific regulatory framework.[5] Italian foundation law has traditionally been very hostile to 'enterprise foundations'.[6]

---

3 The theory of the *Unternehmen an sich* became known to Italian audiences thanks to the publication of W. Rathenau, 'La realtà della società per azioni. Riflessioni suggerite dall'esperienza degli affari' [1960] *Riv. soc.* 912–947.

4 J. le Goff, *Lo sterco del diavolo. Il denaro nel Medioevo*, Laterza, Bari 2012 (5th ed.), passim, illustrates the influence of Catholicism over the antagonism against profit-driven economic activities.

5 On Italian foundation law in general, see, amongst others, C.M. Bianca, *Diritto civile*, 1, *La norma giuridica e i soggetti*, Giuffrè, Milan 2002 (2nd ed.), pp. 343 ff.; F. Galgano (1), 'Delle persone giuridiche', in *Commentario Scialoja-Branca*, Zanichelli-Foro it., Bologna-Turin 1969, *sub* art. 16, pp. 185 ff.; F. Galgano (2), 'Fondazione, 1) Diritto civile', in *Enc. giur. Treccani*, Ed. Enc. It., Rome 1989; P. Rescigno (1), 'Fondazione (dir. civ.)', in *Enc., Dir.* XVII, Giuffrè, Milan 1968, pp. 791–814; P. Rescigno (2), 'Le fondazioni: prospettive e linee di riforma', Cedam, Padua 1989, pp. 480 ff.; A. Carrabba, *Scopo di lucro e autonomia privata. La funzione nelle strutture organizzative*, Esi, Napoli 1994, pp. 319 ff.; V. Iudica, 'Fondazioni, fedecommesserie, trusts e trasmissione della ricchezza familiare. Limiti e prospettive del sistema successorio' [1994] II *Nuova giurisprudenza civile commentata* 47 ff.; A. Zoppini, *Le fondazioni. Dalla tipicità alle tipologie*, Jovene, Napoli 1995, pp. 54 ff.

6 On enterprise foundations specifically, under Italian law, see, amongst others, R. Costi, 'Fondazioni e impresa' [1968] I *Riv. dir. civ.* 1 ff.; P. Rescigno, 'Fondazione e impresa' [1967] *Riv. soc.* 812 ff.; A. Zoppini, above n. 5, p. 61; A. Zoppini, 'Considerazioni sulla fondazione di impresa e sulla fondazione fiduciaria regolate da una recente legge francese' [1991] 1 *Riv. dir. comm.* 573–597; D. Vittoria (1), 'Le fondazioni culturali ed il consiglio di amministrazione. Evoluzione della prassi statutaria e prospettive della tecnica redazionale' [1975] *Riv. dir. comm.* 297–348; D. Vittoria (2), *Le fondazioni culturali e il consiglio di amministrazione*, Jovene, Napoli 1976, pp. 56 ff.; A. Barba, *Associazione, fondazione e titolarità di impresa*, Jovene, Napoli 1996, pp. 95 ff.; G. Ponzanelli, *Gli enti collettivi senza scopo di lucro*, Giappichelli,

However, such an aversion has been constantly on the wane over the last few decades so that the latest approach, even though it does not yet qualify as 'welcoming', is no longer as markedly 'hostile' as it was at the outset.[7]

This chapter is structured along a chronological timeline of the evolution of the law of foundations: first, the law of foundations as etched in the (very few) provisions of the Italian Civil Code of 1942 is described (section 2). Then, the scholars' evolution that occurred in Italy during the Republican age, with specific reference to the late 1960s (section 3). Subsequently, the most significant legal enactments are examined: (i) the 1990s laws on banking foundations (section 4); (ii) the 2000 law on recognition of legal personality and on the requirements of the foundation's 'purpose' (section 5); and (iii) the 2017 Code for the Third Sector (section 6). The final section is dedicated to the conclusions drawn from the preceding discussion (section 7).

2. FOUNDATION LAW IN THE ITALIAN CIVIL CODE

2.1. INTRODUCTION: THE PERSISTENCE OF THE CIVIL CODE'S OLD RULES

Nowadays, the Italian regulation of foundations is still governed by few and rather incomplete articles of the Italian Civil Code of 1942. It is true that, from the entry into force of the Civil Code until today, certain important special foundation laws have been enacted that have somehow enriched Italian foundation legal regime. Yet, the provisions of the Civil Code have never been amended. It is worth mentioning that, upon the approval of the 'enabling act' (*legge-delega*) that led to the approval of the Code for the Third Sector, the government was originally delegated by the Parliament not only to organically regulate the so-called third sector,

---

Turin 2000 (2nd ed.), pp. 177 ff.; A. Cetra, *L'impresa collettiva non societaria*, Giappichelli, Turin 2003, passim; G. Baralis, 'Enti no profit: profili civilistici' [1999] *Riv. notar.* 1091 ff.; G.F. Campobasso, 'Associazioni e attività di impresa' [1994] II *Riv. dir. civ.* 581 ff.

7 A survey of 'corporate foundations' (i.e. foundations that are established by corporations, but that do not necessarily own enterprises) that also includes some information about 'enterprise foundations' is provided by Fondazione Bracco and Fondazione Sodalitas, *Le fondazioni di impresa in Italia – Rapporto di ricerca 2019*, https://www.sodalitas.it/public/allegati/_%E2%80%9CLe-fondazioni-d%E2%80%99impresa-in-Italia%E2%80%9D,-Rapporto-di-ricerca,-2019_2019917184724996.pdf.

but also to coherently revisit the by then outdated regime provided by the Civil Code.[8] As the government failed to fulfil this task, the provisions of the Civil Code technically remain still in force.[9]

We can anticipate our conclusions: the law of foundations set by the Civil Code, as interpreted by the early commentators, represented an insuperable obstacle to the spreading of 'enterprise foundations' in Italy. Here, in brief, are the reasons for this.

2.2. THE LEGACY OF BOURGEOIS IDEOLOGY IN THE INTERCONNECTED REGULATION OF 'FOUNDATIONS' AND 'PROPERTY'

The regime of the 1942 Italian Civil Code testifies to the influence of two different cultural backgrounds: (i) a 'bourgeois' background that can be traced back to the influence that the French Civil Code of 1804 exerted on the Italian Civil Code of 1865 and then on the Code of 1942; and (ii) an 'authoritative' background that traces back to the specific cultural climate of the two decades of fascism in which the Civil Code of 1942 was drafted.

The bourgeois-liberal ideology did not look favourably upon foundations, since it aimed at modifying the property regime to overcome the feudal regime in order to free the market once and for all. There is indeed a strong systematic link between the Civil Code's regulation of foundations and that of property.[10]

In simplified terms, the feudal regime of property was based on the distinction between the superior property right of the lords (*dominum emines*), giving the lord the right to claim a perpetual rent from its ownership (the land) and the so-called right to use (*dominium utile*), which gave the vassal the right to manage, and benefit of, the asset in exchange for the payment of the census (the rent). The two rights circulated separately, so that the property was, in fact, a divided property (*dominium divisum*).[11] Clearly, such regulation impedes the productive exploitation of the land. As the rent due to the owner of the *dominum eminens* was set once and for all, and, as such, was exempted from market negotiation,

---

8 See article 1, para. 2, a) of the Enabling Act ('legge-delega') no. 196 of June 6, 2016.

9 See section 6 below.

10 R. Costi, above n. 6, p. 2, highlighted the connection between the legal regime of property on the one hand and the legal regime of foundations on the other hand.

11 The theory of *dominium divisum* in largely addressed in P. Grossi, *Il dominio e le cose*, Giuffrè, Milan 1992.

a proper management of the costs and revenues of land use, according to rationally capitalistic criteria, was basically impossible. For example, under market conditions, a deterioration in land productivity would have led to a reduction in rent; on the other hand, the feudal regime of *dominum indivisum* radically prevented such an effect, thereby worsening the position of the land exploiter.

The bourgeois regime of property overcomes the inefficiencies of the feudal regime through a revolutionary unification of property regulation: no more separation between *dominum eminens* and *dominum utile*, but rather a sole 'property right' consolidating the right to benefit from the good in the manner deemed most appropriate and the right to sell it on the market or dispose of the leasehold only.[12] Hence, the 'rent' always and in any case due to the holder of *dominus eminens* is abolished, thus creating the conditions for that legal regime, welcomed by capitalistic bourgeoisie, that linked the value of the good's use to the changing dynamics of the market.

The bourgeois regime of property – systematically regulated in the Napoleonic Code of 1804 for the first time – clearly celebrates the liberal ideology of the 'efficient self-interest' that was described in scientific terms by Adam Smith shortly before (1776): since every 'owner' is naturally oriented to the maximization of personal interests (according to the *homo oeconomicus* paradigm) and since the interaction of self-interested owners is naturally oriented towards achieving the best allocation of resources, the more the law incentivizes the 'efficient' bourgeois property regime, the more it will procure that scarce resources are destined to their best use. Clearly, the ideology that presides over such regulation of property rights postulates that the efficient use of property can be achieved only with the consolidation in the same individual of the 'management power' (control) on the one hand, and the 'right to the related economic benefits' (ownership) on the other. Since every individual is naturally driven by self-interest (*homo oeconomicus*), the allocation of the economic benefits to the manager itself secures the utilization most wanted by the market.

Certainly, this bourgeois ideology of property right inspires important provisions originally drawn up by the French Napoleonic Code and still in force today in Italian law under the Civil Code of 1942:[13] (i) the provision

---

12 C.B. Macpherson, *Libertà e proprietà alle origini del pensiero borghese – La teoria dell'individualismo possessivo da Hobbes a Locke*, Milan, 1973; P. Grossi, 'La proprietà e le proprietà nell'officina dello storico', in P. Grossi, above n. 11, p. 648–665.

13 M.V. de Giorgi, 'Fondazioni di famiglia e attività d'impresa' [2005] II *Nuova giurisprudenza civile commentata* 80.

allowing the constitution of the right of usufruct (which, in a certain way, mirrors the division between *dominium eminens*, mere property, and *dominium utile*, usufruct), but, notably, only for the maximum duration of the usufructuary's life or, in event that the usufructuary is a legal entity, for a maximum duration of 30 years; (ii) the provision that, coherently, in the case of the constitution of the usufruct by will, forbids the so-called subsequent usufruct (meaning the transfer of the right of usufruct from a first usufructuary to a second usufructuary); (iii) the provision that allows the constitution by will of a perpetual allowance only to the extent that it serves a 'public utility' purpose and, additionally, that enables the release of the allowance payer (thus ultimately allowing the termination of a potentially perpetual obligation); (iv) lastly, the provision, once again in the field of successions, that prohibits the so-called fideicommissum (meaning the testamentary disposition by virtue of which, following the death of the heir, the assets are transferred to another individual chosen by the testator), with the sole exception of a fideicommissum established by the caretaker of an individual unable to act and therefore in need.[14] Indeed, (i) a perpetual separation between mere property and usufruct, or (ii) the constitution of perpetual burdens in the absence of a public utility purpose, if allowed, would have jeopardized the 'efficient self-interest' ideology that, on the contrary, postulated the consolidation of 'management power' (control) and related 'economic benefits' (ownership) in the same hands.

In light of the above, one could easily understand why foundations were doomed to face a strong opposition. The bourgeoisie's hostility to foundations can be explained by two correlated reasons. First, the allocation of an asset to a legal entity constituted for its perpetual conservation and use for the benefit of certain individuals was thought to pave the way for a subtle reinstatement of the feudal type of property:[15] once the property

---

14 L. Ghidoni, 'Il legato di usufrutto universale', in G. Bonilini and V. Barba (eds.), *Le disposizioni testamentarie*, Utet, Turin 2012, pp. 682 ff.

15 A. Zoppini, 'Quattro tesi per una rilettura delle norme sulle fondazioni', in G. Ponzanelli, above n. 2, p. 78 ('[T]he preposition of an asset to an end – the Idealtypus of the foundation – seemed to the bourgeois legislator, educated to the physiocratic doctrine, incompatible with a political program aimed at promoting the free circulation of profit and the rational exploitation of capital and had, on the other hand, evocated the memory of the 'divided property' and the eminent domain') ('La destinazione di un patrimonio allo scopo, in questo si risolve l'Idealtypus della fondazione, era sembrato al legislatore borghese educato alla dottrina fisiocratica incompatibile con il programma politico vòlto a favorire la libera circolazione della ricchezza e il razionale sfruttamento della ricchezza ed aveva, semmai, evocato il ricordo della 'proprietà divisa' e del dominio eminente').

of the good is transferred to the foundation, such a good is inevitably withheld from circulation and thus its allocation to the most 'efficient' owner is prevented. Second, there was a fear that the disentanglement between the 'management power' and 'claims on economic benefits' could generate inefficient results, according to the same rationale underpinning the perceived efficiency of the 'bourgeois property': a manager with no interest in the results of the management and with no control by an 'owner' has no incentive to ensure the most profitable management of the assets.[16]

The bourgeois-liberal ideology's hostility to foundations – as evidenced, for example, by the French physiocrat Turgot, who advocated for their total prohibition[17] – is at the root of the eloquent silence on the subject by the French Civil Code, which inspired the first unitary Italian Civil Code of 1865 and, later on, the 1942 Code.[18] The Italian legislature of 1942 did not follow the French path of total silence, but addressed foundations with few and inconsistent provisions.

Foundations are permitted, provided they are established by public deed (Article 14 of the Civil Code (CC)); the deed of foundation is qualified as irrevocable even by the founder himself (Article 15 CC); recognition of legal personality – following which the contributed assets are part of a 'separate patrimony' – is subject to the issuance of a licence and is therefore left to the discretion of the public administration; the

16 P. Rescigno (1), above n. 5, p. 803 ('[T]he revolt against this institution, during the Enlightenement and the French revolution, was also based on the risk that through foundations, multiplied by the human desire to achieve immortal deeds, many resources and particular properties would be, in the end, absorbed, in order to achieve goals storically obsolete or no longer felt as useful in society')('La rivolta contro l'istituto, nell'età dell'Illuminismo e della rivoluzione francese, prese a motivo proprio il pericolo che attraverso le fondazioni, moltiplicate dalla vanità umana di dare immortalità ad opera dell'uomo, rimanessero a lungo andare assorbite tutte le risorse e le proprietà particolari, e poste al servizio di scopi storicamente superati o non più avvertiti come utili nell'ambiente sociale').

17 R. Turgot, 'Fondation. Article de l'Encyclopédie' (vol. VII, 1757), in G. Schelle (ed.), *Oevres de Turgot*, Librairie Félix Alcan, vol. I, Paris 1913, p. 593.

18 A. Zoppini, above n. 15, pp. 69–70 ('[T]he reasons for this adversion – which penetrated indistinctly into all legal systems that had the French one as a model – can be summarized essentially in the convergence between the physiocratic dogma, the fear of intermediate bodies hypertrophy, and the conceptual (before than practical) rejection with the fractioning of an asset owned by a single individual')('I motivi di questa avversione – che indistintamente è penetrata negli ordinamenti che hanno avuto a riferimento il modello francese – possono compendiarsi essenzialmente nella convergenza tra il dogma fisiocratico, il timore dell'ipertrofia dei corpi intermedi, il ripudio concettuale, prima ancora che pratico, della possibilità di frazionare il patrimonio imputato ad un solo soggetto').

purchase of real estate properties is subject to the authorization of the public administration (Article 17 CC). Lastly, the public administration has the power to transform or even dissolve, a foundation in the event of the impossibility or 'poor usefulness' of its purpose (Articles 27–28 CC).

Actually, the provisions of the Civil Code do not specify what the purpose of the foundation might be. However, according to an almost unanimous consensus among interpreters of the Civil Code of 1942, foundations could pursue only purposes of 'public utility'.

Such an interpretation, even in the absence of a clear legislative provision, was inferred (i) from the provisions, which are still effective today, that permit a fideicommissum in favour of an entity (such as a foundation) only insofar as it is intended to protect a 'needy' individual (Article 692 CC), as well as (ii) from further provisions that admit perpetual allowances only to the extent that they are intended for 'public utility' purposes.

In summary, foundations represented a danger to the bourgeois-liberal ideology that inspired the 1942 Civil Code: there was a risk of the reinstatement of a property regime dangerously similar to the feudal regime and a further risk of an inefficient property regime. However, foundations were not completely neglected (as they were in the French system); on the contrary, they are explicitly tolerated, but only to the extent that, at least according to the prevailing interpretation, they were justified by the pursuit of 'public utility' – a purpose that, generally, should have been fulfilled by the state, but that, exceptionally, could be entrusted to those 'intermediate bodies'[19] that were looked upon suspiciously by the liberal culture,[20] This distrust rested on the following assumption: private citizens naturally pursue the objective of maximizing their own interests and, thanks to the interaction of selfish individuals, the market achieves

---

19 Organized groups of private citizens, other than profit-driven companies, that pursue collective ends.

20 P. Rescigno (1), above n. 5, p. 793 ('The refusal of the so-called intermediate bodies, and the function that they had absolved up until that point, was mainly aimed against corporativism and, on the other side, Church institutions and activities')('La negazione dei corpi sociali cosiddetti intermedi, e della funzione ch'essi avevano assolta in un lungo arco di tempo, era diretta a colpire soprattutto l'organizzazione corporativa e, in altra parte della realtà sociale, le istituzioni e le attività della Chiesa'); G. Ponzanelli, 'Terzo Settore: la legge delega di riforma' [2017] 5 *Nuova giur. civ.* 726 ('The discipline of the Code was characterized by great hostility against intermediate bodies, and would later reveal its structural limitations against this social phenomenon, that spread more and more') ('La disciplina codicistica era caratterizzata da una forte ostilità nei confronti degli enti intermedi e, in seguito, ha accentuato i suoi limiti strutturali nel confronto con un fenomeno sociale che si faceva sempre più diffuso').

the best allocation of resources; instead, it is the state, and the state alone, that naturally pursues 'common good' as its objective.[21]

2.3. THE HERITAGE OF THE FASCIST CULTURE: THE SUBJECTION OF FOUNDATIONS TO 'POLICE LAW'

The Civil Code's regulation of foundations also drew inspiration from a second ideology which is related to the specific cultural climate of the fascist era in which the 1942 Code was approved – a cultural climate whereby, notoriously, the state took an authoritarian and dirigiste approach in relation to private activities.

In this cultural context, it is no surprise that public interference on private activity was (and still is) particularly strong under the Civil Code – especially with reference to 'entities' that were thought to pose a threat to the productive utilization of goods.

---

21 This was, for instance, the view of A. Solmi, *L'idea fascista nel nuovo codice civile*, Soc. editrice del Foro Italiano, Rome 1940, pp. 91 ff. P. Rescigno (1), above n. 5, p. 797 addresses this original approach with these critical words: ('one would read, on the official comments to the new laws, that the assumption, by the State, of all the duties that had something to do with the general interest, reduced the field in which juridical persons 'of private character' could operate (and therefore the system of norms set forth by the Civil Code was aimed at controlling the residual space of action of that activity, rather than promoting its expansion)') ('accadeva di leggere, nei commenti ufficiali ai nuovi testi legislativi, che l'assunzione, da parte dello Stato, di tutti i compiti che toccassero in qualche misura l'interesse della generalità rendeva assai ristretta l'area in cui potessero muoversi le persone giuridiche 'di carattere privato' (e perciò il sistema di norme predisposte nel codice civile voleva servire piuttosto a controllare quell'àmbito residuo di libera attività, che a favorirne l'espansione)'). More recently, a similar comment has been made by D. Preite, 'Lo scopo negli enti del primo libro del codice civile: nuovi sviluppi in dottrina e in giurisprudenza', in G. Ponzanelli, above n. 2, p. 285 ('for the traditional liberal culture that inspired the Civil code the market operated as an instrument of efficient production and resource allocation, as a place of intersection and coordination of people that aimed at economical and egoistical objectives, in particular the maximisation of their profit. The State, on the other hand, was the instrument for the expression of the sum of each individual will. Consequently, entities that did *not* aim at the aforementioned goal appeared extraneous, and almost an obstacle, to both the efficiency of the market and the regular functioning of the State') ('per la tradizionale cultura liberale che ha ispirato il codice civile il mercato operava come strumento di efficiente produzione ed allocazione di risorse in quanto luogo di incontro e coordinamento di soggetti miranti a scopi economico-egoistici ed in particolare alla massimizzazione del loro profitto. Lo Stato risultava a sua volta strumento ed espressione della somma di volontà individuali. Gli enti che *non* mirano allo scopo suddetto apparivano conseguentemente estranei e quasi di intralcio sia all'efficiente operare del mercato che al normale funzionamento della politica e dello Stato').

As mentioned earlier, the subordination of recognition of juridical personality to a licensing procedure was already capable of vesting the governmental authority with discretionary power on the establishment of a foundation. However, the 1942 Civil Code goes well beyond that. Indeed, it vests the governmental authority with: (i) the power to control and supervise the foundation's assets; (ii) the power to appoint and substitute the directors in the event of the impracticability of the provisions of the bylaws; (iii) the power to annul the resolution, *inter alia*, on the grounds that they are contrary to 'public order and decency'; (iv) the power to dissolve the foundation in the event of unlawful management; (v) the power to authorize a liability action against the directors and to appoint an extraordinary commissioner to replace them; (vi) the power to order the coordination of the activity of multiple foundations or the unification of their management; (vii) the power to transform or dissolve the foundation in the event of supervening impossibility of purpose or 'scarce utility' and, lastly, (viii) the power to allocate, in the event of dissolution of the foundation, the remaining assets to entities having 'similar purposes' (Articles 25–32 CC).

The fact that this regulation stemmed not only from the liberal ideological distrust towards 'intermediate bodies', but also from the specific cultural atmosphere of the fascist era is blatant. Foundations are subject to what has been disdainfully called 'police law'.[22]

However, attention should be paid to one important aspect: the governmental authority's control and supervision over the management of foundations was not only the result of the specific political and cultural climate, but also a response to the real need to regulate entities without owners. Indeed, in the presence of a (substantial) 'owner' of reference in collective institutions (as is the case with associations or, typically, commercial companies), the incentive for efficient management is closely

22 P. Rescigno (1), above n. 5, p. 797 ('the political climate that saw the birth of the Civil Code naturally lead to adopting, and to some extent also exaggerating, that idea of foundations ... which can be characterized as "police law" ... so that when, on the one hand, the novelty of the Italian Civil Code (in contrast with the Napoleonic Code and the post-unitary Code) was highlighted, it was only about the new discipline of private legal persons, while on the other hand the aim was to minimize the extent of the innovations') ('il clima politico che vide nascere il codice civile vigente era naturalmente portato a far propria, ed anzi ad irrigidire, quella concezione delle fondazioni ... che può dirsi di "diritto di polizia" ... [c]osì, mentre veniva sottolineata la novità del codice civile italiano (rispetto al code Napoléon e al codice italiano post-unitario), consistente nella disciplina legislativa delle persone giuridiche private, dall'altro lato si cercava di ridurre al minimo la portata dell'innovazione').

linked to the incentives of such naturally selfish owners. In the inherent absence of an 'owner' instead (as in the unique case of foundations) – the risk of a manager (the holder of the power, but devoid of risks) acting unlawfully arises from the relevant utter separation between ownership and control. Liability rules ensure the alignment between management and the purpose pursued; yet, whereas an 'owner' (i.e. the principal) exists, the manager (i.e. the agent) is 'disciplined' by the risk of paying damages; when the 'owner' does not exist, such a mechanism runs the risk of short-circuiting. Thus, a governmental authority vested with the function of controlling and supervising the foundation's management was meant to fulfil the objective need to preserve the functionality of the management. In other words, the governmental power of control and supervision acted as a 'substitute' to the private owner control that could be deemed to be structurally lacking in private foundations thus conceived.[23]

2.4. THE ORIGINAL SCHOLARSHIP'S OPINION OPPOSING 'ENTERPRISE FOUNDATIONS'

Given that this was the legislative framework set by the Civil Code of 1942, it is no surprise that the scholarship's concern of the time focused on 'whether Italian foundations could carry out economic activities' and, specifically, 'whether they could carry out profit-driven economic activities'. The responses to both these queries were negative.

---

23 R. Costi, above n. 6, p. 47 ('for the protection of their interests, the administrative authority – an external body – intervenes, which operates to prevent that this autonomy in the management would lead to an abuse against those for whom the activity should be carried out. To summarise the contraposition between the two organisational models [i.e. company vs. foundation], we argue that, while the corporation is the expression of liberty and autonomy, the institution is the expression of the authority; or, in other words, that while in the corporation there is a tendential coincidence between power and risk, in the foundation there is power without risk, and a risk without power) ('[a] tutela dei loro interessi interviene un organo esterno al gruppo, l'autorità amministrativa, che vigila per impedire che tale autonomia di gestione si traduca in un abuso ai danni di coloro a vantaggio dei quali tale attività deve svolgersi. Volendo esprimere in estrema sintesi la contrapposizione dei due moduli organizzatori [i.e. company vs. foundation] diremo che mentre nella corporazione si esprime il momento della libertà e dell'autonomia, nella istituzione si esprime il momento dell'autorità; o anche che, mentre nella corporazione v'è una tendenziale coincidenza fra potere e rischio, nella fondazione … v'è un potere senza rischio e un rischio senza potere'). For a similar opinion, see D. Vittoria (1), above n. 6, pp. 334–335.

According to the scholarship of the time,[24] there was a rigid distinction between, on the one hand, those entities governed by the First Book of the Civil Code (namely, together with foundations, 'associations' and 'committees') and, on the other hand, the entities governed by the Fifth Book of the Civil Code (namely, individual and collective enterprise – hence, commercial companies).

The argument ran as follows: the former (foundations, associations and committees) are totally precluded from carrying out 'economic activities' (i.e. activities directed at the production and exchange of goods or services, according to the definition of 'entrepreneur' provided by Article 2082 CC), which were the prerogative of the latter entities (in particular, commercial companies), to the extent that the pursuit of profit was prohibited for the former and were set as a mandatory purpose for the latter.

In other words, a *summa divisio* was thought to exist between entities governed by the First Book of the Civil Code ('foundations', 'associations' and 'committees') and those governed by the Fifth Book ('individual enterprises' and 'companies'): liberal organizations pursuing idealistic, altruistic or public utility purposes in the former case, and economic activities for profit-making egoistic purposes in the latter case.[25]

Based on such classifications, the widespread opinion was that foundations could not carry out any activity other than mere acts of charity,[26] thereby legitimizing 'dispensing foundations' only. Foundations could never pursue any profit-making purpose (which, instead, was a distinctive trait of companies, as prescribed by Article 2247 CC), but only 'public utility' purposes (inherently idealistic and altruistic).

As a result of such an opinion of the predominant scholarship at the time, the Italian jurisdiction was not only hostile to enterprise foundations, but also quite repressive: in the eyes of the first interpreters of the Civil Code, a foundation owning an enterprise and therefore carrying out a profit-driven economic activity was an oxymoron, a mix of 'sacred' (the pursuit of the altruistic 'public utility' purpose, which was primarily

---

24 A. Falzea, 'Brevi note sui caratteri differenziali fra società e associazione' [1947] III *Giur. compl. Cass. civ.* 987; E. Zanelli, *La nozione di oggetto sociale*, Giuffrè, Milan 1962, pp. 53–95; M. Bianca, above n. 5, pp. 334–351.

25 This traditional view is examined in critical terms by G. Ponzanelli, 'Le nuove frontiere del primo e quinto libro del codice civile', in G. Ponzanelli, above n. 2, pp. 3–9.

26 This opinion was drawn directly from Article 16 CC which imposes on the bylaws of the foundations to provide for 'criteria and procedures for the supply of allowances' (unofficial translation), thus making purportedly clear that the foundations that the Italian Civil Code had taken into account were charity foundations only.

reserved for the state) and 'profane' (the pursuit of the selfish goal of profit, naturally sought by individuals).

In this context, it was simply impossible for enterprise foundations to find shelter in Italy: for one thing, they might run the extremely serious risk of being declared unlawful (with the consequent denial, *ab origine*, of legal personality), and also they would have been subject to pervasive public powers of interference, a strong deterrent for anyone intending to assign the management of an enterprise to a foundation.

3. THE NEW CLIMATE IN REPUBLICAN ITALY: THE OPENING BY SCHOLARSHIP AND THE RESISTANCE OF CASE LAW

3.1. THE OPINION OF SCHOLARS

The strong 'hostility' towards 'enterprise foundations' marked by the regulatory framework and by its scholarly interpretation began to fade, at least from an academic point of view, by the end of the 1960s, mainly thanks to the contributions of two distinguished legal scholars.[27]

Three main factors affected the academic debate on the matter. First, after the diffusion of foundations created in Liechtenstein (Anstalten) by Italian citizens, scholars had begun to question whether such foreign foundations were compatible with Italian jurisdiction, with favourable opinions beginning to erode the negative attitude of the recent post-war period.[28]

Second, following the Republican Constitution of 1948 and its acknowledgment of the so-called 'intermediate social entities' (that are now explicitly deemed worthy of legal protection), and along with the gradual diffusion of a less state-centric culture, a more favourable attitude towards such 'intermediate bodies' had started to gain momentum.[29]

---

27 These scholars are notably P. Rescigno (1), above n. 5, pp. 790–814 (a distinguished professor of private law), and R. Costi, above n. 6, pp. 1–49 (a distinguished professor of business law). An analysis of their respective views underlining both the converging and diverging elements thereof is provided by A. Zoppini, above n. 15, pp. 62–63 and, particularly, fn. 4.

28 See L.M. Baiada, 'L'Anstalt, il suo riconoscimento nel diritto italiano e le conseguenze in caso di intestazioni di comodo' [1985] *Rass. dir. civ.* 513–530.

29 D. Vittoria (1), above n. 6, p. 299; P. Rescigno (1), above n. 5, pp. 793–795.

Third, certain German scholars' opinions promoting an innovative use of foundations[30] began to spread in Italian legal culture. Notably, in Germany, in the aftermath of World War II, a certain stance developed to promote the use of foundations for the socialization of 'large companies' intended to benefit the entire community.[31] As testified by the coeval US experience, such large companies were characterized by 'owners' relegated to the irrelevant role of minority shareholders without effective influence on management. This called for the emergence of a new 'owner' – indeed, the foundation – capable of overcoming the agency problem between potentially self-referential managers (agents) and the entire constituency of the shareholders or, better, of the stakeholders in general (employees, consumers, local communities).[32] This pro-foundation German stance was favourably viewed by those Italian scholars who tried to rejuvenate Italian foundations.[33]

---

30 R. Gordeler and P. Ulmer, 'Der Stiftungszweck in der Reform des Stiftungsrechts, zugleich Überlegungen zur Behandlung von Unternehmensstiftungen un Familienstiftungen im Künftigen Stiftungsrecht [1963] *Die Aktiengesellschaft*, 8, 11, pp. 292 ff. and pp. 328 ff.; J. Plagemann, 'Stiftungsunternehmen' [1962] *Aktiengesellschaft*, p. 199; H. L. Steuck, *Die Stiftung als Rechtsform für witschaftliche Unternehmen*, Duncker&Humblot, Berlin 1967, pp. 59 ff.

31 A. Weber, *Sozialisisierung zugleich als Friedenssicherung*, Lambert Schneider, Heidelberg 1947, pp. 8 ff.; A. Mitscherlich and A. Weber, *Freier Sozialismus*, Lambert Schneider, Heidelberg 1946, p. 31.

32 R. Costi, above n. 6, p. 4 ('The Stiftungsunternehmen rose as a general instrument for the general organisation of the enterprise during the socialisation programs advanced in Germany immediately after the war, as a formula that would prevent the reconstruction of private industrial empires, while also allowing the irrenounceable rationalisation of production through big productive units. The shape of the foundation could bind the management of the enterprise to some general interests, such as those of the consumers, the workers and in general the national economy') ('Lo Stiftungsunternehmen assurse a strumento generale di organizzazione dell'impresa nell'ambito dei programmi di socializzazione proposti in Germania nell'immediato dopoguerra come formula che avrebbe impedito il riformarsi di imperi industriali privati, pur consentendo l'irrinunciabile razionalizzazione della produzione attraverso la concentrazione in grandi unità produttive. La forma della fondazione avrebbe potuto … vincolare l'esercizio dell'impresa ad alcuni interessi di carattere generale come l'interesse dei consumatori, dei dipendenti e in generale dell'economia nazionale').

33 P. Rescigno (1), above n. 5, pp. 811–812 ('the tendency … to declare the legitimacy of such foundations [i.e. enterprise foundations] tried to justify itself on the grounds of positive law, but most of all it wants to claim the "configuration" of the foundation as the best one for the actual configuration and concrete mode of acting of the enterprise. In short, the foundation is considered the most adequate tool, more than any other, to accommodate the developments of modern capitalism. With regard to this "configuration", it claims both the full legitimacy and the intrinsic ability to bend

It was thus precisely at the end of the 1960s that a very innovative scholarship orientation went so far as to propose a revolutionary interpretation of the norms of the Civil Code. Since the Code did not explicitly require the pursuit of a public utility purpose, it was concluded that even a completely 'selfish' foundation would not have been incompatible with Italian law.[34]

---

and adapt to the needs and the hidden "institutional" enterprise ideologies. The idea of the "enterprise as such" reduced too much, or even tried to erase, the interest of the "proprietors", meaning the shareholders, ... to transfer to the production facilities, the workers and managers the interest of the company. The foundation seems to fulfil such needs, since the property is just formally attributed to the foundation but, in practice, it presents itself as a "property witout subject"') ('La tendenza ... a dichiarare la piena legittimità di siffatte fondazioni [i.e. enterprise foundations] cerca di giustificarsi sul terreno del diritto positivo, ma soprattutto vuole rivendicare alla "forma" della fondazione la migliore rispondenza all'attuale modo di configurarsi e di concreto operare dell'impresa capitalistica. In breve, la fondazione viene considerata lo schema idoneo, più di ogni altro, a dar veste legale agli sviluppi del capitalismo contemporaneo. Della "forma" descritta si rivendica, dunque, oltre che la piena legittimità la capacità intrinseca di piegarsi alle esigenze e alle ideologie nascoste nelle dottrine "istituzionali" dell'impresa. L'idea della "impresa in sé" riduceva in un margine troppo esiguo o addirittura mirava ad annullare l'interesse dei "proprietari" e cioè degli azionisti ... per trasferire all'organismo produttivo, ai lavoratori, ai managers l'interesse dell'impresa. La fondazione sembra rispondere all'indicato orientamento, per il fatto che la proprietà è solo formalmente imputata al soggetto fondazione e nella sostanza si presenta come una "proprietà senza soggetto"'); R. Costi, above n. 6, pp. 2–3 ('Of such relevance [i.e. the relevance of enterprise foundations] it was aware of the german doctrine that, in the years immediately following the Second World War, amply debated the *Stiftungsunternehmen* in both political and juridical forums, adopting it as the typical operative instrument for some economic policies officially adopted by the country. The Italian doctrine did not perceive the importance that the structural model of the foundation could have both with regards to the general enterprise doctrine and to that of property; on the other hand, it believed that it could conclude that positive right would postulate a substantial incompatibility between enterprise and foundation, in the sense that this could not be constituted with the sole purpose of exercising an entrepreneurial activity. This argument cannot be shared: we believe that even in our legal system a *Stiftungsunternehmen* can be hypothesised.') ('Di tale rilevanza [i.e. the relevance of enterprise foundations] si è resa conto quella dottrina tedesca nella quale, sin dagli anni immediatamente successivi alla seconda guerra mondiale, lo *Stiftungsunternehmen* è stato al centro di ampi dibattiti giuridici e politici assurgendo spesso a ruolo di strumento operativo tipico di alcuni programmi di politica economica ufficialmente proposti per quel paese; la dottrina italiana generalmente non ha avvertito l'importanza che il modello strutturale della fondazione può assumere sia sul piano della teoria dell'impresa, sia su quello della proprietà, ed ha anzi creduto di poter concludere che il diritto positivo avrebbe sancito una sostanziale incompatibilità tra impresa e fondazione, almeno nel senso che questa non potrebbe essere costituita al solo scopo di esercitare un'impresa. Tale impostazione non può essere condivisa: noi crediamo infatti che anche nel nostro ordinamento sia perfettamente ipotizzabile uno *Stiftungsunternehmen*').

34 R. Costi, above n. 6, pp. 13–15 ('the structure of the foundation ... can be used, just like that of the corporation, to achieve the most diverse goals, and, in particular, it is

Thus, a use hitherto totally unknown to the practice was revealed: that of an enterprise foundation constituted by an entrepreneur who, on the one hand, entrusts the management of its enterprise to the foundation, but, on the other hand, does so with the aim of making his descendants the beneficiaries of the foundation's allowances (and therefore indirectly of the enterprise's profits). In other words, for the first time, the enterprise foundation was suggested as an efficient estate planning tool: an absolute separation between 'ownership' and 'control' could reconcile the need for economically providing for the heirs with the need for institutionally professional management of the enterprise.

Although this was a minority view at the time, it certainly marks the great schism between the legal culture associated with the Civil Code of 1942 and the legal culture that was emerging in post-war and post-fascist republican Italy.

Although some legal scholars have gone so far as to support the complete acceptance of 'family foundations'[35] and, in particular, 'family foundations that have control over a business' (industrial family foundations), the position that prevailed throughout these years falls somewhere between the two.[36]

True, foundations are entities with an 'altruistic' aim. However, nothing prohibits a foundation from obtaining the resources needed to fulfil these 'altruistic' goals by operating an 'egoistic' business. Nor could one argue that this would have blurred the boundaries between 'foundations' and 'companies'. In the case of 'companies', profit is 'the ultimate end': profit is pursued in order to be distributed to the 'owners'. Conversely, in the case of 'foundations', profit is a mere means to an end: it is pursued only for fundraising purposes, so that the funds can be then used for the ideal purpose.[37]

---

not true that the foundation must always pursue an interest that does not involve the founder') ('la struttura della fondazione ... può essere usata, così come quella della corporazione, per raggiungere i più diversi scopi e in particolare non è vero che la fondazione debba sempre perseguire un interesse estraneo al fondatore').

35 R. Costi, above n. 6, pp. 13–15.

36 P. Rescigno (1), above n. 5, pp. 812–813, paved the path for this direction. See also G. Ponzanelli, above n. 25, pp. 3 ff.; G. Ponzanelli (2), 'Enti senza scopo di lucro', *Dig. disc. priv., sez. civ.*, VII, Utet, Turin 1991, p. 468; P. Schlesinger, 'Categorie dogmatiche e normative in tema di non profit organizations', in G. Ponzanelli, above n. 2, pp. 275–290.

37 F. Galgano, 'Delle associazioni non riconosciute e dei comitati', in A. Scialoja and G. Branca (eds.) *Commentario del codice civile*, *sub* arts. 36–42, Zanichelli-Il Foro Italiano, Bologna-Rome 1967, p. 84; P. Morandi, 'La fallibilità degli enti non profit'

The opening regarding the admissibility of business activities carried out under private law foundations is also the result of the proper interpretation of the definition of 'business' activity.

Although some scholars[38] held that the 'pursuit of profit' was an unavoidable requirement for the attribution of the status of entrepreneur to a person engaging in economic activity, the majority view is rather that in order to qualify as an 'entrepreneur', the objective goal of producing revenues that are at least adequate to cover costs (so-called 'profit in an objective sense', which substantially corresponds to a 'break-even requirement') is sufficient, with the subjective goal of making extra profits for distribution to the enterprise's owners (so-called 'profit in the subjective sense') being only additional.[39] This conclusion, bolstered by the lack of any 'profit' requirement in the code definition of 'entrepreneur' (Article 2082 CC), led the majority scholarship to hold that:

- An individual who *ex ante* plans a productive activity of goods and/or services at symbolic or below-market prices and is thus by definition unable to cover costs with revenues is not an 'entrepreneur';
- instead, an entity – including 'public bodies' (*enti pubblici*) or, more precisely, foundations – that engages in economic activity with the goal of functioning in compliance with the 'break-even requirement' and is therefore self-sustaining via market activity alone, without the need for subsidies (public or private), is an 'entrepreneur'.

The attribution of the status of 'entrepreneur' to foundations engaging in economic activity in accordance with the 'break-even requirement'

[1998] I *Contratto e impresa* 344 ('[it is possible] to distinguish between the ultimate, or institutional, aims of the entity, and the intermediate ones: the former remains of an ideal nature, otherwise a corporation would be formed, while the latter can be pursued for profit, since they are merely instrumental.') ('[è possibile] distinguere fra gli scopi ultimi o istituzionali dell'ente e quelli intermedi: i primi rimarrebbero comunque di natura ideale, configurandosi altrimenti una società, mentre i secondi possono avere carattere lucrativo, essendo perseguiti in via puramente strumentale'); G.F. Campobasso, above n. 6, pp. 584–585.

38 For example, A. Rocco, *Diritto commerciale, Parte generale,* S.A. Fratelli Treves Editori, Milan, 1936, pp. 255 and 261; A. Arena, *Introduzione allo studio del diritto commerciale e titoli di credito*, Giuffrè, Milan 1936, pp. 43 ff.

39 This stance was originally adopted by the following scholars: W. Bigiavi, *La professionalità dell'imprenditore*, Cedam, Padua 1948, p. 75; A. Pavone La Rosa, *Il registro delle imprese*, Giuffrè, Milan 1964, pp. 103 ff.; G. Ferri, *Manuale di diritto commerciale*, Utet (2nd ed.), Turin 1965, p. 44; F. Roversi Monaco, *Gli enti di gestione*, Giuffrè, Milan 1967, p. 210. Nowadays, this position appears to be accepted by substantially all Italian scholars: G. F. Campobasso, above n. 6, p. 585.

(or, even more so, with the 'means goal' of pursuing profits to be allocated to the altruistic 'end goal') was, and still is, legally relevant for the following reasons.

The title of 'entrepreneur' (and, in particular, that of 'commercial entrepreneur') comes with all the ensuing legal regime, comprising, *inter alia*, its exposure to bankruptcy.[40] Therefore, once a foundation is given the title of 'entrepreneur', the ensuing consequence should be that in the event of insolvency, it has to be declared bankrupt and made subject to all bankruptcy proceedings. Yet, as to the legal tests to be met in order for a foundation to be declared bankrupt, opinions of scholars are divided.

In particular, while some scholars[41] have expressed the view that whether a foundation is 'exclusively or predominantly' involved in business activity as opposed to its other activities is not decisive in relation to its bankruptcy regime (and therefore that a foundation could go bankrupt even when its involvement in business activity is merely 'ancillary'), other scholars have instead taken the view that foundations could only go bankrupt if their business activities represent their 'exclusive or prevalent' purpose.[42] This conclusion (probably refutable) is reached on the basis of the application by analogy of a rule governing 'public bodies' ('enti pubblici') (Article 2201 CC). Because such a rule makes 'public bodies' subject to the legal regime of (commercial) 'entrepreneurs' only on condition that their business activity represents their 'exclusive or main purpose', then (so runs the argument) the same test should also apply to foundations.

The scholarly opinion of those years also raised another extremely relevant issue: that of the 'governance system' of foundations. Since the meagre regulation of the Civil Code mandated the existence of a board of

40 This is the opinion of the large majority of Italian scholars (see the two following footnotes). *Contra*, however, M. Greco, 'L'esonero dal fallimento degli enti non profit', in U. Apice (ed.), *Imprenditori anomali e fallimento*, Cedam, Padua 1997, pp. 215–220, who instead expressed the view that, despite the foundation being qualified as 'commercial entrepreneur', it would nevertheless be exceptionally exempt from bankruptcy.

41 This is, for example, the opinion of G. Ponzanelli, above n. 6, p. 185; L. Degani and R. Mozzanica, 'Fondazioni e attività di impresa: l'applicazione dello statuto dell'imprenditore', [2009] *Enti non profit* n. 7, pp. 9–11; P. Morandi, above n. 37, pp. 336 ff.; F. Rivellini, 'L'esercizio di attività economica degli enti no profit' [2017] *Diritto. it*, pp. 1–5; S. Cerrato, 'Origami giuridici: il fallimento delle fondazioni' [2016] 1 *Giur. It.* 128 ff.; G. F. Campobasso, *Diritto commerciale. Diritto dell'impresa*, Utet, Turin 1993, p. 84.

42 This is instead the opinion, for instance, of F. Galgano, 'L'imprenditore commerciale', in F. Galgano (ed.), *Trattato di diritto commerciale e diritto pubblico dell'economia*, Cedam, Padua 2004, pp. 86; F. Galgano, above n. 37, pp. 84 and. 102.

directors only (without any mention of an assembly-type body or a body to which control over the administration was entrusted), it was debated whether the bylaws could provide for a regime such as to ensure the founder (or other person identified in the bylaws) the power to revoke directors and to appoint new ones. The conclusion was mostly negative.[43] Once the assets had been allocated to the altruistic purpose identified in the bylaws, the founder could have well nominated himself as a director for life of the entity, but could not reserve to himself or other persons the power to appoint the members of the foundation bodies. In essence, the only system compatible with Italian law would have been that of co-optation, i.e. a regime in which only the directors have the capacity to appoint their successors (with the understanding that the ineffectiveness of the relevant bylaws would have triggered the power of appointment by the government authority).

3.2. THE OPINION OF CASE LAW

While scholarship had eventually widely accepted 'enterprise foundations' and had consequently inferred the ensuing applicability thereto of the legal regime of (commercial) entrepreneurs, case law proved much less clear-cut on the point. Although Italian courts have generally abandoned the original rigid stance against the admissibility of 'enterprise foundations',[44] some courts have nevertheless continually failed to draw consistent conclusions from the premise that enterprise foundations are admissible and compatible with Italian law.

---

43 P. Rescigno (1), above n. 5, p. 807 (bodies of the foundation are neither the founder, … nor the beneficiaries. In line with the extraneity in the management of the entity, the founder, while he can reserve the right to nominate members for life of the council, he cannot reserve the power to nominate one or all of the administrators in occasion of each subsequent renovation of the council; neither can he reserve the right to dismiss the board of directors) ('Non sono organi della fondazione né il fondatore … né i beneficiari. Per la rilevata estraneità all'amministrazione dell'ente, il fondatore, mentre può riservarsi all'atto della fondazione la nomina a vita di membri del consiglio, non può attribuirsi il potere di nominare uno o più o tutti gli amministratori ad ogni successiva rinnovazione dell'organo; né può riservarsi la facoltà di sciogliere il consiglio di amministrazione'); R. Costi, above n. 6, pp. 44 ff. This approach started to be criticized in the mid-1970s: see, for example, D. Vittoria (1), above n. 6, pp. 309 ff.

44 Exemplary early court decisions denying the admissibility of 'enterprise foundations' include: App. Rome, 5 June 1957, in *Foro it.*, 1957, I, c. 1274; Trib. Rome, 11 June 1954, in *Dir. fall.*, 1954, II, p. 455; App. Turin, 23 January 1952, in *Giur. it.* 1952, I, 2, c.81. More recently, see Cass. Civ., 8 January 1991, n. 81, in *Società*, 1991, p. 767; Cass. Civ., 11 September 1997, n. 8963, in *Foro it.*, 1998, I, c. 2532.

When facing 'foundations carrying out economic activities', for example, certain courts felt the need to requalify such entities as either 'de facto companies' or 'de facto associations' among the founders and/or directors.[45] The consequences of this approach are quite significant.

If it is assumed that a foundation that carries out (commercial) business activities is legitimate, then, in the event of bankruptcy, the foundation is solely and exclusively responsible for its debts and, thus, the principle of limitation of liability continues to apply.

If, on the other hand, the foundation is requalified as a 'de facto company' or as a de facto 'association', then those who are consequently qualified as 'de facto partners' or as 'de facto associates' (acting in the name of the entity) become *personally* and *fully* responsible for the entity's (the company's or association's) debts.[46]

Such a case law position has clearly represented, and continues to represent, a considerable Sword of Damocles hovering over enterprise foundations. The prospect of the requalification of an enterprise foundation as a 'de facto company' or as a 'de facto association' exposes all individuals with important management functions (be they formalized or not) to the serious risk of *personal* bankruptcy and, hence, of potential *personal* indictment for bankruptcy crimes (fraudulent bankruptcy and simple bankruptcy).

It is not difficult to see how such uncertainty concerning the underlying legal framework has been, and continues to be, a substantial deterrent to the establishment of enterprise foundations.

If, in addition, we also consider the strong limitation in term of governance rules imposed by strict interpretation of the scholarship – i.e. the asserted incompatibility of the provision of assembly bodies given by the Civil Code with foundation legal regime; the impossibility of

---

45 Amongst others: Trib. Milan, 17 June 1994, in *Foro it*, 1994, I, c. 3544; Trib. Milan 16 July 1998, in *Giur. it.*, 1999, 1678; Trib. Alba, 24 March 2009, n. 3, in *Nuova Giurisprudenza Civile Commentata*, 2009, I, pp. 1099–1102; Trib. Biella, 22 May 2015, in *Giur. it*, 2016, 124; Cass Civ., 16 March 2004, n. 5305, in *Dir. Fall.*, 2005, II, 843. *Contra*, however, App. Palermo, 7 aprile 1989, in *Giur. comm.*, 1992, II, p. 61; Cass. Civ., 18 September 1993, n. 9589, in *Fall.*, 1994, p. 151. A thorough analysis of this case law is provided by M. Perrino, 'Esercizio indiretto dell'impresa "scolastica", associazione e fallimento' [1992] II *Giur. comm.* 69–100 and also by A. Cetra, 'L'associazione non riconosciuta che esercita un'impresa commerciale non è una società di fatto fra gli associati' [1999] II *Giur. comm* 442–448.

46 Partners of a commercial partnership (*società in nome collettivo*) are always personally liable for the company's debts vis-à-vis third parties pursuant to Articles 2267 and 2291 CC. Persons acting in the name of an association are subject to the same legal regime pursuant to Article 38 CC.

entrusting the founder or third parties with the power to renew the board of directors (with the consequent risk of government interference)[47] – it is clear why, despite the evolution of the scholarship interpretation of the admissibility of enterprise foundations, the regulatory regime (as resulting from scholarship and case law) turned Italy into a scarcely fertile land for the diffusion and success of industrial foundations.

4. FOUNDATIONS ORIGINATED FROM BANKING REFORMS

4.1. THE AMATO REFORM AND THE 'INVENTION' OF BANKING FOUNDATIONS

In the changing cultural context that began in the late 1960s and followed thereafter, at the beginning of the 1990s, the so-called Amato reform[48] made use of foundations to carry out the privatization of Italian banks that had hitherto been owned by public bodies according to a state-centric model intended to ensure political control of the national financial system.[49]

On the contrary, the need to reform the banking system according to a market-centric and competition-oriented model stemmed from the pressure exerted by those bodies of the European Community that were institutionally in charge of favouring the liberalization of the financial systems of Member States. The Italian legislature followed the lead of the EU institutions, yet it did so in such a way as to shield Italian banks against a potential foreign invasion. The Italian political class of the time feared that a too abrupt transition from a public financial system (controlled and protected by the state) to a private financial system (exposed to international competition) would have made Italian banks easy prey for more solid and better equipped foreign financial institutions. A foreign

---

47 See above n. 43.

48 On the Amato reform, see, amongst others, P. Schlesinger, 'Le c.d. "fondazioni bancarie"' [1995] I *Banca borsa tit. cred.* 421 ff.; P. Rescigno 'La fondazione ed i gruppi bancari' [1992] *Banca, Impresa, Società* 389 ff.; G. Barbetta, 'La legge Amato e le Fondazioni bancarie: nuovi soggetti nel mondo delle imprese senza fine di lucro' [1992] *Econ. e cred.* 247 ff.; F. Capriglione, 'Privatizzazione e mercato: le fondazioni bancarie' [1996] I *Banca borsa tit. cred.* 336 ff.; D. Lucarini Ortolani 'Privatizzazione e fondazione bancaria' [1995] *Foro it.*, V, cc. 120 ff.; G. Pagliari, *Le fondazioni bancarie. Profili giuridici*, Giuffrè, Milan 2004.

49 M. V. de Giorgi, 'Fondazioni bancarie e linee evolutive della disciplina comune' [2004] II *Nuova giurisprudenza civile commentata* 643 ff.

invasion would have exposed the national industrial sector (which has always been heavily reliant on a highly politicalized banking sector) to worldwide financial turbulence.[50]

The 1990 reform implemented the privatization of banks through two fundamental steps: (i) the transformation of banking businesses into joint-stock companies governed by private law; and, above all, (ii) the transformation of the public state bodies that owned the public banking companies into foundations pre-ordained to hold the controlling shareholdings in the newly established banking companies.

Therefore, for the first time, Italian law itself made use of foundations as an organization model institutionally entrusted with the operation and control of what were formerly public banks. The two potentially conflicting needs mentioned above were thus fulfilled. On the one hand, the obligation to privatize and liberalize the banking sector was met; on the other hand, newly privatized Italian banks would not fall into the hands of global players due to the allocation of bank shareholdings in institutions statutorily designated to their long-term detention.[51]

A similar reform was only conceivable thanks to the evolution in the scholarship opinion that began in the 1960s, which, with respect to 'foundations', recognized the compatibility between: (i) the pursuit of ultimate goals of public utility; and (ii) the exercise, as a mere means to an end, of business activities and, more specifically, banking businesses.

This is precisely the scheme adopted by the Amato reform for banking foundations: on the one hand, the essential 'object' of the activity is the management or administration of the controlling stake in the privatized bank (i.e. holding the majority of the voting rights in the banking company), which, in turn, seeks to maximize profit like any enterprise; yet, on the other hand, the ultimate 'purpose' of the entity is the destination of profits for public purposes of general importance, namely in the domains of scientific research, education, art and health.[52]

---

50 R. Costi, 'L'ambiguo ruolo delle fondazioni bancarie' [2012] 4 *Diritto della banca e del mercato finanziario* 49–62.

51 The original distinctive goal of the newly created foundations was to maintain their control over the newly privatized Italian banks, which was translated into the slogan 'never below 51%' (on this point, see F. Cavazzuti, *Privatizzazioni, imprenditori e mercati*, Il Mulino, Bologna, 1996). In more general terms, the Amato reform modelled the foundations as a new legal entity that would have ensured the permanence of a public ownership of the share capital of the newly privatized banks: S. Rizzini Bisinelli, 'Fondazioni bancarie: strumenti innovativi per la dismissione di partecipazioni' [2000] 5 *Le Società* 542.

52 F. Merusi, 'Il prologo. Il progetto di trasformazione delle banche pubbliche spiegato ad un viaggiatore persiano', in F. Merusi, *Dalla banca pubblica alla fondazione*

To justify the political decision to privatize the banking system through the formation of banking foundations (BF), the Amato reform was followed by a declaration of the significance of encouraging private non-profit organizations to take over functions traditionally handled by the state at a time when the public welfare system looked financially unsustainable. However, the fundamental logic underlining such a 'creative' approach was to denationalize and liberalize the national banking system while retaining the controlling shareholdings in privatized banks in the hands of Italian nationals.

4.2. THE CIAMPI REFORM AND THE GOVERNANCE OF BANKING FOUNDATIONS

Less than ten years after their creation, in 1999 the Italian legislature intervened again on BF regulation with a major reform known as the Ciampi Reform.[53]

The Ciampi Reform addressed two objectives. First, it was intended to abandon the merely 'formal' privatization (as accomplished in the 1990s) in order to embrace a 'substantial' privatization by imposing on BFs partial divestment of their controlling shareholdings in banking companies. Second, the time was ripe to proceed with a more substantial regulation of the governance of those entities that had become major providers of significant resources.

As for the first objective, the Ciampi Reform established that BFs pursue 'social utility purposes and the promotion of economic development exclusively' and imposed the obligation to gradually divest their controlling banking shareholdings.

---

privata, Giappichelli, Turin 2000, pp. 23 ff.; M. Tanzi, 'Sulle c.d. fondazioni bancarie: alcune considerazioni critiche' [2013] III *Banca borsa tit. cred.* 266; M. Clarich and A. Pisaneschi, 'Fondazioni bancarie e regioni – commento' [2002] 2 *Giorn. dir. amm.* 139; A. Zoppini, 'Verso la definitiva separazione tra enti conferenti e banche' [1999] 4 *Il corriere giuridico* 411 ff.

53 On the Ciampi reform, see, amongst others, G. Oppo, 'Le fondazioni (ex) bancarie: una strana vicenda legislativa', in S. Amorosino-F. Capriglione (eds.), *Le 'fondazioni' bancarie. Dalla legge n. 218/90 al D.Lgs. n. 153/99*, Cedam, Padua 1999, pp. 1–11; G. Mucciarelli, *Attività e impresa nelle fondazioni bancarie*, Giuffrè, Milan 2005, pp. 7–59; G. Pagliari, above n. 48, pp. 157–241; A. Pavone La Rosa 'Fondazioni bancarie e disciplina dell'impresa commerciale' [2000] I *Banca borsa tit. cred.* 1 ff.; E. del Prato 'Fondazioni bancarie e categorie civilistiche' [2002] VI *Banca borsa tit. cred.* 739 ff.

As for the second objective, it provided, for the first time, an analytical regulation of banking foundation governance which, until then, had remained unchanged from the extremely inadequate Civil Code norms.

The governance of banking foundations as resulting out of the 1999 law can be summarized as follows.

First of all, a 'tripartite model of organization' divided into three fundamental bodies is to be adopted: (i) a founders' council; (ii) a board of directors and (iii) an audit committee. The founders' council is constituted to ensure adequate representation of local public and private entities (regions, municipalities, universities, religious institutions, etc.). It is entrusted with the task of determining 'programs, priorities, and objectives of the foundation' in line with the statutory purpose and it is granted with the power to appoint, revoke and exercise liability actions against the members of the board of directors. The board of directors is in charge of managing the foundation's assets and implementing the strategic guidelines established by the founders' council. The audit committee, composed of individuals qualified to practise as auditors, is tasked with overseeing the legitimacy of the management activity (formal legitimacy control which cannot amount to a control on the merits), as well as the obligation to notify the supervisory authority if any management irregularities are detected.[54]

Banking foundations regulation is relevant for our purposes in two different ways.

First of all, the full compatibility between the status of a 'non-profit organization' and the exercise of profit-driven business activities is unequivocally confirmed. Just as nothing prevents an individual entrepreneur from allocating, for unquestionable personal preference, the profits they derive from their business to general utility purposes, their status as 'entrepreneur' remaining unaffected as a result, nothing prevents an entity that, by law, must pursue altruistic purposes, from operating profit-driven businesses, its qualification as an 'entrepreneur' remaining unquestioned by the same token.

Second, and even more importantly, the full legitimacy of what the Italian scholarship calls 'participation foundations' – i.e. foundations that mix the 'objective element' of a 'dedicated estate' (allocation of assets to a specific purpose) with the 'personalistic element' of an associative

---

54 On the governance of banking foundations, see A. Zoppini, 'L'autonomia statutaria nelle fondazioni di origine bancaria' [2000] *Banca borsa tit. cred.* 399–406.

body – is also unequivocally confirmed.[55] This replaces the old scholars' opinion under which there was no room for party autonomy to provide for founders themselves or other bodies that, although not founders, were nonetheless interested in a certain allocation of the benefit provided by the entity, to appoint the members of the board of directors of the foundations.[56] Indeed, in the case of BFs, it is legitimate that the power to appoint and dismiss the directors of the foundation is entrusted to certain public and private bodies identified in the bylaws. It must be deemed equally legitimate, then, for an enterprise foundation (other than a banking foundation) to reserve the power to appoint directors to the founders or other bodies that are best equipped to ensure a supply of benefits in line with the ideal purposes of the entity as outlined in the bylaws.

---

55 Authors who supported the admissibility of so-called 'fondazioni di partecipazione' (participatory or associative foundations, i.e. foundations with an assembly of founders), and did so also before the enactment of the TSC, include E. Bellezza and F. Florian, *Le fondazioni di partecipazione*, La tribuna, Piacenza 2006, passim; A. Zoppini, 'Profili evolutivi della fondazione di partecipazione nella moderna prassi e nella legislazione speciale', in Fondazione Italiana per il Notariato, *Fondazioni di partecipazione*, Il Sole-24 ore, Milan 2007, p. 21; M. Maltoni, 'La fondazione di partecipazione: natura giuridica e legittimità' [2007] X(2) *Quaderni della fondazione Italiana per il Notariato – 'Fondazioni di partecipazione'*, 25–31; A. Fusaro, 'La fondazione tra modello tradizionale e modello partecipativo quale strumento per la tutela delle categorie svantaggiate' [2011] *Vita not.*, 1089; *contra*, however, A. Zoppini, above n. 15, pp. 102–103.

56 This original position was, for example, expressed by P. Rescigno (1), above n. 5, p. 802 ('[T]he will of the founder is interpreted as an objectivised statement, given to the board of the foundation and destined to give the criterion used to judge the way in which the activity has been carried out, as well as its conformity. The founder remains extraneous to the entity that has been created on the basis of legal recognition, also because of its act of private autonomy; this justifies the opinion that the founder, if the act is an *inter vivos*, cannot reserve themself rights that affect the life and administration of the entity (in particular, it cannot reserve itself the right to nominate, wholly or partially, members of the bodies of the foundation). Decoupled from him, the "will of the founder" remains to guide the life of the foundation') ('La volontà del fondatore viene intesa come qualcosa di obiettivato, affidato alle tavole della fondazione e destinato a fornire il criterio di giudizio dell'attività svolta e della conformità allo scopo. Il fondatore rimane estraneo all'ente che è nato in virtù di riconoscimento, sulla base, tra l'altro, dell'atto di autonomia privata da lui compiuto; e per questo si giustifica l'opinione che il fondatore, se si tratta di negozio fra vivi, non possa preservarsi poteri che incidano sulla vita e l'amministrazione dell'ente (in particolare, non possa attribuire a sé per il futuro la nomina, in tutto o in parte, degli organi della fondazione). Staccata dal fondatore, rimane a indirizzare costantemente la vita della persona giuridica la "volontà del fondatore"')'. Needless to say, this stance concerning the legal constraints on the governance of a foundation made its adoption quite unfit for the purposes of the establishment of an enterprise foundation.

In turn, the legislative acknowledgement of the compatibility of a 'participatory' form of governance with the status of a foundation triggers several consequences:

- First of all, the effects of the absence of an 'owner' acting as 'controller' in the common principal-agent relationship is mitigated and the governmental authority's influence on the governance structure and management choices of the entity becomes redundant and can be gotten rid of for good (although the governmental authority is still left with the control over the legitimacy of the entity's management);
- second, in the event of insolvency, the 'requalification' of a 'foundation' into an 'association' or 'company' is precluded and the bankruptcy of any person in any capacity involved in the management of the bankrupted entity is avoided, thus superseding the case law examined above.

5. FURTHER REGULATORY EVOLUTION: THE LAW ON LEGAL PERSONALITY RECOGNITION AND THE 'PURPOSE' OF FOUNDATIONS

5.1. BEYOND THE LICENCE REGIME AND THE 'LAWFULNESS' OF THE PURPOSE AS SOLE REQUIREMENT

A significant step forward in the evolution of the Italian law of foundation occurred in 2000 with a law that reformed the procedure for recognizing legal personality of, *inter alia*, foundations.[57]

Two novelties are important for our purposes. The first is that the recognition of legal personality is no longer subject to a governmental authority's licence grant,[58] but to an authorization subject to a mere

57 D.P.R. 10 febbraio 2000, n. 361 ('Regulation regarding the simplification of recognition procedures for private legal persons and of the approvation of changes to the articles of association and the statute') ('Regolamento recante norme per la semplificazione dei procedimenti di riconoscimento di persone giuridiche private e di approvazione delle modifiche dell'atto costitutivo e dello statuto'). Pertinent comments on this law can be found in A. Zoppini, 'Riformato il sistema di riconoscimento delle persone giuridiche' [2001] 18(3) *Corr. giur.* 291–297; and G. Ponzanelli, above n. 6, passim.

58 Before the enactment of the law at stake, an author had even expressed the view that the traditional 'licence regime' was to be considered incompatible with the Italian Constitutional Charter: V. Mariconda, 'Libertà di modelli organizzativi e statutari per le fondazioni e funzione notarile' [1997] I *Riv. notar.* 638.

legitimacy control. The 'statist philosophy' underlying the Civil Code ('the state is master of legal persons') gives way to a more contemporary 'liberal philosophy' ('private citizens are free to adopt any legal scheme consistent with lawful purposes').

Second, with specific regard to 'foundations', the recognition of legal personality is made subject not to the existence of a 'public utility' purpose – which was often assumed as implicit in the case law and also in many scholars' opinion (despite it not being required in any Civil Code rules),[59] – but of a purpose simply qualified as 'lawful'.[60]

According to the majority of commentators, this change is significant because it confirms the full, and now unquestionable, legitimacy not only of foundations that operate a business and then allocate profits to social utility purposes, but also of those that allocate profits for 'selfish', but in any case 'lawful' purposes (for example, benefiting the employees of a certain company).

This precise regulatory evolution has recently led Italian scholars to conclude that the key principle of foundations, far from being that of a presumed 'altruistic purpose', should rather be reduced to the mere prohibition of disbursement of profits to the founder itself, also known as the non-distribution constraint.[61] Without prejudice to this limit, Italian

59 The traditional view had instead hitherto been that the purpose of the foundation could not be anything but 'altruistic': see, for example, P. Rescigno (1), above n. 5, p. 806; G. Sicchiero, 'Le fondazioni di partecipazione' [2020] 1 *Contratto e impresa* 34.

60 A. Zoppini, 'Le fondazioni' in D. Carusi, *Associazioni e fondazioni. Dal codice civile alle riforme annunciate (Convegno di studi in onore di Pietro Rescigno)*, Giuffrè, Milan 2001, p. 72 ('the identification – from which the legislator moved in 1942 – of legal persons, regulated in the First Book of the Civil Code, and non-profit entities, pursuing public utility, has now declined; a textual indication of this trend can be found in the new discipline for the recognition (D.P.R. 10 Febuary 2000, n. 361), which requires only the "sufficiency" of the assets and the "lawfulness" of the purpose, thereby acknowledging that the requirement of the "public utility" is entirely absorbed by the other provisions that the lawmaker gave as sector-specific rules, outside of the Civil Code') ('l'identificazione – da cui muoveva il legislatore del '42 – tra le persone giuridiche regolate nel primo libro del codice civile e gli enti non lucrativi che realizzano uno scopo di pubblica utilità è ormai venuta meno; un'indicazione testuale in questa direzione si rinviene anche nella nuova disciplina del riconoscimento (D.P.R. 10 febbraio 2000, n. 361), che ai fini della personificazione si limita a richiedere, oltre alla "sufficienza" dei patrimonio, la "liceità" dello scopo, confermandosi così che la rilevanza della "pubblica utilità" è interamente assorbita dalle fattispecie che il legislatore ha previsto quali discipline di settore collocate fuori dal codice').

61 See, amongst others, G. Ponzanelli, above n. 25, pp. 4–5 and 7–8; A. Zoppini, above n. 15, pp. 67–68; P. Manes, 'Le nuove prospettive in materia di fondazioni' [2018] 1 *Contratto e impresa* 267.

foundations are currently deemed to be legitimized in order to pursue any purpose, whether 'altruistic' or 'selfish'.

The identification of the key trait of foundations, not so much with regard of the aims pursued (altruistic or selfish), but rather regarding the so-called non-distribution constraint makes it possible to distinguish 'foundations' and 'commercial companies' in the following terms.

In commercial companies (entities with an ownership structure), it is the 'ownership' of the capital conferred that assigns both (i) the title to participate in the appointment of directors, and (ii) the participation in the profit distribution. On the contrary, in 'participatory'-based foundations (entities with a non-proprietary structure, but with an assembly of participants/founders who appoint and dismiss the directors), (i) the right to participate in the appointment of directors, on the one hand, and (ii) the right to participate in the profit distribution, on the other hand, are structurally non-coincidental and independent from 'ownership'. The first right (appointment of directors) is attributed under the bylaws to the founders/participants, the former being considered the 'former owner', in some sense, as they make contributions to the foundation free of charge and not in exchange for shareholdings. The second right (profit distribution) is given to those beneficiaries who are chosen by the foundation's board of directors based on the criteria outlined in the bylaws.

In other words, as accurately pointed out by the liberal scholars of the 1960s who were favourable to 'family business foundations', the governance structure of a foundation determines an absolute split between 'ownership' and 'control': 'control' is vested in individuals who are 'no longer owners' and therefore 'no longer legitimized' to participate in the profit of the company. Conversely, 'ownership' (i.e. the right to receive the economic benefits of the company) is vested in individuals completely devoid of any voice over the management of the company. Beyond this fundamental difference, once the traditional discrepancy trait based on 'purpose' disappears, the contrast between 'foundation' and 'commercial company' is enormously reduced.

5.2. ABSENCE IN ITALIAN BUSINESS LAW OF AN IMPERATIVE PRINCIPLE OF CORRELATION BETWEEN 'RISK' AND 'POWER'

The fact that a 'foundation' can determine an absolute split between 'ownership' and 'control' requires a thorough examination of its systematic compatibility with Italian law.

Such an arrangement could raise doubts from the same perspective, which, historically, underlines the bourgeois regime of the right to property. In fact, in an 'enterprise foundation', the lack of coincidence between individuals who appoint directors ('participants' and 'non-owners') and individuals who benefit from the entrepreneurial activity ('beneficiaries') creates exposure to the risk of negligence domino effects: (i) negligence by the 'participants' who, being by definition disinterested in management, may not appoint carefully the 'best' directors; and (ii) negligence by the 'directors' who, as an emanation of uninterested parties, could feel free from any 'control' mechanism (with a consequent exacerbation of the so-called agency problem). The managerial efficiency of a company with a similar atypical 'owner' (or, better, a 'non-owner') structure ends up depending on the ability of the 'participants' to become effective interpreters of the interests of the 'beneficiaries'. In other words, one should assume that the 'altruism' of the uninterested 'participants' (the 'founders' of the entity that originated from their free disbursements) is functionally equivalent to the 'selfishness' of the owners concerned (the 'founders' of a company who incorporated it with contributions in exchange of the shareholdings entitling them to the right of profit). Therefore, one could say that the managerial efficiency of a profit-driven company held by a foundation holds up insofar as the *homo oeconomicus* paradigm is replaced by the *homo reciprocans* paradigm.[62] In particular, *homo reciprocans* is that individual who, on the one hand, acts rationally to ensure that the management of the company pursues the maximum profit – and therefore, in this respect, likewise a *homo oeconomicus* – but does so not for personal benefit, but

---

62 Behavioural economics marked the downfall of the *homo oeconomicus* paradigm in favour of other types of economic agents affected by psychological, cognitive, emotional, cultural and social factors. There is probably no single paradigm capable of effectively describing the behaviour of a social agent in every situation, but there is awareness of the inadequacy in that respect of the *homo oeconomicus* paradigm. For an overview of the new paradigms emerged, see E.J O'Boyle, 'Requiem for Homo Economicus' [2007] 10 *Journal of Markets and Morality* 322.
According to Herbert Gintis et al., *Homo reciprocans* is 'neither the selfless altruist of utopian theory, nor the selfish hedonist of neoclassical economics. Rather, he is a conditional cooperator whose penchant for reciprocity can be elicited under the proper circumstances'. See S. Bowles, R. Boyd, E. Fehr and H. Gintis, *Homo reciprocans: A Research Initiative on the Origins, Dimensions, and Policy Implications of Reciprocal Fairness*, Cambridge University (Massachussets) 1997, p. 5; on empirical evidence of *homo reciprocans*, see also E. Fehr and S. Gächter 'Reciprocity and Economics: The Economic Implication of *homo reciprocans*' [1998] 42 *European Economic Review* 845–859; T. Dohmen, A. Falk, D. Huffman and U. Sunde, '*Homo reciprocans*: Survey Evidence on Behavioural Outcomes' [2009] 119 *Economic Journal* 192–612.

rather to allocate the business' profit to a category of beneficiaries identified not by their capital holding (i.e. as 'owners'), but by their belonging to that category of individuals that the founders wanted to benefit.

Indeed, if one examines the fundamental principles of Italian company law, the compliance with law of a governance structure of a corporation that determines an absolute split between 'ownership' and 'control' could be questioned at first. For example, under company law, as regulated in 1942, the law of joint-stock companies was governed by the mandatory 'one share, one vote' principle, which aimed precisely at correlating 'ownership' and 'control' on the assumption that only a management influenced by a self-interested profit-seeking individual can ensure the adequate structure of incentives that guarantee efficiency.[63]

If we focus instead on the evolution of company and business law over the last 20 years, then one will notice that the correlation 'ownership'/ 'control' initially prescribed by the Civil Code of 1942 has now been substantially overcome.

In a nutshell, over the last two decades, the most significant regulatory evolutions in this sense are as follows. First of all, with respect to joint-stock companies (*società per azioni*), after the organic reform of 2003 and the more modest reform of 2016, it is now possible, thanks to the combination of multiple voting shares (with the limit of three votes per share) and no voting shares (issuable to an extent that does not exceed half of the share capital), that a person holding a relatively small minority of the capital (precisely 12.5%) exercises legal control over the company.[64]

Second, and above all, in a limited liability company (*società a responsabilità limitata*), thanks to the admissibility of 'particular rights'

63 L. Calvosa, *La partecipazione eccedente*, Giuffrè, Milan, 1999, 160; G. Ferri, 'Potere e responsabilità nell'evoluzione della società per azioni' [1956] *Riv. soc.* 35 ff.; G. Frè, 'Della società per azioni', in *Commentario Scialoja-Branca*, Zanichelli-Foro it., Bologna-Turin 1972, *sub* art. 2351, pp. 198 ff.

64 This rule seems to establish only a residual link between 'ownership' and 'control'. See, amongst others, A. Pisani Massamormile, 'Azioni e altri strumenti finanziari partecipativi' [2003] *Riv. soc.* 2195; A. Angelillis, M. L. Vitali, 'Commento *sub* art. 2351' in P. Marchetti-L.A. Bianchi-F. Ghezzi-M. Notari (eds.), *Commentario alla riforma delle società*, Egea, Milan, 2008, pp. 371 ff.; P. Spada, *Appunto in tema di capitale nominale e conferimenti*, Consiglio Nazionale del Notariato, Commissione Studi d'Impresa, Studio n. 127–2006/I, p. 7; J. Sodi, 'L'assegnazione delle partecipazioni non proporzionale ai conferimenti nelle società di capitali' [2009] *Studi e materiali*, 587; R. Guglielmo-M. Silva, *I diritti particolari del socio – Vicende della partecipazione tra regole legali ed autonomia statutaria*, Consiglio Nazionale del Notariato, Commissione Studi d'Impresa, Studio n. 138–2011/I, passim; E. Barcellona, *Rischio e potere nel diritto societario riformato fra* golden quota *di s.r.l. e strumenti finanziari di s.p.a.*, Giappichelli, Turin 2012, pp. 122 ff.

to quota holders (whatever the size of the quota), it is now possible for a holder of a minimal fraction of capital to control the company. Thus, Italian law now seems to admit an almost absolute decoupling between 'ownership' and 'control.[65]

Finally, with the introduction in 2017 of the new 'social business' model (which can also be organized in the form of a joint-stock company), Italian law has admitted the existence of a company operating in specific sectors of social utility with the purpose of disbursing profit in favour of categories of beneficiaries identified in the bylaws rather than to the owner of the company (founders, shareholders or directors are prohibited from receiving profit) or the reinvestment in the company itself.[66]

This regulatory evolution is clear evidence that the Italian legal system certainly tolerates a governance structure based on an absolute split between management power and the expectation of profits distribution and that therefore no longer postulates any necessary correlation between 'ownership' and 'control' to safeguard the efficiency of the company. The recognition of the sociological relevance of the individual's orientation

---

65 On the admissibility under Italian law of the so-called 'golden quota', see, amongst others, A. Santus and G. De Marchi, 'Sui 'particolari diritti' del socio nella nuova s.r.l.' [2004] 1 *Riv. not.* 75; R. Rosapepe, 'Appunti su alcuni aspetti della nuova disciplina della partecipazione sociale nella s.r.l.' [2003] *Giur. comm.*, 4, 479; R. Guglielmo, 'Diritti particolari dei soci nelle s.r.l. e voto non proporzionale' [2010] 3 *Riv. not.* 589; M. Maugeri, 'Quali diritti particolari per il socio di società a responsabilità limitata?' [2004] 6 *Riv. soc.* 1483; M. Cavanna, 'Partecipazione e "diritti particolari" dei soci', in M. Sarale (ed.), *Le nuove s.r.l.*, Zanichelli, Bologna, 2008, 125; R. Santagata, 'I diritti particolari dei soci', in A.A. Dolmetta and G. Presti (eds.), *S.r.l. Commentario dedicato a Giuseppe B. Portale*, Giuffrè, Milan 2011, 291; A. Blandini, 'Categorie di quote, categorie di soci', in G. Rossi (ed.), *Collana della Rivista delle Società*, Giuffrè, Milan 2009, 95 ff., particularly p. 97; M. Maltoni, 'La partecipazione sociale', in C. Caccavale, F. Magliulo, M. Maltoni and F. Tassinari (eds.), *La riforma della società a responsabilità limitata*, IPSOA, Milanofiori-Assago, 2007, 2nd ed., 218: V. de Stasio, 'Commento *sub* art. 2468. Quote di partecipazione', in P. Benazzo and S. Patriarca (eds.), *Codice commentato delle s.r.l.*, Utet, Turin 2006, 137; R. Genghini, 'Le modifiche statutarie', in *Il nuovo ordinamento delle società. Lezioni sulla riforma e modelli statutari*, IPSOA, Milan 2004, para. 4.5; E. Fazzutti, 'Commento sub art. 2468. Quote di partecipazione', in M. Sandulli and V. Santoro (eds.), *La riforma delle società*, Giappichelli, Turin 2003, pp. 57–58; P. Revigliono, 'Commento sub art. 2468. Quote di partecipazione', in G. Cottino, G. Bonfante, O. Cagnasso and P. Montalenti (eds.), *Il nuovo diritto societario, Commentario*, Diretto da Zanichelli, Bologna-Rome 2004, 1807; L. Salvatore, 'La nuova s.r.l.: la disciplina dei conferimenti e delle partecipazioni sociali' [2003] *Contratto e impresa* 239–240; R. Rordorf, *I sistemi di amministrazione e controllo nella nuova s.r.l.* [2003] *Società* 666–667.

66 N. de Luca, 'Tipi societari e impresa sociale: profili notarili' [2019] II *Riv. Notariato* 449 ff.

both to the selfish pursuit of personal interests (according to the *homo oeconomicus* paradigm) and to altruistic and solidarity interests (according to the *homo reciprocans* paradigm) led Italian law to grant private autonomy significant leeway: individuals are free to adopt a governance structure that fully decouples control rights from economic rights.

Not only does the current regulatory framework not oppose such organizational structures, but it actively encourages them. At a time when the welfare state is proving unsustainable for the public treasury, the legal system can only praise the initiative of those private individuals who combine the desire to start a profitable (or at least economically sustainable) business with the desire to share the company's profits with others (the beneficiaries). As a consequence, the favourable impact is twofold. First, a profitable or economically viable business contributes to collective wellbeing by allowing the better allocation of resources. Second, since any company profit is not intended to enrich 'capital', but to allocate wealth in accordance with a solidarity-based paradigm, the private sector contributes to the task of redistribution of wealth that the contemporary state is struggling to achieve.

5.3. THE LEGITIMACY OF FAMILY BUSINESS FOUNDATIONS AND NON-EXISTENCE OF THE NON-DISTRIBUTION CONSTRAINT

The above considerations pave the way to a reassessment of the admissibility under Italian law of the so-called family business foundations.[67] These foundations operate a business with the purely 'selfish' purpose of benefiting the founder's family members.

Once it is established that (i) foundations are simply required to pursue a 'lawful' purpose (and not necessarily a 'public utility' purpose)

67 On family foundations under Italian law, see, for example, P. RESCIGNO (1), above n. 5, pp. 810–811; E. MOSCATI, 'Associazioni e fondazioni: finalità fiduciarie e loro rilevanza' [1995] *Nuova giurisprudenza civile commentata* II, pp. 25 ff.; A. ZOPPINI, 'Fondazioni e trust quali strumenti della successione ereditaria', in P. RESCIGNO (dir.), *Trattato breve delle successioni e delle donazioni*, I, Cedam, Padua 2010, pp. 147–195; G. IORIO, *Le fondazioni*, Giuffrè, Milan 1997, pp. 181 ff.; A. PALAZZO, 'Il diritto delle successioni: fondamenti costituzionali, regole codicistiche ed istanze sociali' [2004] *Vita not.* 116; M.V. DE GIORGI, 'Fondazioni di famiglia' [1973] II *Riv. dir. civ.* 295 ff. Italian scholars who expressed the view that family foundations are to be deemed to be compatible with Italian law include P. MANES, above n. 61, p. 265 and p. 269; M.V. DE GIORGI, above n. 13, p. 79 (but on the condition that the purpose of the family foundation also serves some public benefit).

and that (ii) the absolute separation between 'ownership' and 'control' does not violate any principle of public order under Italian law, there is one inevitable conclusion: no systematic reason prevents the admission or legitimacy of 'family business foundations' with a purely 'selfish' (lawful) purpose.

Notably, if under Italian law there are no reasons for preserving the efficiency of a business when a person holding a minimal quota of the capital exercises control over an entity organized as a 'limited liability company', and if, always under Italian law, there are no reasons for preserving the efficiency of the 'social business' company, where 'shareholders' have no claim over profit and yet exercise control over a social enterprise organized in a corporate form, then one unquestionable conclusion can be drawn. No need for the preservation of business efficiency exists when the management of a family business is handed over to a foundation whose management body is required, under the bylaws, to allocate the profit to the descendants of the founder.

There are also further reasons to believe that family business foundations pursue interests 'worthy of protection' (under Italian law, freedom of contract is always protected when the interests pursued are deemed worthy of protection: Article 1322 CC).[68]

The separation of 'control' and 'ownership' in a family business foundation aiming at distributing profit to the founder's family members ensures unity and continuity to the company's strategic management by shielding it from the risk of heirs' conflict. Furthermore, while the heirs are effectively 'deprived' of management power (unlike the dangerous scenario where this power is placed directly in their hands via the shares in the company), they are not 'deprived' of the right to receive profit, as the family foundation's bylaws mandate for the disbursement of the foundation business's profit in their favour.

Furthermore, the fact that family (business) foundations are undoubtedly legitimate under Italian law from the specific point of view of the absolute decoupling between 'ownership' and 'control' is evident (and undisputedly so nowadays) following the implementation in Italy of The Hague Convention on 'trusts'.[69] Even in a 'trust', one observes a decoupling between 'ownership' and 'control' entirely analogous to that entailed by a foundation. Therefore, if a foreign trust which assigns: (i) management

68 P. Manes, above n. 61, pp. 267–268.

69 The Hague Convention of 1 July 1985 on the Law Applicable to Trusts and Their Recognition was enacted in Italy with law no. 364 of 16 October 1989.

power to the trustees ('managers', but 'non-owners'); and (ii) the associated economic benefits to the 'beneficiaries' ('quasi-owners', but not 'managers') is deemed fully compliant with Italian law,[70] then no valid reason could exist any longer to question the admissibility of a family (business) foundation which substantially replicates the same governance format.

True, certain limits on the constitution of 'family business foundations' derive from Italian inheritance law, which, like other continental legal systems, assigns a reserved portion of the estate to specified groups of individuals (spouses, children and, in some situations, parents). Since, in most cases, the family business (more often the controlling shareholding in a profit-making company) represents almost the entirety of the founder's assets, the gratuitous assignment of such business to a foundation could be challenged by the reserved heirs for violation of their reserved portion under certain conditions. The problem only arises in cases where the potential founder of the foundation has family members who qualify as 'reserved' heirs.[71]

But these inheritance law-related limitations are not insuperable. One could easily think of certain suitable structures to reconcile (i) the need to achieve the desired decoupling between 'ownership' and 'control' and (ii) the need to protect the foundation from the risk of claims from 'reserved' heirs. In particular, it is possible to turn the company that owns the enterprise into a corporation structure that entitles the holder of a special share (representing a minimal fraction of capital) to full control. This is possible by using both the 'limited liability company' structure (where full control can be attributed to a shareholder with so-called 'particular rights') and the 'limited partnership limited by shares' structure (where the power to manage the company can be attributed to a shareholder[72] whose office as director is irrevocable without their consent). Basically, both the 'limited liability company' structure and the 'limited partnership limited by shares' structures allow the creation of so-called golden shares. Such shares represent a minimal fraction of the capital and are thus endowed with an irrelevant economic value for succession purposes (under Italian law, the testator may always freely dispose of

---

70 See, amongst others, A. Gambaro, 'Problemi in materia di riconoscimento degli effetti dei *trusts* nei paesi di civil law' [1984] I *Riv. dir. civ.* 93 ff.; M. Zaccheo, *Gestione fiduciaria e disposizione del diritto*, Giuffrè, Milan 1991, passim; U. Morello, 'Fiducia e trust: due esperienze a confronto' [1990] *Quadrimestre* 239 ff.

71 A. Zoppini, n. 67, p. 153; G. Iorio, n. 67, pp. 82 ff.

72 Because such a shareholder can also be a legal entity, this governance layout can last 'forever'.

at least a quarter of the estate) while incorporating the right of full control. Therefore, such a golden share could be transferred to the family foundation to ensure that (i) control is transferred according to the rules set out in the foundation bylaws, regardless of the fate of all other non-golden shares, which, instead (ii) enshrine economic rights that circulate in accordance with ordinary 'proprietary' rules. A family foundation, certainly immune from the hereditary disputes, could therefore ensure the unity of the strategic management of the family business, despite being the owner of a substantially insignificant fraction of its capital.

We have now reached the final turning point in the evolution of Italian foundation law: the admissibility under Italian law of family foundations that are potentially identical to a foreign law trust postulates the inapplicability to Italian foundations (whether enterprise foundations or not) of any 'non-distribution constraint', the last alleged mandatory barrier to a true freedom of choice regarding the incorporation of a foundation. Traces of such legal constraints cannot be found in the foundations regime under the Civil Code or in general principles of Italian private law.

Certainly, as mentioned above, Italian law expressly provides a prohibition on the disbursement of profits to founders, shareholders and directors of 'social enterprises'. However, this circumstance reinforces rather than denies the absence of any non-distribution limitation in the case of foundations. First of all, under the 'ubi lex voluit, dixit' principle, when the law intended to establish a prohibition on the disbursement of profits to certain categories of individuals, it did so explicitly. Second, under a teleological perspective, the rationale behind the regime of social businesses differs from the rationale behind the regime of foundation. In the former case, the company is not an ordinary company under the law, as its bylaws mandate to pursue general interests. In the latter case, the contrary is true, as the foundation may well be the owner of an 'ordinary' non-social business.

In conclusion, (i) the legislative amendment of 2000 which legitimized the foundations to pursue any 'lawful purpose' (and not necessarily 'public utility' purposes), (ii) the existence of numerous indexes suggesting that a total split between 'ownership' and 'control' does not contradict any Italian mandatory rule, (iii) the recognition by Italian law of a legal structure (i.e. the trust) that is very similar, in this respect, to family foundations are all elements that consistently point towards the following conclusion. Not only should it be undisputed that a foundation may have as its activity the exercise of an enterprise (including a profit-driven enterprise), but an enterprise family foundation should also be considered an effective estate planning tool that enables the founder/entrepreneur to reconcile both (i) their wish to ensure the unity and professionalism of the business contributed to the foundation (as their 'alter ego') and (ii) their wish to have their descendants benefit from the enterprise's profit. And this would be fully compatible with Italian law, albeit within the limits of inheritance law.

6. THE 'THIRD SECTOR CODE' AND THE 'NOT-FOR-PROFIT FOUNDATIONS': TOWARDS THE REPEAL OF THE RULES OF THE CIVIL CODE?

The study of Italian foundation law would not be complete without addressing the recent organic reform of the not-for-profit sector that resulted in the approval of the 'Third Sector Code' in 2017.[73]

As mentioned above, the Parliament that entrusted the government with the task of organically regulating the 'Third Sector Code' had also delegated to it the additional task of overhauling the provisions of the First Book of the Civil Code that regulate 'foundations', 'associations' and 'committees'.[74] Unfortunately, this opportunity was not taken, so the regime of 'generic' private law foundations (those that do not qualify as 'not-for-profit sector entities') continues inexorably to be, on the one hand, outdated and in need of repeal and, on the other hand, woefully inadequate and resulting in a lack of 'legal certainty'.[75]

The not-for-profit sector code draws its fundamental source of inspiration from the decline of the welfare state and from the ordoliberalist orientation that, again due to pressures from the EU, the same Italian Constitutional Charter has now adopted.[76]

The 2001 reform of Title V of the Italian Constitution (devoted to territorial public bodies known as 'Regions', 'Provinces' and 'Municipalities') provided the opportunity to enhance the so-called principle of

---

73 A comprehensive history of the evolution of the law of the third sector in Italy is provided by P. Consorti, L. Gori and E. Rossi, *Diritto del Terzo Settore*, Il Mulino, Bologna 2021, passim.

74 L. Gori and E. Rossi, 'La legge delega n. 106 del 2016 di riforma del terzo settore' [2016] 2, *Osservatorio sulle Fonti* 6.

75 L. Gori, 'Il sistema delle fonti nel diritto del terzo settore', in [2018] 1 *Osservatorio sulle Fonti* 15.

76 S. Benvenuti and S. Martini, 'La crisi del welfare pubblico e il "nuovo" Terzo Settore: la via tracciata dalla legge-delega n. 106/2016' [2017] 2 *Osservatorio Costituzionale* 1–21.

subsidiarity to constitutional status. The last paragraph of Article 118 of the Constitution establishes that: 'The State, regions, metropolitan cities, provinces and municipalities shall promote the autonomous initiatives of citizens, both as individuals and as members of associations, relating to activities of general interest, on the basis of the principle of subsidiarity.' This is a complete game-changer with respect to the traditional aversion of the liberal state and, even more so, of the authoritarian fascist state, to the so-called intermediate bodies. When the principle of subsidiarity is interpreted not only in a 'vertical' sense (i.e. the higher-level territorial body can only intervene when the lower-level body is unable to pursue the general interest), but also in a 'horizontal' sense (i.e. the public authority only pursues general interest objectives when private initiative is unable to accomplish, on its own, the aim of ensuring the 'common good').[77] this sanctions a total inversion of the traditional hierarchical order. Thus, private initiative is considered to be meritorious not only when it ensures the most efficient allocation of resources thanks to the competitive dynamics of 'selfishness' (according to the *homo oeconomicus* paradigm), but also when it efficiently organizes objectives of solidarity thanks to the spontaneous dynamic of 'altruism' (according to the *homo reciprocans* paradigm).

In 2012, after the well-known sovereign debt crisis, which jeopardized the single currency's survival, and in response to strong pressures from

---

[77] M. Romano, 'I limiti all'autonomia statutaria nelle fondazioni di partecipazione alla luce della riforma del terzo settore' [2019] 2 *Le nuove leggi civili commentate* 355–358 and, in particular, p. 357 ('[F]rom the combined reading of art. 118 with art. 117 Const., the central role of private initiative emerges as a means of granting the civil and social rights given to every citizen by the Constitution; many of these rights coincide with the sectors of activity in which non-profit organisations traditionally operate.') ('Dal combinato disposto dell'art. 118 con l'art. 117 Cost. emerge questo ruolo centrale dell'iniziativa privata nell'assicurare il soddisfacimento dei diritti civili e sociali riconosciuti a ciascun cittadino in attuazione dei principi costituzionali; numerosi di questi diritti coincidono proprio con i settori di attività in cui tradizionalmente operano gli enti non profit') and p. 358 ('[T]he transposition of the principle of horizontal subsidiarity in our legal system surely represented a new challenge for non-profit entities, for which a new horizon opened: their initiative has gained priority over the one of the public hand, to which a mere role of integration and organisation of the private initiative is left')('Il recepimento del principio di sussidiarietà orizzontale nel nostro ordinamento ha rappresentato indiscutibilmente una nuova sfida per gli enti non profit per i quali si è aperto un nuovo ampio orizzonte: la loro iniziativa ha assunto una rilevanza prioritaria rispetto a quella della mano pubblica, alla quale resta quindi riservato un ruolo di supplenza e di organizzazione dell'intervento privato'). See also G.U. Rescigno, 'Principio di sussidiarietà orizzontale e diritti sociali' [2002] *Dir. pubbl.* 10 ff.

Member States in Central and Northern Europe,[78] the achievement of a net financial balance was made a constitutional principle, effectively outlawing the deficit spending that had financed Italy's welfare structure (and not always in a virtuous way).[79]

The (horizontal) principle of subsidiarity and the principle of net financial balance have shifted the expectations raised by the traditional welfare state to the so-called not-for-profit sector[80] – hence the need to revisit the entire non-profit regime through an organic reform that has given rise to the 'Third Sector Code' (TSC), the expressed purpose of which is, not surprisingly, that of 'supporting the autonomous initiative of citizens who contribute, even in associated form, to pursuing the common good'[81] (Article 1 TSC).

As far as our purposes are concerned, the TSC defines 'third sector entities' (TSEs) as those entities that 'set up for the pursuit, on a non-profit basis, of civic, solidarity and social utility purposes by carrying out, exclusively or principally, of one or more activities of general interest'[82] (Article 4 TSC). Such TSEs may also carry out business activities, but only on an ancillary basis. In fact, the enabling law specifies that foundations (not from the third sector) that primarily or exclusively carry out business activities will be governed by a law that, as of today, has not yet been approved.[83]

Moving on to the aspects that are relevant for our purposes, the TSC provides that the legal form of the TSE can be, *inter alia*, that of the 'foundation'. It then provides, with specific reference to third sector foundations (TSFs), an articulated regime that is even more detailed than that reserved for BFs in the 1990s.[84]

First of all, it is expressly confirmed that the bylaws of the TSF may envisage a 'participatory body';[85] furthermore, it is also implicitly

---

78 I. Ciolli, 'I Paesi dell'Eurozona e i vincoli di bilancio. Quando l'emergenza economica fa saltare gli strumenti normativi ordinari' [2012] 1 *Rivista AIC* 1 ff.

79 S. Benvenuti and S. Martini, above n. 76, pp. 1–2.

80 G. Ponzanelli, above n. 6, pp. 726–727 ascribes the growth of the third sector to both a government and a market failure. See also A. Zoppini, above n. 15, pp. 80–81.

81 Unofficial translation.

82 Unofficial translation.

83 Article 3, letter d of the Enabling Act ('legge-delega') no. 106 of 6 June 2016.

84 G. Donadio, 'La disciplina generale delle associazioni e delle fondazioni del Terzo Settore' [2017] 3 *Non Profit* 127; E. Rossi, 'Il rompicapo dei controlli sugli enti del Terzo Settore' [2017] 3 *Non Profit* 271.

85 This further attests to the admissibility under Italian law of the so-called 'fondazioni di partecipazione' (participatory or associative foundations): see above n. 55. After the enactment of the TSC, the same stance has been generally taken by most Italian

confirmed that the TSF may even adopt an associative structure 'open' to the entry of new participants. If the foundation's bylaws provide for such a 'participatory body', then, unless otherwise specified, the regime provided for third sector associations' assembly becomes applicable. The assembly is therefore essentially competent on the following matters: (i) the appointment and revocation of the corporate bodies; (ii) the appointment and revocation, where required, of the statutory auditors; (iii) the approval of the financial statements; (iv) the promotion of liability action against members of corporate bodies; (v) amendment of the bylaws and (vi) the resolution of dissolution, transformation, merger or division.

The board of directors remains a necessary body, whether appointed by the assembly (if any) or according to the specific rules of the bylaws. It is composed of directors with general representation powers (hence, limits that are not registered in the Single National Register of the Third Sector cannot be raised as exceptions) and subject to the same rule on conflicts of interest envisaged for directors of commercial companies.

The audit committee, a compulsory body for the TSF, is subject to a regime substantially similar to that envisaged for those of joint-stock companies: (i) it must be composed of individuals with particular requirements of professionalism and independence; (ii) it oversees compliance with the law and the bylaws, as well as compliance with the principle of 'correct administration'; (iii) it monitors compliance with the civic, solidarity and social utility purposes pursued by the entity and, finally, (iv) it certifies the correctness of the 'economic-financial' statements, as well as of the 'social' financial statements (the preparation of which is compulsory). Moreover, the financial statements of the TSF are subject to a compulsory audit by an external auditor or by an auditing firm when certain size thresholds are exceeded.

Lastly and, again, by analogy with the provisions regarding joint-stock companies, a certain percentage of participants may report 'reprehensible facts' to the audit committee (which, when the complaint is raised by a qualified minority, must report it to the assembly). Additionally, with authorisation from a certain percentage of the participants, the audit

scholars, including G. Sicchiero, 'Le fondazioni di partecipazione' [2020] 1 *Contratto e impresa* 20–63; P. Manes, above n. 61, pp. 267 and 269; and M. Romano, above n. 77, pp. 368–370 ('[T]he legislator [has] indirectly confirmed that participatory foundations are not atypical foundations, and that the foundation is a model upon which statutory autonomy can be implemented, even though there are precise limits') ('Il legislatore [ha] indirettamente confermato che la fondazioni di partecipazione non sono fondazioni atipiche, e che la fondazione è un modello sul quale l'autonomia statutaria può innestarsi, seppure con limiti precisi').

committee, the auditor or the public prosecutor may act before the competent court to report 'serious management irregularities'. This report may also lead to the judicial revocation of the corporate bodies and the appointment by the court of one or more administrators.

These rules are extremely important as they mark the definitive abandonment, in the case of TSF, of that 'police right' of authoritarian origin, which authorized governmental authority to intervene *ex officio* in the control and supervision of foundations. A much more liberal protection mechanism left essentially to private initiative now takes its place, eliminating that 'threat' of public intervention in the management of foundations that acted as an enormous deterrent on the spreading of such a model.

Fundamental to our purposes and highly debated by the first interpreters of the TSC, is the question arising from the inclusion (Article 3, paragraph II TSC) of the principle according to which the rules of the Civil Code continue to apply to TSE (and, therefore, also to the TSF) (i) 'insofar as not provided for by this Code [i.e. the TSC]' and (ii) only 'to the extent compatible'.[86]

In reality, since the regime dictated by the TSC is more detailed than that set by the Civil Code, the aforementioned provision should entail, even regardless of the 'compatibility' clause, the substantial total repeal (or rather the inapplicability) of the Civil Code regime to all 'third sector entities', including 'not-for-profit foundations'.[87]

A fundamental question for our purposes is whether the legal regime dictated by the TSC is applicable by analogy to entities that cannot be qualified as belonging to the third sector: this would be the case for a foundation that does not carry out activities of 'general interest' for 'civic, solidarity and social utility' purposes (as required for foundations that are TSEs), but rather exclusively or mainly carries out a business activity with non-altruistic (yet 'lawful') purposes.[88]

The early commentators provided a non-uniform response to this question: both the pro-analogy and anti-analogy[89] opinions have adherents.

---

86 Unofficial translation.

87 M. Romano, above n. 77, pp. 366–367.

88 G. Ponzanelli, above n. 20, p. 728; P. Consorti, 'Profili generali della riforma del 2017', in P. Consorti, L. Gori and E. Rossi, *Diritto del Terzo Settore*, Il Mulino, Bologna 2021 (2nd ed.), p. 60.

89 M. Romano, above n. 77, p. 367. Early commentators questioned whether and to what extent the provision contained in the new decree could by analogy also apply to entities carrying out non-altruist purposes (i.e. not qualifying as third-sector entities). In this regard, on the one hand, some scholars are of the opinion that those rules of

Naturally, should the opinion of those supporting the application by analogy of the TSC discipline to foundations outside the Third Sector prevail and, in turn, the application of the TSC regime renders the one dictated by the Civil Code structurally inapplicable, as the case should be, the consequences would be enormous. It would mark the end of what remains of the outdated 'police law' of the 1942 Civil Code.

Unfortunately, the fact that the legislature of the TSC chose not to intervene on the rules of the Civil Code and, instead, delegated the regime of foundations that wholly or predominantly engage in economic activity to another yet-to-be-approved law makes this conclusion not entirely clear. As long as the relevant areas of regulatory uncertainty exist on such an important front as the relationship between private activity and public control, the terrain of Italian law will remain 'fertile' ground only to a limited extent for purely private company foundations, albeit far less 'sterile' than it originally was.

7. CONCLUSION

Italian foundation law has undergone an extraordinary evolution from the Civil Code of 1942 to date. Due to (i) solicitations from the more vanguard scholarship of the 1960s and (ii) special legislation enacted in recent decades (a) on 'banking foundations' in the 1990s, (b) on the recognition of legal personality and 'purpose' in 2000 and (c) on the regime of the 'third sector' in 2017, the following conclusions can finally be drawn:

- Foundations can legitimately exercise 'business activities' not only on an ancillary or instrumental basis, but also on an 'exclusive or prevalent' basis; in other words, 'enterprise foundations' have today acquired 'citizenship rights' even in Italy.
- Despite the initial resistance to the founder's right to, directly or indirectly (through an ad hoc body), appoint and dismiss directors,

the TSC that protect the general interest can be applied by analogy (in this sense, see G. Posio 'Norme del CTS applicabili a tutte le fondazioni di partecipazioni', in G. Sicchiero (ed.), 'Le fondazioni di partecipazioni' [2021] Ipsoa 2512 ff.; G. Iorio, 'Il codice del terzo settore e le associazioni: i riflessi civilistici della nuova disciplina' [2018] *Ianus* 17, pp. 23 ff.). On the other hand, other scholars argued instead that, in light of the specific purposes of third-sector entities, it is not possible to extend the application of TSC's special provision by analogy (in this sense, see G.D. Mosco, 'L'organizzazione degli enti del Terzo settore tra codice civile, leggi speciali e autonomia privata' [2021] 2 *LUISS Law Review* 81).

foundations can now adopt the so-called associative model, which contemplates the devolution of authority to an assembly body that appoints and removes directors.
- Since the foundation can now pursue any 'legitimate purpose' and since it can no longer be argued that our law mandatorily prescribes a necessary correlation of 'ownership' and 'control' in the management of businesses, there are no longer any obstacles to consider legitimate even purely 'selfish' foundations such as family business foundations – there is no rule that imposes the so-called non-distribution constraint for foundations.
- By way of analogy with the tripartite model of the organization initially adopted for the BF and now replicated for the TSF, the governance of any foundation (even if not belonging to the 'third sector') should preferably be articulated in three bodies: (i) the 'board of directors', which has always been required by law, but also (ii) the 'audit committee' (now required) and (iii) the 'founders' council' (not required, but admitted).
- Since the regime of private controls envisaged for the TSF replaces public control prescribed under the Civil Code, if the regime of TSC is generally applied to foundations outside the 'third sector', the threat of *ex officio* interference by governmental authorities provided by those articles of the code that are still formally in force no longer exists.

In a nutshell, the Italian legal infrastructure is already less hostile towards, if not moderately welcoming towards, enterprise foundations. In order to overcome the doubts that still exist among practitioners, a limited reform of the Civil Code clarifying the private nature of the Italian legal regime by the explicit repeal of all those rules of fascist inspiration is certainly desirable.

The evolution of foundation law that has been examined here appears to be inextricably connected with the concurrent evolution of property rights and, in particular, of the rights of ownership of enterprises, to which the former appears inevitably linked.

The changed attitude towards foundations indeed appears to be strongly interconnected with the changed 'sociological' context. The evolution from (i) the original rules of the Civil Code, strongly influenced by the Napoleonic Civil Code of the early nineteenth century to (ii) the new law on 'subsidiarity' (including in the horizontal sense) and 'third sector', which, on the contrary, appears to be influenced by the constitutionalism of ordoliberal inspiration, which encourages private entrepreneurial initiative not only for self-interested purposes, but also 'common good' purposes, albeit pursued via profit-driven activities.

The nineteenth-century law, which still casts its long shadow over the Civil Code of 1942, was intended to discourage *ancien régime* forms of ownership – i.e. land ownership protecting the rent of an unproductive class (the old nobility) – and to favour the new revolutionary ownership; ownership of capital oriented to entrepreneurial uses for the benefit of the new bourgeoisie. Therefore, such laws intended to supplant a socio-anthropological model rooted in *homo gaudens* (the noble *rentier*) with a new model of *homo oeconomicus*, incarnated in the new hero of modernity (the bourgeois entrepreneur). In this context, any organization – such as foundations – capable of jeopardizing the market-oriented use of property was seen with suspicion and relegated to the market's periphery.

Contemporary law, in a phase in which the capitalist model has by now found maximum diffusion and is certainly no longer threatened by the 'unproductive' pressures of a class of 'passive' owners, has a completely different need now. Indeed, today the need is that of encouraging private individuals to make up for that function of guarantor of the 'common good' of the welfare state, which the contemporary state, heavily indebted and constitutionally limited by 'ordo-liberal' budget constraints, is no longer able to appropriately fulfil. In brief, the contemporary need is no longer to safeguard the *homo oeconomicus* paradigm, but on the contrary to ensure its 'happy' coexistence with the *homo reciprocans* paradigm – hence the legislative favour not only for 'social businesses', but also for those 'businesses' which, although not 'social' (as they do not pursue aims of 'social utility'), can nonetheless contribute to the 'common good' both indirectly, through the exercise of a profitable economic activity (like any profit-making enterprise with a traditional ownership structure) and directly through the concurrent pursuit (not compulsory, but certainly permitted) of ends that can benefit the whole community, under the peculiar ownership structure of a 'foundation'.

Many scholars, myself included, stand by in the hope that our legislature will run the 'last mile' and finally make Italian law favourable to 'enterprise foundations' to the same extent as the most advanced (at least under this respect) Scandinavian or Northern European laws are.

ARE ENTERPRISE FOUNDATIONS POSSIBLE IN THE UNITED STATES?

Ofer ELDAR*

ABSTRACT

This chapter discusses the ability of entrepreneurs to form enterprise foundations in the US and the hurdles for forming them. The US regime for tax-exempt private foundations is very restrictive and does not practically allow them to have substantial ownership of for-profit firms. As a result, there is a perception that enterprise foundations are not feasible in the US. However, enterprise foundations, broadly defined as industrial firms controlled by any nonprofit firm, need not involve ownership by a private foundation (as it is defined in the US Tax Code) and could also be owned by other types of nonprofits. Such enterprise foundations are unlikely to benefit from key tax exemptions (such as tax-deductible donations or income tax exemptions), which probably explains their unpopularity.

* I thank Henry Hansmann, Peter Molk, Anne Sanders, Steen Thomsen, and participants at the Enterprise Foundations workshop for valuable comments. Brendan Smith also provided excellent research assistance.

The chapter evaluates recent developments to liberalize the law of enterprise foundations, such as the "Newman's Own" exception and the perpetual purpose trust.

1. INTRODUCTION

While enterprise foundations are common in some European countries, they have historically been extremely rare in the US. Enterprise foundations, broadly defined, include industrial companies controlled by a non-profit, including any entity – whether a corporation or a trust – that has no owners.[1] The only known example of an enterprise foundation until recently has been the Hershey Company, a chocolate manufacturer, which is controlled by the Hershey Trust, a charitable trust that operates a school for orphans.[2]

The question of whether enterprise foundations are feasible in the US is particularly timely. As I and others show, the number of founder-controlled companies going public has recently risen dramatically. Between 2017 and 2019, almost 20% of initial public offerings were dual-class firms that allocated control to the firm founders.[3] One of the motivations for adopting a dual-class structure is to enable founders to pursue their vision uninhibited by the pressure of sophisticated investors.[4] In fact, some of these firms, such as Lemonade and Allbirds, are benefit corporations that purport to pursue a public benefit which is not limited to seeking profits.[5]

Founders may wish to ensure that the business firm they control will continue to pursue their legacy or vision after their death. Enterprise foundations – if legally feasible – may provide a mechanism for accomplishing

---

1 See S. Thomsen, "Foundation Ownership around the World" in this volume, section 2.

2 See J. Klick and R.H. Sitkoff, "Agency Costs, Charitable Trusts, and Corporate Control: Evidence from Hershey's Kiss-off" (2008) 108 *Columbia Law Review* 749.

3 D. Aggarwal, O. Eldar, Y. Hochberg, and L. Litov, "The Rise of Dual-Class Stock IPOs" (2022) 144 *Journal of Financial Economics* 122, 124.

4 Z. Goshen and A. Hamdani, "Corporate Control and Idiosyncratic Vision" (2016) 125 *Yale Law Journal* 560, 588–591.

5 For analysis of benefit corporations, see O. Eldar, "Designing Business Forms to Pursue Social Goals" (2020) 106 *Virginia Law Review* 937, 964–968; M.B. Dorff, J. Hicks, and S.D. Solomon, "The Future or Fancy? An Empirical Study of Public Benefit Corporations" (2021) 11 *Harvard Business Law Review* 113.

"immortality" for founders' visions.[6] Without employing an entity to control the corporation, it is largely impossible to ensure that the firm is committed in perpetuity to pursuing the founder's vision or a defined public benefit.[7] In fact, in at least one notable case, Delaware courts have invalidated an antitakeover device that the firm's founders adopted partly as an attempt to protect the mission of the firm in perpetuity.[8]

The general perception is that the formation of enterprise foundations in the US is prohibited by tax penalties.[9] The primary restriction is the tax on excess business holdings by private foundations, which are essentially nonprofits that are controlled by their main donors. The main exception to this tax permits private foundations to invest in for-profits that further the foundation's purpose through program-related investments. A simple example would be investing in a bank that makes loans to low-income individuals. Thus, for all practical purposes, the tax on excess business holdings prevents private foundations from holding a controlling stake in industrial for-profits.

However, enterprise foundations in the broader sense need not involve ownership by a private foundation and could also be owned by other types of nonprofits. The restrictions on other tax-exempt nonprofits that do not qualify as private foundations are much less severe. For example, the Mozilla Corporation, a for-profit firm that operates the Firefox web browser, is owned by the Mozilla Foundation (which, confusingly, is not a private foundation), a tax-exempt nonprofit devoted to improving and protecting the internet. The exempt nonprofit may need to pay taxes

---

6 However, It should be noted that it is unclear whether private foundations actually do a good job of fulfilling their founders' visions; see B. Galle, "The Quick (Spending) and the Dead: The Agency Costs of Forever Philanthropy" (2021) 74 *Vanderbilt Law Review* 757 (showing empirical evidence suggesting that managers of private foundations depart significantly from the preferences of the organization's major donors after their deaths).

7 On the use of control mechanisms to commit an organization to a social purpose, see O. Eldar, "The Role of Social Enterprise and Hybrid Organizations" (2017) *Columbia Business Law Review* 92, 154–157.

8 *eBay Domestic Holdings, Inc. v. Newmark*, 16 A.3d 1, 34 (Del. Ch. 2010) ("Jim and Craig contend that they identified a threat to craigslist and its corporate policies that will materialize after they both die and their craigslist shares are distributed to their heirs. At that point, they say, 'eBay's acquisition of control [via the anticipated acquisition of Jim or Craig's shares from some combination of their heirs] would fundamentally alter craigslist's values, culture and business model, including departing from [craigslist's] public-service mission in favor of increased monetization of craigslist.'" Ibid, 32).

9 H. Hansmann and S. Thomsen, "The Governance of Foundation-Owned Firms" (2021) 13 *Journal of Legal Analysis* 172, 174.

known as unrelated business income tax (UBIT) on any income from the for-profit business if unrelated to its purpose,[10] but it may in principle continue to operate and control it.

Moreover, if the nonprofit is not tax-exempt, there seem to be very few restrictions on its control of a business firm. The only potential limitations on control are embedded in states' corporate laws. Although these do not appear to be burdensome and are rarely enforced,[11] there is little evidence that entrepreneurs use nontax-exempt nonprofits to control industrial corporations, particularly those that are publicly listed.

While the regulatory system for forming enterprise foundations appears not to have resulted in many such organizations, two recent developments could potentially spur the growth of enterprise foundations in the US. The first one is the adoption of another exception to the tax on excess business holding, which permits private foundations to hold 100% of the voting rights of an industrial corporation without incurring the tax, subject to certain requirements relating to the foundation's independence from its founders and donors.[12] It is unclear how many private foundations have taken advantage of this exception, except that it was passed specifically to assist Newman's Own Foundation, a private foundation that received a contribution of 100% of Paul Newman's food and beverage firm.

The second development relates to changes in trust laws under certain US states' laws that permit the creation of a perpetual purpose trust.

---

10 UBIT is defined as "the gross income derived by any organization from any unrelated trade or business regularly carried on by it," less certain deductions and modifications (I.R.C. §512). The major modifications – including income from dividends, interest, annuities, royalties, rents, sale of non-inventory property – largely serve to exclude most passive income from being UBTI (ibid, §512(b)). As defined in section 513, an unrelated trade or business is one "the conduct of which is not substantially related … to the exercise or performance" by the organization of its exempt purpose or another 501(c)(3) purpose, with certain carveouts (I.R.C. §513). "Trade or business" includes "any activity which is carried on for the production of income from the sale of goods or the performance of services" (ibid, §513(c)). Whether a trade or business is "regularly carried on" hinges on the "frequency and continuity with which the activities productive of the income are conducted and the manner in which they are pursued" (Treas. Reg. §1.513-1(c)(1)). In general, activities conducted year-round will be considered regularly conducted, as will activities conducted seasonally when seasonal operation is the norm for the field. Whether a trade or business is "substantially related" depends on the causal relationship between the conduct of the business and the achievement of the organization's exempt purposes, other than through the production of income (Treas. Reg. §1.513-1(d)).

11 P. Molk and D.D. Sokol, "The Challenges of Nonprofit Governance" (2021) 62 *Boston College Law Review* 1497, 1522–1525.

12 See below, nn. 60–62.

Historically, it was largely impossible to set up a perpetual purpose trust, particularly if the purpose was not charitable. However, some states, such as Delaware, have recently enabled entrepreneurs to set up perpetual purpose trusts, and such trusts may control industrial business corporations.[13] To date, control by perpetual purpose trusts has primarily been used as a substitute to employee stock option plans which are subject to hefty regulation and to ensure that controlled business corporations distribute a sizable share of their profits to the employees. But this structure could potentially be used by founders to create public firms that are controlled by a trust whose purpose is to promote the founder's values. In fact, very recently the founder of Patagonia, a manufacturer of environmentally friendly clothing, transferred control to a perpetual purpose trust.[14]

It remains to be seen whether the developments in US law will lead to further evolution of enterprise foundations in the US. Given that creating an enterprise foundation through a perpetual trust appears to be possible, the lack of tax exemptions for such trusts (unless they qualify as charitable) may potentially hinder the evolution of enterprise foundations. Likewise, if founders want to maintain control over the business firm (or let their heirs do so), the requirements for satisfying the exceptions to the tax on excess business holdings may be insufficient to spur the growth of enterprise foundation through US private foundations.

This chapter describes in detail the law that regulates the formation of enterprise foundations under US law. The basic takeaway is that contrary to the perception that legal institutions prohibit enterprise foundations, it is possible now to create enterprise foundations in the US. The "catch" is that if founders are interested in the tax exemptions afforded to tax-exempt nonprofits, these requirements are very restrictive.

I do not take a normative stance on whether the requirements under US law should be relaxed to allow private foundations to control business firms more freely while benefiting from tax exemptions, as is the case in some European jurisdictions. This question depends, on the one hand, on whether ownership of a business firm would distract private foundations from serving their purposes, and, on the other hand, whether businesses

---

13 S.N. Gary, "The Oregon Stewardship Trust: A New Type of Purpose Trust That Enables Steward-Ownership of a Business" (2020) 88 *University of Cincinnati Law Review* 707, 711–712.

14 All voting power was allocated to a perpetual trust, and the non-voting stock that carries 98% of the economic interest was transferred to a non-exempt nonprofit; see: https://www.patagonia.com/ownership/.

owned by private foundations are likely to operate efficiently.[15] I leave these questions for further research.

2. PRIVATE FOUNDATIONS

To understand the restrictions on private foundations' control, it is first necessary to understand what a private foundation is. A private foundation under US law is defined by the Tax Code and is not simply any nonprofit entity that does not have owners. The definition itself is somewhat complex. The starting point is that a private foundation is a section 501(c)(3) tax-exempt organization, and thus it is organized for a tax-exempt purpose (charitable, religious, educational, scientific, or literary). It is further subject to the prohibition on inurement, which means that none of the organization's earnings may inure to any private shareholder or individual.[16]

Every tax-exempt organization is a private foundation unless it falls into one of the excluded categories under section 509(a) of the Tax Code.[17] Importantly, the code excludes organizations that are not controlled directly or indirectly by a disqualified person,[18] and do not receive more than a third of their funding from such a person.[19] A disqualified person is defined to include a substantial contributor to the organization, or an entity in which such a contributor has more than 35% beneficial interest.[20] Accordingly, the result of this convoluted definition is that a tax-exempt nonprofit that is highly dependent on a private entrepreneur that contributes a substantial amount of his or her wealth to the organization is classified as a private foundation.

---

15 See H. Hansmann and S. Thomsen, above n. 9, pp. 182–184 (describing empirical evidence that business firms owned by foundations do not perform worse than investor-owned firms). Cf. J. Klick and R.H. Sitkoff, above n. 2 (showing that stock markets reacted positively to the news that the Hershey Trust would sell its controlling stake in the Hershey Company and negatively to the news that that the sale was canceled).

16 I.R.C. §501(c)(3) (defining tax-exempt charitable entities as those in which "no part of the net earnings … inures to the benefit of any private shareholder or individual").

17 The first category includes certain specified types of organizations, such as hospitals, churches, and universities. I.R.C. §509(a)(1); I.R.C. §170(b)(1)(A).

18 I.R.C. §509(a)(3).

19 I.R.C. §509(a)(2).

20 26 U.S. Code §4946.

2.1. EXCESS BUSINESS HOLDINGS

The private foundation faces substantial restrictions on owning and controlling operating companies. The most significant one is the excise tax imposed by section 4943.[21] The base for the section 4943 tax is the "excess business holdings" of any private foundation in a "business enterprise". "Business enterprise" is defined by exclusion in the statute: it does not include (1) a business that is a "functionally related business" or (2) a trade or business for which at least 95% of its gross income is derived from passive sources.[22]

A functionally related business is one which is not an unrelated trade or business[23] or which is part of an aggregate of activities related to the exempt purpose of the organization.[24] Conversely, if the business in question *is* an unrelated trade or business, this exception will not apply, and it will be treated by default as a business enterprise unless the passive income exception applies.[25] Passive sources for purposes of the second exception mostly track the passive income exclusions from unrelated business taxable income in section 512, most notably dividends, interest, annuities, royalties, rents from real property and incidental personal property, and gains or losses from disposition of property besides inventory.[26]

If a trade or business qualifies as a business enterprise, excess business holdings are calculated as the private foundation's excess interest in the enterprise over its "permitted holdings".[27] Permitted holdings are generally calculated as an aggregate of the interest held by the private foundation and

---

21 For the purposes of section 4943, "private foundation" includes certain deemed private foundations: notably, donor-advised funds and certain supporting organizations. See I.R.C. §4943(e)–(f).

22 Ibid, §4943(d)(3); see also Treas. Reg. §53.4943-10 (noting that a trade or business need not result in a profit to be a business enterprise).

23 Defined in I.R.C. §513 as a trade or business which is not substantially related to the exercise or performance of the organization's purpose.

24 Ibid §4942(j)(4).

25 Treas. Reg. §53.4943-10(a)(1) ("'[B]usiness enterprise' includes the active conduct of a trade or business, including … an unrelated trade or business under section 513").

26 I.R.C. §4943(d)(3) (citing I.R.C. §512(b)(1)–(3), (5)). For example, operating a donated apartment complex that generates more than 95% of gross income from rents could be an unrelated trade or business, but it would fall within the passive sources exception and would not be a section 4943 business enterprise (I.R.S. P.L.R. 201422027 (May 30, 2014)). Notably, revenue from services besides rents in that remaining 5% (such as revenue from coin-operated laundry machines) could still be subject to UBIT, §4943 notwithstanding.

27 I.R.C. §4943(c)(1).

"disqualified persons".[28] Disqualified persons include, broadly speaking, substantial contributors or insiders of the foundation who were able to exercise "substantial influence over the affairs of the organization" at any time during the preceding five years, as well as certain family members and controlled entities.[29]

How permitted holdings are calculated depends on the entity form of the enterprise. For corporations, permitted holdings are generally 20% of the voting stock minus the percentage of voting stock owned by disqualified persons.[30] Two exceptions apply: first, where a third person has "effective control of enterprise" (essentially, real control over management of the enterprise[31]), the threshold is 35%;[32] and, second, a 2% *de minimis* rule applies under which a foundation will not be treated as having excess holdings if it owns less than 2% of voting stock and 2% of total share value of the corporation.[33] Additionally, as long as disqualified persons do not together own more than 20% or 35% (depending on the applicable threshold) of voting stock, all nonvoting stock held by the private foundation will be permitted holdings.[34]

The initial excise tax is 10% of the value of excess holdings in an applicable business enterprise.[35] The tax is imposed on the last day of the private foundation's taxable year, but its calculation uses the excess holdings amount from the day in the foundation's taxable year on which excess holdings in that enterprise were at their greatest (by value).[36] Additionally, if excess holdings are still maintained at the end of the "taxable period",

---

28 Ibid.

29 Ibid, §4943(f)(4).

30 Ibid, §4943(c)(2).

31 Treas. Reg. §53.4943-3(b)(3)(ii).

32 I.R.C. §4943(c)(2)(B).

33 Ibid, §4943(c)(2)(C). When different classes of voting stock exist, the percentage of voting stock owned is determined by reference to the relative power of each class to vote for directors, disregarding treasury stock and authorized but unissued stock (Treas. Reg. §53.4943-3(b)(1)(ii)). The example from the regulations: a private foundation holding 20% of a stock class entitled to elect three directors and no stock from the class entitled to elect five directors is treated as holding 7.5% of voting stock (20% of the class having 37.5% of the voting power) (ibid).

34 I.R.C. §4943(c)(2)(A). For unincorporated businesses, the tests are analogous. For partnerships, the corporate tests apply with the substitution of "profits interest" for "voting stock" and "capital interest" for "nonvoting stock" (ibid, §4943(c)(3)(A)).

35 Ibid, §4943(a)(1). This was raised from an earlier rate of 5% by the Pension Protection Act of 2006, and some regulations have not been updated yet to match the new, higher rate (Treas. Reg. 53.4943-2(a)(1)(i)).

36 Treas. Reg. §53.4943-2(a)(2).

a penalty tax of 200% of excess holding value is applied.[37] The taxable period begins on the first day on which there are excess holdings and ends on the earlier of two dates: the date of mailing of a notice of deficiency or the date on which the initial 10% tax is *assessed*.[38] Various grace periods may apply to permit the foundation to dispose of excess holdings before the tax comes into effect in circumstances where the foundation did not know or had no reason to know that it acquired excess business holdings.[39]

The general effect of this substantial tax penalty is that private foundations cannot, for all practical purposes, have a controlling ownership stake in a business firm. As discussed above, evaluating the policy rationale for this outcome is beyond the scope of this chapter. But it is worth noting that when adopted in 1969 through the Tax Reform Act, there was robust debate regarding its desirability.

The center of the debate was a 1965 Treasury report which found that around 14% of private foundations had ownership of at least 10% of an outstanding class of stock of a corporation.[40] The report expressed concerns about the involvement of private foundations in active commercial businesses on several grounds. The managers of foundations, often their main donors, were arguably managing the business firm in a way that compromised the interests of the foundations, for example, by refusing to distribute dividends.[41] Controlling the business firm arguably also enabled the foundations' insiders to cause the business firm to enter into self-dealing transactions with these insiders and their affiliates.[42] Investment of tax-exempt funds by foundations in active commercial ventures put taxable businesses at a competitive disadvantage.[43]

On the other hand, others argued that restrictions on foundation control of business firms would be harsh and undiscriminating.[44] They argued that most foundations ran business firms without any tax abuse or abusive acquisitions, and that the tax advantages offered to private foundations

37 I.R.C. §4943(b).

38 Ibid, §4943(d)(2). "Assessment" is used here as the term of art referring to statutorily required recording of tax liability (Treas. Reg. §301.6203-1 (method of assessment)).

39 Treas. Reg. §53.4943.

40 Senate Comm. on Fin., 89th Cong., Treasury Department Report on Private Foundations 31 (1965).

41 Ibid, 39.

42 Ibid, 15–16.

43 Ibid, 31.

44 Senate Comm. on Fin., 91st Cong., Tax Reform Act of 1969, H.R. 13270: Part A – Testimony to be Received Tuesday, October 7, 1969 107 (Comm. Print 1969) (statement of James Irvine Foundation).

were limited.[45] Moreover, the restrictions would harm small community-oriented foundations capitalized by a substantial ownership interest in a local business, and thus would be detrimental to foundations' ability to serve communities' needs.[46] Nonetheless, opponents of foundations' control of business firms prevailed, and the tax on excess business holding was adopted.

2.2. PROGRAM-RELATED INVESTMENTS

The main exception until recently to the tax on excess business holding has been investments that qualify as program-related investments (PRIs). A PRI is defined as a foundation investment, the primary purpose of which is to accomplish religious, charitable, scientific, literary, and/or or educational purposes, and no significant purpose of which is the production of income or the appreciation of property.[47] An investment qualifies if it significantly furthers the accomplishment of the private foundation's exempt activities, and if the investment would not otherwise have been made.[48] While any investment may qualify as a PRI, so can an investment that provides the foundation with control over a business corporation. Accordingly, there are generally no limitations on private foundations if they invest in businesses that serve an exempt purpose.

The advantages of PRIs go beyond the exemption from the tax on excess business holdings. The income from PRIs is itself tax-exempt because the income flows from a related business and thus is not subject to the Unrelated Business Income Tax (UBIT), which is discussed is more detail below. Moreover, PRIs qualify towards foundations' mandatory distribution requirements, despite the fact they can yield some income. Foundations must annually satisfy statutorily imposed minimums for expenditure made in furtherance of their charitable purposes which generally equal at least 5% of their assets.[49] Undistributed income is subject to a 30% tax.[50] Amounts invested as PRIs thus help foundations avoid this tax penalty.

---

45 Ibid, 119–121.
46 Ibid, 116–117.
47 26 U.S.C. §4944(c); 26 C.F.R. §53.4944-3(a)(1).
48 26 C.F.R. §53.4944-3(a)(2); "Program-Related Investments" *IRS*: https://www.irs.gov/charities-non-profits/private-foundations/program-related-investments.
49 26 U.S.C. §4942(e)(1).
50 Ibid, §4942(a).

Despite the advantages associated with PRIs, few foundations make them in practice.[51] The reason is that investments that purport to qualify as PRIs create substantial legal risks for foundations. If a specific investment fails to qualify as a PRI, it may result in failure to meet the foundation's minimum distribution requirements, leading to substantial tax payments.[52] Moreover, because such investments tend to carry high risk and lower return, they could be viewed as jeopardizing the foundation's financial ability to carry out its exempt purpose,[53] and as jeopardizing investments, they would be subject to a 10% tax.[54] In extreme cases, the investment may result in the foundation losing its tax-exempt status if the investment violates the prohibition on private inurement by creating a private benefit for the shareholders of the business firm that received the investment.

The ultimate responsibility of verifying that an investment qualifies as a PRI rests with the foundation itself. Private foundations must exercise "expenditure responsibility" by monitoring the firm that received the investment to ensure that the funds are used for their intended purposes, obtaining reports on how the funds are spent, and making detailed reports to the IRS.[55] The PRI rules and several private letter rulings by the IRS mitigate the uncertainty of verifying and monitoring PRIs by providing specific examples of qualifying investments. These refer mainly to businesses that transact with disadvantaged individuals or businesses, in circumstances where conventional sources of funds are unwilling to provide funds at reasonable rates. Examples include a business that employs a substantial number of low-income persons or an investment firm organized for investing in businesses in low-income communities.[56] Nonetheless, there remains substantial legal uncertainty for foundations when making PRIs because there may be reasonable disagreements as to whether different businesses would further the purpose of the foundation, and whether these businesses can obtain capital at reasonable terms from other sources. Accordingly, it is not surprising that most foundations are reluctant to assume this responsibility.[57]

---

51 O. Eldar, above, n. 5, p. 959.
52 Ibid, p. 960.
53 Treas. Reg. §53.4944-1(a)(2)(ii).
54 26 U.S.C. §4944(a)(1).
55 I.R.C. §4945(d)(4); Treas. Reg. §53.4945-5(a)(2); Treas. Reg. §53.4945-4(a)(2).
56 O. Eldar, above, n. 5, p. 961.
57 Ibid, 960.

In summary, PRIs provide an exception that permits private foundations to invest in and control business firms, but this exception is relatively narrow because it is confined to businesses that serve a foundation's tax-exempt purposes. Moreover, due to the legal uncertainty associated with making PRIs, relatively few foundations make use of them.

2.3. THE "NEWMAN'S OWN" EXCEPTION

In 2018, the Tax Code was amended under the Philanthropic Enterprise Act of 2017 to allow for another exception to the tax on excess business holdings.[58] Interestingly, the law was passed specifically to assist Newman's Own Foundation, a private foundation that received a contribution of 100% of Paul Newman's for-profit food company, called Newman's Own, that paid all of its profits to charity. The foundation faced the risk of paying the tax on excess business holdings because its holdings exceeded the permitted threshold of 20% of the voting rights in the for-profit good company. Paul Newman himself apparently lobbied for the legislation.

The exception at section 4943(g) mirrors the situation faced by the Newman's Own Foundation. The provision exempts from the excise tax all holdings in a business enterprise that meets three tests: (a) "ownership," (b) "all profits to charity" and (c) "independent operation".

The "ownership" test has two requirements: the private foundation must have held 100% of voting stock in the business enterprise during the taxable year; and all its ownership interests must have been acquired by means other than purchase.[59]

The "all profits to charity" test requires that the business enterprise distribute its net operating income (calculated as gross minus deductions, tax, and a working capital allowance) to the parent foundation within 120 days of the close of its taxable year.[60]

The "independent operation" test requires three markers of independence: first, no substantial contributor[61] to the private foundation

58 Pub. L. No. 115-123, §41110, 132 Stat. 64 (2018); I.R.C. §4943. The exception does not apply to certain deemed private foundations that are otherwise subject to the excise tax. I.R.C. §4943(g)(5) (donor-advised funds; certain supporting organizations; certain charitable and split-interest trusts).

59 Ibid, §4943(g)(2).

60 Ibid, §4943(g)(3).

61 Defined at I.R.C. §4958(c)(3)(C). Generally speaking, a donor of more than $5,000 and more 2% of the organization's total contributions in a year counts as a substantial contributor.

or family member of the same may be involved in the business;[62] second, at least a majority of the board of directors of the foundation must be persons who are not directors or officers of the business enterprise or family members of substantial contributors and, third, there must be no loans outstanding from the business enterprise to substantial contributors, their family members, or the private foundation itself.[63]

Taken as a whole, these requirements are designed to address the concerns that underlie the policy rationale for the tax on excess business holdings discussed above. As the foundation is the sole owner of the business firm, there is no risk that tax-exempt funds will be used to benefit other shareholders. There is also no risk that profits from the business will be locked in the for-profit entity and will be unavailable to the foundation. Moreover, the main donors are not permitted to control both the foundation and the business firm, and thus there is little risk they would be able to utilize both to their personal advantage.

Finally, the income from the for-profit is generally taxable as UBIT if it is unrelated to the purpose of the foundation. For example, the income from selling food products is clearly unrelated to the charitable purpose of the Newman's Own Foundation, and thus is taxable at the normal corporate tax rate.

Overall, the "Newman's Own" exception is relatively narrow in scope, but it does provide foundations an opportunity to generate income from business activity. In particular, the exception may be used by philanthropists who wish to bequeath their ownership stake in business firms to private foundations, and for foundations to operate such firms to generate more income and increase their funds.

3. TAX-EXEMPT ORGANIZATIONS THAT DO NOT QUALIFY AS PRIVATE FOUNDATIONS

It is important to remember that the heavy restrictions on controlling a for-profit business firm apply only to private foundations. These restrictions do not apply to nonprofits that do not qualify as private foundations. The IRS issues a section 509(a) ruling with respect to every tax-exempt

62 Specifically, they may not be a "director, officer, trustee, manager, employee, or contractor of the business enterprise (or an individual having powers or responsibilities similar to any of the foregoing)". Ibid, §4943(g)(4)(A).

63 Ibid, §4943(g)(4).

organization in order to determine whether the organization is a private foundation, or alternatively, a public charity. If the organization is a public charity, it is not subject to the tax on excess business holding.

Public charities include certain types of specified organizations, such as hospitals and churches, and educational organizations, such as schools and universities.[64] A more general category that appears to have been overlooked in the earlier literature is an organization that normally receives a substantial part of its support from a governmental unit or from the general public described in section 170(b)(1)(A)(vi) of the Tax Code. The "substantial part of its support" requirement is generally met if the organization receives at least 33.33% of its support from the government and the general public.[65] The Mozilla Foundation discussed above is an example of such an organization. Thus, the tax on excess business holdings does not apply to its ownership of the Mozilla Corporation.

Paradoxically, the most well-known example of a public charity that controls a business firm, the Hershey Trust, is not representative of general practice, but is viewed as a unique anomaly. The trust owns a controlling stake through a dual-class structure in the Hershey Chocolate Company. The trust that received its assets, including the ownership stake in the chocolate company from Milton Hershey in 1918, would be treated as a private foundation. But because the trust's role is to support a school for orphan children, it qualifies as a "supporting organization" to an educational organization under section 509(a)(3) – an exception that Congress apparently created specifically for the Hershey Trust.[66]

Nonetheless, this ownership structure by public charities is subject to some, albeit milder, restrictions.[67] The most direct one is the UBIT.[68] This tax amounts to the normal corporate tax rate imposed on trade or business which is not regularly carried on and is not substantially related to the exempt purposes of the organization.[69] The Hershey Chocolate company's business is clearly unrelated to the purpose of the Hershey Trust.

---

64 I.R.C. §509(a)(1); I.R.C. §170(b)(1)(A).

65 Treas. Reg. §1.170A-9(f)(ii)(2). Alternatively, the IRS may conduct a multifactor analysis based on "facts and circumstances", but including whether at least 10% of the support of the organization is sourced from the public. Ibid, §1.170A-9(f)(ii)(3)–(3)(i).

66 E. Brody, "Whose Public? Parochialism and Paternalism in State Charity Law Enforcement" (2004) 79 *Indiana Law Journal* 937, 987–988.

67 I.R.C. §4944(c).

68 Ibid, §511. The investment in the for-profit would also be subject to a 10% tax if it is so risky so as to jeopardize the ability of foundation to carry out its exempt purpose. I.R.C. §4944.

69 Above n. 10. Note that the UBIT also applies in the case of private foundations, whether or not there is excess business holding.

The Mozilla Corporation does in some years generate business income from licenses and various services it sells, and this income may be unrelated to the purposes of the nonprofit parent, and to that extent that income is taxable.[70] More drastically, if the unrelated business activity is too substantial, the organization will be deemed not to be operating exclusively for exempt purposes and will not qualify for tax-exempt status.[71] Thus, operating a business firm is risky for nonprofits even if they are willing to pay tax on the income generated by the business.

There are likewise examples where the for-profit business qualifies as a related business, and therefore the income from the business that flows to the foundation is exempt from income tax. An example is the Greyston Foundation, a nonprofit that is devoted to enhancing employment opportunities in low-income communities by promoting open hiring practices.[72] The foundation is not a private foundation, again because it receives a substantial part of its support from the general public under section 170(b)(1)(A)(vi).[73] The Greyston Foundation owns 100% of the Greyston Bakery, a commercial bakery that is committed to employing people in low-income communities that suffer from systemic unemployment. In this case, the operations of the for-profit subsidiary are likely related to the tax-exempt purposes of the parent nonprofit, and thus they are not typically classified as UBIT.

4. NON-EXEMPT PURPOSE-ORIENTED ORGANIZATIONS

In assessing whether enterprise foundations are possible in the US, it is important to emphasize that it seems entirely possible for organizations that are not tax-exempt to have a controlling stake in for-profit firms.

---

70 The 2019 filing of the Mozilla Foundation states: "The foundation qualifies as a public benefit charitable organization exempt from income taxes on related income under section 501(c)(3) of the internal revenue code and applicable sections of the California revenue and taxation code. The foundation provides for tax, if any, on unrelated business income. In accordance with the accounting standard on accounting for uncertainty in income taxes, no portion of an uncertain tax position will be recognized if the position has less than a 50 percent likelihood of being sustained upon audit by the relevant taxing authority. Also, interest expense, if any, is recognized on the full amount of deferred benefits for uncertain tax positions". Mozilla Foundation, I.R.S Form 990: Supplemental Financial Statements, DLN. 93493321080390 (2019).

71 See Treas. Reg. §1.501(c)(3)-1(c).

72 O. Eldar, above n. 7, p. 114.

73 See above n. 64 for an explanation of the "substantial support" test.

Taking nonprofit corporations first, just like business corporations, they can usually be formed for "any lawful activity".[74] It is generally possible to create a nonprofit whose purpose is to promote some nonpecuniary purpose that is related to the vision of some entrepreneur, and for that nonprofit to have voting control of the business corporation which was owned by that entrepreneur. A recent example is the transfer of all stocks of Tripp Lite, an electrical device manufacturing company, to a nonprofit formed under section 501(c)(4) to promote conservative political causes.[75]

Of course, the management of the nonprofit will be subject to the standard fiduciary duties of loyalty and care, and since the nonprofit corporation was created under the laws of a US state, the state attorney general will monitor whether managers act beyond their powers or engage in self-dealing transactions.[76] Accordingly, it may be difficult for entrepreneurs to maintain control over the nonprofit after the transfer of their ownership interest. However, state monitoring of nonprofits is generally very loose, and it is rare for state attorneys general to expend substantial resources in policing the management of nonprofits.[77]

Instead of using the nonprofit form, it may also be possible to create a limited liability company (LLC), which would be outside the ambit of state attorneys general and not subject to mandatory fiduciary duties under states' corporate laws. The LLC is an entity form that allows entrepreneurs to design all its internal governance arrangements through the LLC agreement.[78] The LLC agreement could lay out a constraint on distributing any profits to individuals, such that the LLC has no owners. The LLC could further be governed by a self-appointing board of directors

---

74 Revised Model Nonprofit Corp. Act §3.01.

75 K. P. Vogel and S. Goldmacher, "An Unusual $1.6 Billion Donation Bolsters Conservatives", New York Times, August 22, 2022.

76 P. Molk and D.D. Sokol, above n. 11, p. 1509.

77 Ibid, 1522–1525. In fact, state attorneys general are more likely to intervene in transactions when it is politically expedient to do so – see J. Klick and R.H. Sitkoff, above n. 2, pp. 755–756 (the Pennsylvania Attorney General intervened and obtained a preliminary injunction of the Milton Hershey School Trust's (Trust) sale of its Hershey Company stake, on the grounds that the sale would harm the local Pennsylvania economy and community).

78 Recently, Facebook's founder, Mark Zuckerberg, chose to organize his charitable activities in an LLC instead of a private foundation, partly to avoid some of the tax complexities and restrictions that foundations entail. See D.B. Reiser, "Disruptive Philanthropy: Chan-Zuckerberg, the Limited Liability Company, and the Millionaire Next Door" (2018) 70 *Florida Law Review* 921, 931–948.

that is entrusted with pursuing the purpose of the LLC, which again will be defined in the LLC agreement. The LLC, which would effectively serve as a nonprofit, could be allocated the controlling stake in a business firm and continue to run it in perpetuity.

The "perpetual purpose trust" or "stewardship trust" is a novel form of ownership that was recently introduced in the US,[79] and may be used to create enterprise foundations. At common law, a non-charitable purpose trust would generally fail due to the lack of ascertainable beneficiaries.[80] The Uniform Trust Code (UTC) modified the common law rule in section 409 to allow for trusts created for a specific noncharitable purpose or a valid, noncharitable purpose selected by the trustee.[81] Although this change allowed creation of purpose trusts, a durational limit remained, prohibiting perpetual trusts.[82] Additionally, §409 UTC gave courts the power to reduce the corpus of a purpose trust to the extent the total is "not required for the intended use."[83] These limitations diminished the business incentives to place a perpetual entity under the control of a purpose trust. However, certain states, notably including Delaware, omitted these restrictions from their trust statutes, permitting perpetual, noncharitable purpose trusts without threat of court-ordered asset reduction.[84]

The perpetual trust has been increasingly used to create a form of employee-owned business by designating employees as the trust's beneficiaries. It is often seen as an alternative to employee stock-ownership plans (ESOPs), which are heavily regulated and highly inflexible.[85]

---

79 See Z. Schlag, D. Razo and C. Canon, *Exiting to Employees through Employee Ownership Trusts*, Common Trust Partners LLC and Purpose Network US, 2021; L. Tyson, S. Thomsen, R. Strand, E. Pelissier, and E. Gurfein, *Perpetual Purpose Trust and Organically Grown Company: Rethinking Corporate Ownership for the Future*, Berkeley Haas Case Series, 2021.

80 S.N. Gary, above, n. 13, pp. 713–716 (citing Restatement (Third) of Trusts §47 (Am. Law. Inst. 2007).

81 Ibid, 717–719 (citing Unif. Trust Code §409 (amended 2010)).

82 Absent additional change, noncharitable purpose trusts remain subject to the duration fixed in the statute – either the default 21 years of the rule against perpetuities or an extended term adopted by the state. Ibid, 720.

83 Ibid. (citing Unif. Trust Code §409(3) (amended 2010)).

84 Ibid, 721.

85 ESOPs are retirement products and thus their benefits are mainly paid to participants near or at retirement age. In contrast, the trust structure allows employees to share in the company's profits throughout the life of the firm. Holding the company's shares through a trust avoids the valuation issues that arise with the circulation of shares in

Although the employees do not own the company directly, they may thereby be able to share in its profits.[86] The trust will also typically specify the conditions under which a sale might happen in order to ensure the protection of the purpose of the trust.[87] Although the trust may hold all the voting stock of the company, the company may retain the ability to raise capital by issuing nonvoting preferred stock.[88] The trust thus ensures that the firm will remain employee-owned throughout its lifetime.

The management of the trust is highly flexible in identifying the key stakeholders that control the business firm and determining the governing structure of the operating company. Typically, the parent trust is managed by a committee. The committee is elected by stakeholders, such as employees and community representatives. The committee's role is then to ensure that the trust upholds its purpose, and it oversees the board of the operating company.[89] The exact scope of decision-making of the committee or the board as well as the power of employees or other stakeholders in decision-making and elections are set by the trust agreement.

Overall, despite the fact that it is growing in popularity in the context of employee-owned firms, it remains a relatively rare ownership model. Very recently, the founder of Patagonia, a clothing company, announced that his family had transferred the ownership of the firm by creating a dual-class structure under which a perpetual purpose trust will have the voting power in the firm and a non-exempt nonprofit organized to protect nature and the environment under section 501(c)(4) will be entitled to 98% of the economic profits.[90] Importantly, the founder's family will keep its influence over the company through the trust's governance structure.

It remains to be seen whether Patagonia and Tripp Lite remain unique examples of a founders willing to part with their wealth, and whether more founders will form enterprise foundations. A major challenge for creating such structures is that at least in the US, the demand for them is often

---

an ESOP under ERISA. A perpetual trust may avoid the lack of diversification inherent in an ESOP by instead applying profits as an employer contribution to a traditional 401(k) plan for the company's employees. See Z. Schlag, D. Razo and C. Canon, above n. 77, pp. 23–24.

86 Ibid, 23.

87 Ibid, 24.

88 S.N. Gary, above, n. 13, p. 729.

89 See Z. Schlag, D. Razo and C. Canon, above n. 74, pp. 40–41.

90 One reason for not seeking a tax-exempt status for the nonprofit firm is to allow it to undertake political and lobbying activities, which are not permitted for tax-exempt nonprofit under section 501(c)(3); see D. Gelles, "The Climate Philanthropists" New York Times, Sep. 16, 2022.

motivated by tax considerations.[91] A disadvantage of non-exempt entities is that any gifts or transfers to the organization would not typically be tax-deductible, including transfer of stocks in the relevant business firm.[92] However, lifetime gifts to section 501(c)(4) nonprofits are exempt from estate and gift taxes.[93] This exemption may have facilitated the transformation of Patagonia and Tripp Lite into enterprise foundations, and in the case of Patagonia, the founder's family got around to maintain its influence by allocating voting control to the trust. Further research is necessary to evaluate which tax exemptions may be critical for entrepreneurs to induce them to form enterprise foundations.

5. CONCLUSION

There is a perception that enterprise foundations are not possible in the US. In this chapter, I have shown that it is actually feasible to form them, yet they are rarely created. The reason appears to be that subject to a few exceptions, there are no tax benefits to forming enterprise foundations in the US. This suggests that at least in the US, without tax benefits, it is generally unlikely that business planners would opt to employ nonprofits to control business firms.

However, some recent innovations may potentially lead over time to the greater popularity of enterprise foundations in the US. It is possible that more private foundations will utilize the "Newman's Own" exception to own and control business firms. The challenge is that the conditions for satisfying the exception, such as the requirement that the foundation should own 100% of the business firm, are quite restrictive.

Likewise, the emergence of the perpetual purpose trust may provide an efficient legal tool for creating enterprise foundations, without subjecting entrepreneurs to the complexities and vagueness of the Tax Code (though without important tax benefits, such as tax-deductible donations or

91 This is generally consistent with the evidence on perpetual trusts. See M.M. Schanzenbach and R.H. Sitkoff, "Perpetuities or Taxes? Explaining the Rise of the Perpetual Trust" (2006) 27 *Cardozo Law Review* 2465 (demonstrating that the demand for perpetual trusts was driven by exemptions from estate tax).

92 I.R.C. §§2501, 2001. See D.B. Reiser, above n. 76, pp. 952–956; Tyson, S. Thomsen, R. Strand, E. Pelissier, and E. Gurfein, above n. 77, p. 5.

93 I.R.C. §§2501(a)(6). See A. R. Sorkin et al., "Philanthropy, The Billionaires' Way" New York Times, Sep. 16, 2022.

exemption from income tax). These trusts are increasingly used to form employee-owned firms, and there are some recent examples of trusts created to control for-profit firms that purport to have a purpose that is broader than merely profit-maximization. Control by a trust that has no investor-owners may be used to ensure that such firms will not sacrifice their missions in order to make more profits.[94]

---

94 O. ELDAR, above n. 7, pp. 154–157. In contrast, legal forms, such as the benefit corporation, do not provide a credible commitment device that ensures that firms pursue social missions effectively; see O. ELDAR, above, n. 5, pp. 964–968.

ENTERPRISE FOUNDATION LAW IN A COMPARATIVE PERSPECTIVE

Concluding Observations

Anne Sanders and Steen Thomsen

1. INTRODUCTION

The chapters in this book demonstrate the remarkable variety in the regulation of enterprise foundations in different legal systems. This concluding chapter provides a comparative overview. We briefly address the following issues: the definition of foundations and especially enterprise foundations in different legal systems (section 2); the admissibility of enterprise foundations (section 3); different notions and practices in relation to the purpose of enterprise foundations (section 4); the flexibility founders enjoy in the creation of foundation charters and their influence on the administration of foundations (section 5); foundation governance (section 6); tax law (section 7) and the economic significance of enterprise foundations (section 8). The concluding remarks summarize the main findings of the chapter and offer suggestions for the legislator.

We typically rely on scales to assess and illustrate similarities and differences between different legal systems. We are of course aware that assessments using such scales oversimplify issues and are somewhat subjective. However, we nevertheless decided to add them in order to improve the readability and foster further comparative debate.

2. DEFINITIONS: WHAT IS AN ENTERPRISE FOUNDATION?

Defining an enterprise foundation is no trivial matter. Depending on the jurisdiction, such a definition may determine whether a given enterprise foundation is legal, how it is regulated and how it is taxed. Failure to grant official recognition to a foundation will prevent it from obtaining legal personhood, and legal liability will revert back to the founders and directors.

2.1. WHAT IS A FOUNDATION?

The European chapters in this volume show a common legal understanding of the foundation as an entity without members or shareholders with legal personality, which is independent from its founder and requires an (in principle) irrevocable transfer of property to pursue a purpose established by the founder under some form of public supervision. Setting up a foundation requires some form of registration, even if the special approval formerly required is no longer technically necessary. A foundation's charter must usually be in writing and may be included in a will.

Table 1. **Foundation definition elements by country**

Separate legal entity (separate from founder) with separate administration	**Without members or shareholders**	**Irrevocable transfer of property to serve a certain purpose**	**Supervision by public authority**
Denmark	Denmark	Denmark	Denmark
Sweden	Sweden	Sweden	Sweden
Austria (private and federal foundations)	Austria (private and federal foundations)	Austria (only federal foundations)	Austria (mainly federal foundations)
Germany	Germany	Germany	Germany
Switzerland	Switzerland	Switzerland	Switzerland
Italy	Italy	Italy	Italy

Source: Compiled by the authors.

A main characteristic of the foundation is that it is founded as a legal entity of its own without members or shareholders. It is administrated and represented by its directors who are meant to realise the foundation's purpose. While all the European legal systems discussed in this book agree on these fundamental principles, there are considerable differences with respect to the purpose a foundation may propose and the ensuing requirements in respect to the foundation's board of directors, especially if the board has to be independent from the founder. Such differences will be discussed below.

However, there is one remarkable exception: while the exclusively charitable Austrian federal foundation lives up to all requirements of a foundation set up above,[1] the Austrian private foundation is a special case: the founder may not only reserve a right to change the charter of the foundation, but may also revoke the gift completely for the 'price' of a tax burden.[2] Moreover, after 100 years, the foundation may be dissolved completely, unless the beneficiaries do not decide to continue the foundation.[3] In addition, public supervision only plays a minor role in relation to Austrian private foundations.[4] In this respect, it may well be argued that the Austrian private foundation is not a foundation in the classic sense; rather, it might be considered as an alternative to the trust, which does not exist in most civil law countries like Austria.

The discussion of the law of foundations in the US shows a different understanding which considers federal tax law as the major source of

1 S. Kalss, Austria chapter in this volume, section 1.1.
2 S. Kalss, Austria chapter in this volume, sections 1.4, 6.
3 Ibid, section 1.4.
4 Ibid, section 2.2.2.

foundation law – a foundation is defined as an entity without owners set up for the purpose of tax exemption for charitable purposes (s. 501(c)(3) of the Internal Revenue Code).[5] The material legal rules – typically states' law – concerning the organization of such entities are not the focus of the discussion. Therefore, this comparative overview will only briefly refer to the US example in relation to a few issues.

However, one issue is worth mentioning: both the German[6] and the US chapters[7] show that alternative legal entities outside foundation law may be used to construct foundation-like entities. In Germany, the charitable limited company – the gGmbH – enjoys the same tax benefits as a charitable foundation, but is easier to set up and is not under public supervision. In the US, LLCs and perpetual purpose trusts[8] are used for comparable reasons.

2.2. ENTERPRISE FOUNDATIONS: LEGAL DEFINITION AND REGULATION

This comparative overview shows that enterprise foundations have a significant presence in the countries covered in this book. However, with the exception of Denmark,[9] there is no special legislation for enterprise foundations and thus no legal definitions. Consequently, defining a foundation as an enterprise foundation is of little legal significance in the different legal systems, but is merely of practical interest. Therefore, most chapters in this book work explicitly or implicitly with the functional definition set up by Thomsen at the beginning of this book. According to this pragmatic view, an enterprise foundation is a foundation with a controlling influence in a business.[10] It does not matter whether the foundation has a charitable purpose and only happens to own a company by chance or for historical reasons. For example, the Swedish chapter describes an enterprise foundation as a grant-making foundation which conducts business or owns shares. A distinction made in a draft Swedish Foundation Act between grant-making and activity-based foundations has not become law.[11]

Probably because of this lack of legal definitions, there is also no discussion in the chapters on whether being an enterprise foundation

[5] O. Eldar, US chapter in this volume, section, 2.
[6] A. Sanders, Germany chapter in this volume, section 1.3.3.
[7] O. Eldar, US chapter in this volume, sections 3, 4.
[8] In the UK, a perpetual purpose trust is possible for a charitable purpose.
[9] R. Feldthusen, Denmark chapter in this volume, section 5.2.
[10] S. Thomsen, Foundation Ownership around the World chapter in this volume, section 2.
[11] K. Olsson, Sweden chapter in this volume, section 1.4.

requires that a foundation holds 100% of shares in a business or whether a majority or even minority of shares is still enough. Danish enterprise foundation law speaks of 'controlling influence', which would include all foundations with a voting majority larger than 51%, but a smaller ownership stake of 20% or less might be sufficient for effective control, depending on the circumstances.[12]

However, there is a discussion in different countries as to whether a foundation may manage a business itself (a direct enterprise foundation) or may simply hold shares in it (an indirect enterprise foundation or holding foundation). The Austrian private foundation may only act as a holding foundation by owning shares,[13] while most other countries permit both.

The European chapters in this volume show that in relation to large enterprises, holding foundations are much more common. In Germany, the Zeiss foundation used to be the most prominent example of a direct enterprise foundation. However, it was restructured because in German law, there is agreement that the foundation does not offer the best structure for managing a business directly.[14] Direct enterprise foundations usually employ the business in question as a way to pursue their purpose directly – e.g. a hospital is managed by a charitable foundation as a means to improve healthcare or a museum runs a museum's shop and café. In contrast, holding foundations are also concerned with financial value creation.

Denmark is not only the sole country that has developed a legal definition for enterprise foundations, but also provides special legislation for enterprise foundations and non-enterprise foundations.[15] These specialized rules take into account the fact that for market participants, interacting with a foundation owning a business may raise the same issues as would be the case for a corporation owning one. The Danish rules concerning enterprise foundations therefore show many similarities with legal entities conducting commercial activities.[16]

In other countries, such as Italy,[17] foundations must simply follow general rules for all entities conducting business.

Like Denmark, Austria offers two legal regimes for foundations,[18] however, the distinguishing factor is not whether the foundation

12 R. Feldthusen, Denmark chapter in this volume, section 6.
13 S. Kalss, Austria chapter in this volume, section 4.
14 A. Sanders, Germany chapter in this volume, section 1.4.
15 R. Feldthusen, Denmark chapter in this volume, section 5.2.
16 Ibid, section 5.
17 T. Horvarth, *Stiftungen als Instrument der Vermögensnachfolge*, Peter Lang, Frankfurt 2010, p. 87–91.
18 S. Kalss, Austria chapter in this volume, sections 1.1, 1.2.

conducts business or not but whether the foundation pursues a private or charitable purpose. While the latter is free to act commercially in pursuit of its charitable purpose, the former faces limitations with respect to the direct involvement in the business. The US offers specialized tax law for foundations undertaking commercial activities. However, other countries discussed in this book offer only one legal regime for foundations. The emergence of specific third-sector rules, as is the case in Italy,[19] with its Third Sector Code, may influence this development in the future.

Most countries (Germany,[20] Italy,[21] Sweden[22] and Switzerland) do not require that a foundation is established with a certain minimum level of capital. The only requirement is that a foundation receives enough capital to be able to pursue its purpose in a sustainable way.

The situation is different in Denmark[23] and with Austrian private foundations.[24] In Denmark, at least DKK 300,000 (approximately €40,000) must be donated to form a foundation. Enterprise foundations use the same capital structure as Danish limited liability companies (*anpartsselskaber*) and joint stock companies (*aktieselskaber*) with a division between base capital and free reserves. An enterprise foundation may only make distributions from its free reserves. In Austria, the initial minimum assets of the foundation are €70,000. The assets need only be actually present at the time of the establishment and registration of the foundation.

While the question of minimum capital may not be decisive, it may be considered an interesting sign of the professionalization of the founding process.

3. ADMISSIBILITY OF ENTERPRISE FOUNDATIONS

Table 2. Admissibility

Full endorsement	Some restrictions	Serious limitations
Denmark	Austria	USA
Sweden	Germany	
Switzerland	Italy	

Source: Compiled by the authors.

19 E. Barcellona, Italy chapter in this volume, section 6.
20 A. Sanders, Germany chapter in this volume, section 2.3.
21 T. Horvarth, above n. 17, p. 67.
22 K. Olsson, Sweden chapter in this volume, section 2.
23 R. Feldthusen, Denmark chapter in this volume, section 5.2.
24 S. Kalss, Austria chapter in this volume, section 5.

All the countries discussed in this book allow enterprise foundations to exist. However, there are differences in relation to the limitations set by the regulatory system. The situation is very clear in Denmark with specific legal rules on enterprise foundations and – in recent years – a political goal to facilitate the formation of enterprise foundations through the tax system. Danish enterprise foundations are not merely tolerated but are also understood as an important policy tool to enable the long-term ownership of important national businesses.

In Sweden, enterprise foundations also play an important role and are admissible after a conscious decision of the legislator in 1993.[25] However, apart from that, the Swedish handling of enterprise foundations is far less transparent than in Denmark. For example, most of the major enterprise foundations – like the Wallenberg Foundations – are considered to be charitable foundations rather than enterprise foundations, even though they are both according to the approach taken in the chapter on Sweden.

In Switzerland, enterprise foundations are admissible without restrictions,[26] so the legal system may be put on the same level as Sweden. However, the discussion in this chapter shows that some recent tax and regulatory issues provide some obstacles to enterprise foundations.

German federal law has clearly allowed enterprise foundations since 2002.[27] Both running the business directly by a foundation as well as serving as a holding are possible, even though there are very few examples of the former. The law allows a foundation to exercise fully its rights as a shareholder. However, running an enterprise may not be stated as a foundation's only purpose because of the so called Verbot der Selbstzweckstiftung, which demands that a foundation may not only pursue the purpose of administering its own property without any effect on the world.[28] This point has been challenged by academic writers, but is not a great hindrance to practitioners. Other, additional purposes can be found and stated in the foundation charter. So far, foundation authorities have been hesitant to force foundations to exercise their shareholders' rights in order to receive maximum dividends for their other (often charitable) purposes. However, the interpretation of such rules may differ among different supervisory bodies and there is no guarantee that the practice will not change in the future.

---

25 K. Olsson, Sweden chapter in this volume, section 1.7.

26 D. Jakob, Switzerland chapter in this volume, section 2.2.1.

27 A. Sanders, Germany chapter in this volume, section 1.2.

28 Ibid, section 2.1.

As mentioned earlier, almost all countries in our sample allow that foundations run businesses directly and indirectly as shareholders. However, the latter approach, in which a foundation owns a company running the business in question is more common for larger business in all examined countries. The former approach may be taken, for example, by a charitable foundation using a business to pursue its purpose, e.g. providing healthcare services through foundation-run hospitals. Yet, in Austria, the Privatstiftung may not engage in entrepreneurial activities itself, although it may hold shares in companies (often through holding companies), but is not allowed to get too involved in the day-to-day running of the organization of its subsidiaries (keine straffe Konzernführung).[29] Nevertheless, the most important decisions may be taken at the foundation level. The federal foundation (Bundesstiftung) which needs to pursue a charitable purpose may hold shares and run a business as long as the dividends are used for that charitable purpose.

In Italy, setting up enterprise foundations was not possible for a long time due to established hostility towards foundations in general and an understanding that owning and leading a business was impossible for a charity-oriented entity like a foundation. However, currently, following critical scholarly work since the 1960s, it is possible to form them, even if the legal environment still cannot be described as welcoming to them. There are still uncertainties in the case law, especially the risk of a foundation to be classified as a de facto company with its directors as personally liable de facto associates.[30]

Placing the US in the chart above is not easy because of the country's unique legal approach to foundations which focuses on federal tax rather than the material state's law structuring the foundation as a legal entity. This is understandable from the perspective of federal tax law, while the organization of corporations of different kinds are regulated by the individual states. Therefore, in the US, the term 'foundation' does not have the same legal meaning as in civil law Europe. In the US foundations are defined in federal tax law as non-profit tax-exempt organizations, which are not covered under certain exemptions. In terms of tax, it is highly unattractive for such foundations to own and control property. However, there are certain exceptions, including the Newman's Own Exception in the Philanthropic Enterprise Act 2017. Moreover, the LLC

[29] S. Kalss, Austria chapter in this volume, section 1.5.
[30] E. Barcellona, Italy chapter in this volume, section 3.2.

and perpetual purpose trust are now used in certain states as a non-tax-exempt alternative.[31]

4. PURPOSE

Foundations do not have shareholders or members. Their direction is determined by a purpose decided by the founder. The extent of the founder's freedom to determine and modify this goal is of crucial importance for the regulatory approach to enterprise foundations.

In the past, legal systems including Italy, Austria and Germany demanded that foundations pursue a charitable goal. However, today, only the Austrian federal foundation still demands such a purpose. Most countries now accept all kinds of purposes as long as they are not harmful to the public. Pursuing charitable goals is generally only demanded as a prerequisite for enjoying tax benefits.

While Italy started with the inadmissibility of enterprise foundations and a requirement that foundations must serve public utility, scholars now claim, after a reform in 2000, that foundations may now pursue any lawful purpose.[32] Germany accepted the lawful foundation that does not necessarily pursue public benefit by federal law in 2002.[33]

Table 3. Do enterprise foundations have to have a charitable purpose?

Yes	No
US (tax law)	Denmark
Austria (federal foundation)	Sweden
	Switzerland
	Austria (private foundation)
	Italy
	Germany

Source: Compiled by the authors.

However, not all kinds of purposes are now acceptable. There are limitations to selfish goals. A foundation may not be set up to support the founder. Nevertheless, supporting a family may be a foundation's

31 O. Eldar, US chapter in this volume, sections 2.3, 4.
32 E. Barcellona, Italy chapter in this volume, section 5.1.
33 A. Sanders, Germany chapter in this volume, section 1.2.

purpose in most countries, with some limitations. In this respect, there is in many countries a noticeable tension with rules against perpetuities and the longstanding rejection of the fideicommissum,[34] which are – for example – forbidden in the Danish Constitution.[35] Fideicommissa were used to preserve noble property over generations. They had no legal personality and consisted of unsaleable property bound for the purpose of preserving the name and glory of a noble family. Liberal forces all over Europe rejected them for some time claiming that they preserved noble privilege and indulgence and impaired economic development in general by withdrawing property from market forces.[36] Thus, it is understandable that foundations set up for the support of a family are viewed with suspicion in many countries.[37]

In Denmark, foundations founded after 1985 may distribute benefits to family members born after the funding of the foundation only on an equal footing with other members of the public.[38] In Sweden, unwritten foundation law requires that a foundation set up for the benefit of family members without any limitation in time requires a certain purpose on which the foundation's board can make a decision, e.g. poverty of family members or financial needs to pay for education. In Germany, family foundations may be used more freely and commentators have remarked that in fact, the family foundation may be used for the same purposes today as fideicommissa in the past.[39] Limitations on the number of years

---

[34] For fedeicommissa in Denmark, see R Feldthusen, *Succession*, Copenhagen, Djøf Forlag, 2001; see for the history in Germany: R. Eckert, *Der Kampf um die Familienkommisse in Deutschland*, Peter Lang, Frankfurt 1992; B. Bayer, *Sukzession und Freiheit*, Duncker & Humblot, Berlin 1999.

[35] R. Feldhusen, Denmark chapter in this volume, section 5.6.

[36] E. Barcellona, Italy chapter in this volume, section 5.1; R. Eckert, above n. 34, pp. 533 et seq.

[37] P. Rawert, 'Der Stiftungsbegriff ud seine Merkmale' in K. Hopt and D. Reuter (eds), *Stiftungsrecht in Europa*, Carl Heymanns Verlag, Cologne 2001, pp. 118–122; H. Kronke, 'Familien- und Unternehmensträgerstiftungen' in K. Hopt and D. Reuter (eds), *Stiftungsrecht in Europa*, Carl Heymanns Verlag, Cologne 2001, pp. 159–173.

[38] R. Feldhusen, Denmark chapter in this volume, section 5.6.

[39] On the 'functional equivalence' with a fideicommisum and a family foundation that requires no further requirements for supporting family members and for a critical view, see D. Reuter in *Münchener Kommentar BGB*, 6th edition, CH Beck, Munich 2012, §81 para 96; A. Dutta, *Warum Erbrecht*, Mohr Sieback, Tüblgen 2014; B. Weitemeyer in *Münchener Kommetar BGB*, 9th edition, CH Beck, Munich 2021 §80 paras 186–192; and R Hüttemann and P. Rawert, in *Staudinger BGB*, Sellier/de Gruyter, Berlin, 2017, 'Vorb. zu §§80 ff.' para 264 et seq.; the differences between a family foundation and fideicommissa and the legality of the former stresses BverfGE 37, 328, 336 and RG 26.5.1905 – Rep. VII 508/04 RGZ 61, 28 para 2.

such a foundation may last have been debated, but have not been introduced so far.[40] In this light, the possibility for the beneficiaries of an Austrian private foundation to wind up the foundation after 100 years[41] seems understandable.

Table 4. May enterprise foundations support a family as its purpose?

Yes (under certain conditions)	Yes, but subject to debate	Only under certain conditions	No
Austria (private foundation) Germany Switzerland	Italy	Denmark Sweden	Austria (federal foundation)

Source: Compiled by the authors.

This is in a way surprising if one considers a foundation a non-profit organization in the sense of Hansmann. Such a non-profit organization is barred from distributing its net earnings to anyone exercising control over it. Hansmann has called this prohibition on distribution of profits the 'nondistribution constraint'.[42] However, a foundation's beneficiaries do not necessarily have control over the foundation and usually do not have a legal claim to support from the foundation.

Since most foundation laws now accept all kinds of lawful purposes, pursuing a lawful business purpose should also be acceptable. However, this issue is slightly unclear or under debate in most countries. In Germany, the predominant opinion among academics and also the legislator is that a business purpose would violate the so-called probation of the Selbstzweckstiftung.[43] A foundation must have an outward-directed purpose and must not simply administer its property. It is claimed that merely managing a business without any additional purpose would be the same as simply administering property. Most countries do not follow this approach clearly, but this is a topic that is still the subject of debate, even though in Germany, it poses few limitations to setting up enterprise foundations in practice. Finding an additional purpose in drafting the

40 A. Dutta, in A. Richter (ed.), *Stiftungsrecht Handbuch*, CH Beck, Munich 2019, §5 para. 35 et seq. with further references.

41 S. Kalss, Austria chapter in this volume, section 1.4.

42 H. Hansmann, 'The Role of Non-profit Enterprises' (1980) 89(5) *Yale Law Journal* 835 et seq.

43 A. Sanders, Germany chapter in this volume, section 2.1; see also P. Rawert, 'Der Stiftungsbegriff ud seine Merkmale' in K. Hopt and D. Reuter, above n. 37, pp. 117–118.

charter is not difficult. However, some scholars claim that supervisory authorities could call upon such 'fake' purposes at any time and demand that a foundation pursues its 'real' purpose, even to the detriment of running the business. Moreover, from an academic perspective, it is interesting to ask why managing and developing a business should not be considered an outward-directed purpose. After all, every business interacts with society through its various stakeholders.

In Sweden, the discussion on admitting a business purpose seemed more focused on the question on whether a foundation with its unchanging purpose and without shareholders may offer a suitable tool for business activities. However, this question was decided in favour of enterprise foundations.[44]

Table 5. May a foundation pursue a business purpose as its sole purpose?

Yes	No
Denmark	Austria
Sweden	Germany (with considerable arguments to the contrary)
Switzerland	
Italy	

Source: Compiled by the authors.

5. FLEXIBILITY AND IRREVOCABILITY

As discussed above, the irrevocable donation of assets is part of the general definition of a foundation. Nevertheless, retaining some flexibility can be of crucial importance in order to adjust a foundation to a changing environment. In most countries, including Germany[45] and Sweden,[46] some parts of the foundation's charter may be changed if the founder has reserved the right for the governing body of the foundation to do so and receives the approval of the supervisory body. In countries like Switzerland and Austria (private foundations, not federal foundations), founders may even reserve the right to change the charter themselves. In Germany, the introduction of such a right was discussed in the recent reform process. However, this step was not taken.[47]

44 K. Olsson, Sweden chapter in this volume, section 1.7.
45 A. Sanders, Germany chapter in this volume, section 2.5.
46 K. Olsson, Sweden chapter in this volume, section 2.
47 A. Sanders, Germany chapter in this volume, section 2.5.

In Italy, the Civil Code explicitly states that the settlement of a foundation can be revoked by the founder only until the foundation has obtained 'legal personality' or has de facto started to operate (Article 15). This has traditionally been interpreted as an indication that, once the foundation exists, as a matter of general principle, the founder has no special prerogatives. Furthermore, if it is held that the fundamental 'purpose' of the foundation cannot be materially changed at all, it is unclear if a founder can preserve the right to themselves or the board to change the charter. If it is at all permissible, such a change would require the consent of the supervisory authority.

However, in Austria, the founder may reserve the right not only to change the charter but also to revoke the foundation in general.[48] This degree of flexibility might be welcome to founders and may encourage them to establish a foundation in the first place. Yet, as mentioned earlier, it might be questioned whether the Austrian foundation can still be called a foundation in the classical sense.

Table 6. Flexibility of the foundation's charter

Founder can preserve right to revoke the foundation	Founder may preserve the right to change the charter of the foundation	Founder may preserve the foundation's board the right to change the charter
Austria (private foundation)	Austria (private foundation)	Denmark
	Switzerland	Sweden
		Austria
		Germany
		Switzerland

Source: Compiled by the authors.

6. GOVERNANCE/TRANSPARENCY

6.1. FOUNDATION GOVERNANCE

Foundation governance is a topic of central importance across Europe. While shareholders or members of a corporation may be expected to ensure that directors do not squander 'their' money, foundations without owners or members are in need of special protection.[49] Traditionally, this

48 S. Kalss, Austria chapter in this volume, sections 1.4, 2.2.1.

49 For a general discussion of this topic, see D. Jakob, *Der Schutz der Stiftung*, Mohr-Siebeck, Tubingen 2006.

protection is provided by supervisory authorities. These authorities are usually limited to legal supervision and do not question business decisions. Supervisory authorities generally have the right to dismiss directors and demand special audits. In Denmark since 2014, enterprise foundations have been under the legal supervision of the Business Authority, which can, for example, request that a special audit is undertaken.[50]

It is interesting to note that in Austria, private foundations are not under the supervision of a foundation authority but are supervised to a limited extent by the commercial court.[51] However, Austrian private foundations have a legal duty to establish internal governance mechanisms. This movement away from public supervision towards internal governance is also noticeable in Germany. Private foundations like family foundations may be exempt from public supervision, as in Bavaria, or may only be subject to limited supervision.

The discussions in this volume show that public supervision is no replacement for internal governance mechanisms and transparent registration in general. How to establish such mechanisms may be considered as one of the most important topics of the law of enterprise foundations.

In many countries, such as Germany, Switzerland, Sweden and Italy, the law is silent about foundation governance. In Germany, for example, only one director is necessary. This director may be the founder or members of the founding family. There is no prerequisite to establish an additional body to supervise the director or directors and no rule demanding that its members or at least some of them should be independent from the founder. The new foundation law of 2021 did not change that, but at least made it clear that additional bodies may be established.[52] In Switzerland,[53] the law is also silent on this and lawyers consult the Swiss Foundation Code as a source of inspiration for best practice and recommendations. In Sweden, foundations may even be administered by another legal entity (attached administration), an opportunity approximately 50% (20,000 foundations) have taken.[54] Swedish foundations are under supervision by the County Administration Board. While the founder can exempt the foundation from supervision, this is not possible for enterprise foundations. This provides at least some special regulation for enterprise foundations.

---

50 R. Feldhusen, Denmark chapter in this volume, section 6.
51 S. Kalss, Austria chapter in this volume, section 2.2.2.
52 A. Sanders, Germany chapter in this volume, section 2.4.
53 https://www.swissfoundations.ch/wp-content/uploads/2021/06/9783727277931.pdf.
54 K. Olsson, Sweden chapter in this volume, section 2.

In Italy, there are governance rules in the 'Third Sector Code' (TSC) applicable to the third-sector foundations, but no specific governance rules are contained in the Italian Civil Code. When dealing with the foundations, the Civil Code simply states that the foundation has its 'directors' (Articles 18 and 25) and implicitly assumes that more than one director makes up a 'board of directors', but nothing more than this. Therefore, nothing in the Civil Code prevents a foundation from having the founder or their family members as directors.

Table 7. Governance regulation

High prerequisites	Some special governance rules	Low prerequisites
Austria	Sweden	Germany
Denmark		Switzerland
		Italy

Source: Compiled by the authors.

The situation is different in Denmark and Austria, where the law demands that some (Denmark) or all (Austria) members of the board of directors must be independent.

In Denmark, each board of directors must at least have three members who must be natural persons. At least one-third of the board of directors must be independent of the founder of the foundation. Moreover, rules are in place to guarantee that the foundation acts independently of its subsidiaries and other companies over which the foundation exerts influence. The majority of board members and the chair and vice-chair of the board cannot be executives of the foundation. Moreover, the management of subsidiaries or companies over which the foundation exerts significant influence may not appoint members to the board of the foundation. The chair or vice-chair of the foundation may also only be an executive of a subsidiary with the special permission of the Business Authority.[55] In 2014, Danish law went a step further: a Committee on Foundation Governance was established, the purpose of which was to issue a set of recommendations upon which enterprise foundations were obligated by law to report, but on a comply-or-explain basis.[56]

Austrian law provides some special rules for the governance of private foundations: its board must have a minimum of three directors, who

55 R. Feldhusen, Denmark chapter in this volume, section 5.5.

56 Ibid, section 7.

must all be natural, independent persons. According to the case law of the Austrian Supreme Court, this independence requires that directors of the foundation cannot be directors of subsidiary companies and cannot be related to the foundation's beneficiaries up to the third degree.[57] The foundation is registered, but supervision is provided by a special auditor who checks the legality of the annual financial statements.[58]

6.2. TRANSPARENCY

Another important topic of European foundation law is transparency and thus the question what information enterprise foundations should be obligated to disclose and to whom such information should be disclosed. These issues are of great importance in order to hold foundations accountable. In public corporations, this is an important task for shareholders. In foundations which do not have shareholders, other actors must ensure that foundations are held accountable.

Again, Danish law is at the forefront of this movement. As enterprise foundations are separate legal entities running a business or controlling an operating company, the disclosure requirements have generally been the same as for other Danish limited liability companies, i.e. public annual accounts and registration in a central public business registry. In 2015 new legislation on enterprise foundations entered into force and with it came additional requirements in relation to disclosure and transparency. It is now a requirement that all transactions with related parties, whether at market value or not, are disclosed in the annual accounts.[59]

In Germany, a federal foundation register will be introduced for the first time in 2026. In terms of transparency, this is definitely a step forward; however, public annual accounts cannot be expected even then.

7. TAX

The tax system may influence the formation of enterprise foundation in various ways.[60] It can provide tax deductions which allow founders to

---

57 S. Kalss, Austria chapter in this volume, section 8.2.

58 Ibid, section 8.3.

59 R. Feldthusen, Denmark chapter in this volume, section 7.

60 S. Thomsen and N Kavadis, 'Enterprise Foundations: Law, Taxation, Governance, and Performance', (2022) 6(4) *Annals of Corporate Governance* 227: http://dx.doi.org/10.1561/109.00000031.

make deductions in their taxable income. It can also provide tax penalties by taxing foundations with business holdings (as is the case in the US) or it can require founders to pay inheritance tax even though they donated their wealth to a foundation (as was the case in Denmark until recently). However, in most cases, foundation law has chosen a middle way in which founders neither receive tax deductions nor are required to pay inheritance or capital gains taxes when establishing an enterprise foundation. However, there may be certain tax benefits for charitable foundations.

All chapters in this book stress the high importance of tax law for enterprise foundations, especially when they are used as tools for succession planning. However, placing countries in a table is particularly hard in this case, as in tax law, a number of different rules work together to create a more or less favourable environment.

The common denominator seems to be that enterprise foundations are taxed at the same rate as companies running a business or holding shares in other companies in Denmark, Sweden and Germany. There does not seem to be a special foundation tax law in most countries. Setting up a foundation may cause inheritance and gift tax. However, there are capital gains and inheritance tax exemptions for foundations with a charitable purpose in Denmark, Germany and Switzerland. In Sweden, there is no inheritance tax at all. In both Germany and Switzerland, double foundations are used to combine the tax benefits of a charitable foundation with the advantages of a family foundation.[61]

In both Denmark[62] and Austria in the past, setting up foundations was to some degree encouraged by the avoidance of capital gains, private wealth and inheritance taxes, which were historically substantial. In Austria, for example, the introduction of private foundations was supported by considerable tax benefits in relation to inheritance tax in the process of succession planning. However, later, with decreasing tax incentives, the number of private foundations dropped. Today, private foundations are often dissolved and their property is distributed to the beneficiaries. The 'price' for this is the tax burden on the donated (currently valued) assets with capital gains tax.[63]

In Denmark, where the formation of enterprise foundations was largely blocked by an onerous tax regime between 1998 and 2018, the tax due on succession to a foundation ownership has recently been lowered and

61 D. Jakob, Switzerland chapter in this volume, section 2.2.3; A. Sanders, Germany chapter in this volume, section 1.5.3.
62 R. Feldhusen, Denmark chapter in this volume, section 8.
63 S. Kalss, Austria chapter in this volume, section 1.3.

foundations have been allowed to succeed in paying taxes with the goal of encouraging the founding of new foundations.[64]

Table 8. Was the tax environment more favourable before?

'Yes, it used to be better'	'Stable'	'It is improving'
Denmark (before 1998)	Germany	US
Austria		Denmark (since 2021)
Switzerland		

Source: Compiled by the authors.

8. ECONOMIC SIGNIFICANCE, CHALLENGES AND OPPORTUNITIES

8.1. ECONOMIC SIGNIFICANCE

Assessing the economic significance of enterprise foundations in the legal systems discussed in this volume is not easy. According to all the data presented by Thomsen[65] and Feldthusen[66] in this book, the economic significance of enterprise foundations in Denmark is impressive. Among the countries discussed here, Denmark takes pole position in terms of the economic significance of enterprise foundations.

However, it is difficult to precisely ascertain the actual significance of enterprise foundations in other countries. Only Denmark registers enterprise foundations separately. Therefore, while in countries like Germany, Switzerland and Sweden, the significance of enterprise foundations also seems to be considerable, to some degree they may fly 'under the radar', without any precise data on their economic importance. In Austria, there are roughly 3,000 private foundations, but not all of them are enterprise foundations in the sense discussed here. So far, Germany has not even established a central foundation register, let alone one for enterprise foundations specifically.

Nevertheless, on the basis of the data presented in this book, it can be assumed that the importance of enterprise foundations is considerable.[67]

---

[64] R. Feldhusen, Denmark chapter in this volume, section 8.

[65] S. Thomsen, Foundation Ownership around the World chapter in this volume, sections 5–7.

[66] R. Feldthusen, Denmark chapter in this volume, section 2.

[67] See also D.J. Schröder, 'Publicly Listed Foundation-Owned Firms around the World: An Overview', unpublished working paper, 2021, https://www.enterprisefoundations.dk/wp-content/uploads/2021/11/Publicly-listed-FoFs-Descriptive-Paper-02112021.pdf.

With respect to listed foundation-owned companies,[68] the economic significance of enterprise foundations in the countries discussed here may be ranked as follows:

Table 9. Economic significance of enterprise foundations owning listed companies from high to low in relation to % of market capitalization

Denmark	Austria	Sweden	Italy	Switzerland	Germany	US
63%	26.1%	18.9%	6.3%	5%	3.8%	1.1%

Source: Compiled by the authors.

In general, the relative positions on the scale correspond with the more or less welcoming regulatory approach to enterprise foundations summarized in this chapter. In particular, the extensive special regulation of enterprise foundations in Denmark and private foundations in Austria corresponds to a high significance of enterprise foundations in both countries.

However, there are two exceptions to this. First, in relation to Italy, the relative position may be surprising given the formerly hostile approach to enterprise foundations. This is no doubt due to the important role of the Italian banking foundations which the Italian government created by privatizing former financial mutuals. Second, the low ranking of Germany on this scale may not provide a full picture of the situation there. The available data on privately owned companies show that German enterprise foundations own firms with an impressive asset volume that surpasses other countries. Given the growing importance of enterprise foundations as a tool of succession planning for small and medium-sized enterprises, it is to be expected that a considerable number of enterprise foundations are difficult to assess.

8.2. HISTORICAL BACKGROUND AND FUTURE CHALLENGES

Discussing the economic importance of enterprise foundations and how this corresponds to the regulatory approach towards them illustrates the importance of the social and historical context in different legal systems. In Denmark and Germany, historical foundations like the Carlsberg Foundation (1876) and the Zeiss Foundation (1889) are closely linked to

68 S. Thomsen, Foundation Ownership around the World chapter in this volume, Table 2.

the public's perception of such foundations.[69] The Swedish discussion also shows a history of foundations, and even if the beginning of enterprise foundations is less clear, they have become influential after the first World War. A closer look also often reveals fascinating developments in the different countries – for example, there are the unique Swedish pension fund foundations (*löntagarfondsstiftelserna*).[70]

The most important insight that the historical perspective may offer is the fact that different policy makers and consequently legal systems have both welcomed and rejected enterprise foundations as the table below (Table 10) shows. Austrian legislators saw potential benefits in strengthening foundations with tax advantages in order to combat foreign competition, such as by Liechtenstein Foundations in Austria.[71] On the other hand, the chapters on Italy[72] and the US show that policy makers have looked and still look at foundations with suspicion.

Table 10. Regulatory approach in the past

Welcoming	Neutral	Hostile/suspicious
Denmark	Sweden	US
Austria	Switzerland	Italy
	Germany	

Source: Compiled by the authors.

The discussions in the chapters in this volume illustrate that the approach to enterprise foundations in any legal system is not fixed. The experience in Denmark and Austria shows that the enthusiasm for foundation building diminishes considerably once the initial tax benefits are removed. Moreover, both the chapters on Austria and Switzerland show that an increasingly challenging regulatory environment and case law of the courts may reduce the attractiveness of a legal system for enterprise foundations. While the Austrian courts' case law make foundation governance difficult,[73] the new case law on asset management in the Swiss Federal Supreme Courts may severely affect enterprise foundations in the future.[74]

---

69 R. Feldthusen, Denmark chapter in this volume, section 1; A. Sanders, Germany chapter in this volume, section 1.2.
70 K. Olsson, Sweden chapter in this volume, section 1.2.
71 S. Kalss, Austria chapter in this volume, section 1.3.
72 E. Barcellona, Italy chapter in this volume, section 2.
73 S. Kalss, Austria chapter in this volume, section 8.4.
74 D. Jakob, Switzerland chapter in this volume, section 3.4.

However, the chapters also show that the regulatory environment is improving in some countries, even if slowly. The German legislator, for example, while improving the regulatory system under the new foundation law, especially by introducing a foundation register, has arguably missed the chance to make an even bigger step towards a more flexible foundation law.[75] In the US, the 'Paul Newman exception'[76] and state legislation on the perpetual purpose trust may lead the way. In Italy, the acceptance of enterprise foundations has changed with the TSC.[77] All this may at least be partly due to an increasing interest in the third sector, and different forms of long-term purpose-oriented businesses organization that do not focus on shareholder value maximization. In that respect, enterprise foundations may offer attractive opportunities in a changing world.

Table 11. Trend in legislation/case law

Legal regime is improving	Stable	Legal regime is getting more difficult
Germany	Denmark	Switzerland
Italy	Sweden	Austria
US		

Source: Compiled by the authors.

9. CONCLUSION

Summarizing all the findings of this book into one table is almost impossible, because a simple ranking oversimplifies the information and paints with much too broad a brush. On the other hand, we still tried to do so, knowing full well that every placement on the table is highly debatable. We are also aware that every such ordering includes a value judgement weighing up different aspects. Moreover, it should be noted that all countries discussed in this book embrace enterprise foundations to varying degrees. Therefore, even in countries such as Germany and Italy, which have been depicted here as relatively lukewarm, enterprise foundations can and are founded. If more legal systems would be included

[75] A. Sanders, Germany chapter in this volume, sections 4.1, 4.3.
[76] O. Eldar, US chapter in this volume, section 2.3.
[77] E. Barcellona, Italy chapter in this volume, section 6.

in the analysis, it is likely that both countries would end up in a much more favourable position.

Denmark is the frontrunner in this respect because it is the only country with a proper legal framework specifically designed for enterprise foundations regulating governance, transparency and also a tax environment which (again) encourages the establishment of enterprise foundations.

Sweden comes second behind Denmark. Even though enterprise foundations mostly fly 'under the radar' there and are not specifically regulated (as they are in Denmark), they still enjoy great freedom of purpose, governance and are subject to favourable tax laws.

Confirming the order of Austria and Switzerland in this sense is especially difficult. Both have a strong tradition in relation to enterprise foundations. In Austria, the private foundation is of considerable economic importance. Moreover, it allows great flexibility to its founders. However, it should not be forgotten that part of the attractiveness of the private foundation was built on tax benefits which have now been removed. Moreover, the case law of the Austrian Supreme Court make governance difficult.

Switzerland is famous for having many enterprise foundations, partly because it allows great flexibility to founders with respect to purpose, governance and charter changes. However, it seems that the regulatory environment is getting more difficult, and the new case law of the Federal Supreme Court on asset management may cause serious problems for charitable enterprise foundations.

In Germany, foundations have become more popular as vehicles to structure the succession of family businesses. However, so far, the legal environment with the split between federal and state foundation law and the lack of a foundation register has left much to be desired. The reform of 2021 was an important step, but could have gone further, increasing flexibility, improving governance and embracing business purposes.

To place Italy as least conductive to enterprise foundations does not fully capture the big step forward that enterprise foundations have made there. The remaining legal uncertainties depicted in the Italian chapter are the reason for this position.

The US should be seen as outside the table because the chapter in this book and this analysis has only looked at federal tax law rather than all the other elements discussed in this chapter. Still, it might be reasonably concluded that tax law discourages founders from setting up foundations.

Table 12. Overall assessment of the legal environment for enterprise foundations

From left to right: most to least favourable						
Denmark	Sweden	Austria	Switzerland	Germany	Italy	US

Source: Compiled by the authors.

9.1. POLICY CONCLUSIONS

Policy makers wishing to encourage the formation of enterprise foundations in their country may use the material in this book as a tentative guide.

They should first and foremost ensure the legality and legitimacy of the enterprise foundation form. Enterprise foundations with a charitable purpose should be possible. In addition, foundation law should recognize that the responsible, long-term-oriented ownership of a business company is a legitimate primary goal for a foundation. Policy makers may or may not want to mandate additional goals like support for the descendants of the founder. Family support is a deviation from pure foundation ownership in the direction of family and may be deliberately limited – for example, as a share of donations or in tax treatment of foundations established with a family purpose. However, admitting a (limited) family purpose is certain to make succession to foundation ownership more popular with founding entrepreneurs and may allow them to sustain some of the positive characteristics associated with family businesses.

Second, policy makers should ensure that the tax treatment of enterprise foundations is reasonably favourable without being overly generous. The idea would be to aim for neutrality so that founders do not establish enterprise foundations for tax reasons, but only when they believe that this is the right approach for the company. This is economically feasible since the supreme economic sacrifice required by founders – donating the bulk of their wealth to foundations – will in any case limit the number of founders who wish to follow this path. The tax system should avoid both income tax exemptions and fines on controlling business ownership, but should also avoid requiring founders to pay wealth taxes (inheritance and capital gains taxes) on funds that they give away to enterprise foundations with a charitable purpose.

Third, policy makers should put in place regulation to ensure the good governance of enterprise foundations which will help ensure their efficiency and legitimacy. This includes governance rules which ensure the independence of the foundation board vis-à-vis the founding family and employees or directors of the company. A majority of the foundation board should be independent. However, involving some members with a material interest in the proceeds of foundation (e.g. as beneficiaries) may provide a good balance. Moreover, a good argument can be made to allow a strong family presence on the board to preserve the character of a family business even in an enterprise foundation. Moreover, regulators should create a foundation register (for all types of foundations), to which enterprise foundations in particular should be required to submit audited annual reports. Appropriate transparency will help assuage ill-founded fears from the general public about mismanagement and shady dealings in enterprise foundations.

Fourth, the authorities should establish an efficient foundation authority which should exercise legality supervision of all foundations and enterprise foundations in particular. Legality supervision would require regulators to protect foundations against abuse by the founding family and company management. However, it should avoid micromanaging the foundation businesses which regulators are ill-equipped to do. In particular, enterprise foundations should be allowed to take risks which may sometimes lead to bankruptcy, although obvious recklessness may be regarded as contrary to the foundation purpose.

9.2. FUTURE RESEARCH AND CLOSING REMARKS

This book is only a first step in our understanding of enterprise foundation law. As pioneers, we are very conscious that many errors must remain and that future research will be needed to weed out mistakes and improve our knowledge of this important area. Furthermore, we have covered a limited number of countries leaving out important foundation countries like the Netherlands, Norway, Liechtenstein, France and Belgium. Future work would do well to take their experience into consideration.[78]

---

[78] For some information in German, see the chapters in the still-excellent K. Hopt and D. Reuter, above n. 37.

Nevertheless, we are happy to present this book to a wider audience and the experience of editing it has only increased our interest in enterprise foundations as a unique and attractive ownership form which has much to teach us about business ownership and much to contribute to the global business community. After all, long-term-oriented, purpose-driven businesses are discussed as promising contributors to the economy of the future. Enterprise foundations are uniquely qualified to play a major role in this endeavour.

INDEX

ABOUT THE EDITORS

Prof. Dr. Anne Sanders, M.Jur (Oxon) holds the chair for Civil law, Company law, the law of Family Businesses and Comparative Judicial Studies at the University of Bielefeld, Germany. She is co-director of the Institute for Family Businesses at the University of Bielefeld (IFUn) and Professor II of the faculty of law of the University of Bergen, Norway (2021–2025). She focusses her research on purpose driven organisations such as foundations, companies and steward owned businesses which are included in the 2021 coalition agreement of the German government.

Prof. Dr. Steen Thomsen, Ph.D., is Novo Nordisk Foundation Professor of Enterprise Foundation Governance at Copenhagen Business School (CBS). He specializes in enterprise foundations and corporate governance as a teacher, researcher, consultant, commentator and practitioner. His publications include more than 30 international journal articles and 5 books on the subject. Steen has served as a board member in several business companies and is currently a founding board member of Boardmeter (which provides software-based board evaluations), the Pluto Foundation (which works to promote biodiversity around the world) and the Finn Nørgaard Association (which seeks to prevent terrorism by social inclusion).

www.ingramcontent.com/pod-product-compliance
Ingram Content Group UK Ltd.
Pitfield, Milton Keynes, MK11 3LW, UK
UKHW021845100926
8556IPUK00019B/1052

9 781839 703065